International Political Economy Series

General Editor: Timothy M. Shaw, Professor and Director, Institute of International Relations, The University of the West Indies, Trinidad & Tobago

Titles include:

Lucian M. Ashworth and David Long (*editors*)
NEW PERSPECTIVES ON INTERNATIONAL FUNCTIONALISM

Robert W. Cox (*editor*)
THE NEW REALISM
Perspectives on Multilateralism and World Order

Frederick Deyo (*editor*)
GLOBAL CAPITAL, LOCAL LABOUR

Stephen Gill (*editor*)
GLOBALIZATION, DEMOCRATIZATION AND MULTILATERALISM

Björn Hettne, András Inotai and Osvaldo Sunkel (*editors*)
GLOBALISM AND THE NEW REGIONALISM

Christopher C. Meyerson
DOMESTIC POLITICS AND INTERNATIONAL RELATIONS IN US–JAPAN TRADE POLICYMAKING
The GATT Uruguay Round Agriculture Negotiations

Isidro Morales
POST-NAFTA NORTH AMERICA

Manuela Moschella
GOVERNING RISK
The IMF and Global Financial Crises

Volker Rittberger and Martin Nettesheim (*editor*)
AUTHORITY IN THE GLOBAL POLITICAL ECONOMY

Justin Robertson (*editor*)
POWER AND POLITICS AFTER FINANCIAL CRISES
Rethinking Foreign Opportunism in Emerging Markets

Michael G. Schechter (*editor*)
FUTURE MULTILATERALISM
The Political and Social Framework
INNOVATION IN MULTILATERALISM

Ben Thirkell-White
THE IMF AND THE POLITICS OF FINANCIAL GLOBALIZATION
From the Asian Crisis to a New International Financial Architecture?

Thomas G. Weiss (*editor*)
BEYOND UN SUBCONTRACTING
Task Sharing with Regional Security Arrangements and Service-Providing NGOs

Robert Wolfe
FARM WARS
The Political Economy of Agriculture and the International Trade Regime

International Political Economy Series
Series Standing Order ISBN 978–0–333–71708–0 hardcover
Series Standing Order ISBN 978–0–333–71110–1 paperback
(*outside North America only*)

You can receive future titles in this series as they are published by placing a standing order. Please contact your bookseller or, in case of difficulty, write to us at the address below with your name and address, the title of the series and one of the ISBNs quoted above.

Customer Services Department, Macmillan Distribution Ltd, Houndmills, Basingstoke, Hampshire RG21 6XS, England

Governing Risk

The IMF and Global Financial Crises

Manuela Moschella

First published 2010 by
PALGRAVE MACMILLAN

Palgrave Macmillan in the UK is an imprint of Macmillan Publishers Limited, registered in England, company number 785998, of Houndmills, Basingstoke, Hampshire RG21 6XS.

Palgrave Macmillan in the US is a division of St Martin's Press LLC, 175 Fifth Avenue, New York, NY 10010.

Palgrave Macmillan is the global academic imprint of the above companies and has companies and representatives throughout the world.

Palgrave® and Macmillan® are registered trademarks in the United States, the United Kingdom, Europe and other countries.

ISBN: 978–0–230–23687–5 hardback

This book is printed on paper suitable for recycling and made from fully managed and sustained forest sources. Logging, pulping and manufacturing processes are expected to conform to the environmental regulations of the country of origin.

A catalogue record for this book is available from the British Library.

A catalog record for this book is available from the Library of Congress.

10 9 8 7 6 5 4 3 2 1
19 18 17 16 15 14 13 12 11 10

Printed and bound in Great Britain by
CPI Antony Rowe, Chippenham and Eastbourne

Contents

Acknowledgements

Over the past years, I was fortunate enough to meet many people and visit several institutions that contributed to the completion of this book. Now time has come to acknowledge their contribution. First, I want to express my profound gratitude to Christopher Gilbert, my former dissertation advisor, who encouraged me to work on the IMF and its approach to capital liberalization. His advice, encouragement, and insight have been crucial to the development of the book. At the University of Trento, I also record my gratitude to Andrea Fracasso for his close and thoughtful reading of the entire manuscript. Mark Beittel, Giorgio Fodor, and Mark Gilbert also offered me precious advice. Many friends and colleagues also supported the development of my book project. Among them, Barbara Guastaferro has been a special welcome source of advice and intellectual challenge.

Many institutions have provided me with space and financial support throughout the past years, and I am in their debt as well. The University of California Washington Centre (UCWC) and the School of Advanced International Studies (SAIS) of the Johns Hopkins University, in particular, provided me assistance during my field research at the IMF. The staff of the IMF, including the staff of IMF Archives has been extraordinary helpful in assisting my research.

Special thanks go to the International Centre for Business and Politics (CBP) of the Copenhagen Business School, where I spent a semester thanks to a generous fellowship granted by the GARNET research network. At CBP Professor Leonard Seabrooke deserves special mention not only for reading portions of my book but also for offering such good advice.

This book and the ideas that it advances have benefited immeasurably from the insights of a number of individuals I met and collaborated with at various stages in the process of writing. For the insights received before and during conferences and workshops, I want to thank Fulvio Attinà, Jacqueline Best, André Broome, Ralf Leiteritz, Bessma Momani, Susan Park, Antje Vetterlein, and Kate Weaver. At the UCWC, James Desveaux made a big difference to my experience in Washington. Still, I'm extremely grateful to Mark Blyth, whose works has inspired me since the beginning, and to Erik Jones and Sven Steinmo who offered me incisive criticism and critical advice on the overall argument as well as on specific chapters.

Parts of Chapters from 1 to 5 as well as parts of Chapter 7 appeared in the journal article 'When ideas fail to influence policy outcomes: the IMF and orderly liberalization,' *The Review of International Political Economy* (*RIPE*), 16 May 2009. These parts have been reprinted with the permission of Taylor & Francis.

Finally, I'm profoundly grateful to the persons whose unfailing support led me to the end of this journey, that is to say, my parents and my sister. However, this book would not have been possible without the sustained interest and support of my partner. For these and another thousand reasons, this work is dedicated to Marco.

1
Introduction: The IMF and Global Financial Governance

This book investigates the changing nature of the policies adopted to promote global financial stability. Specifically, the book investigates the evolution of the policies that member countries requested the International Monetary Fund (IMF) to follow in the aftermath of the Mexican crisis (1994–95), the Asian crisis (1997–98), and the subprime crisis (2007–8). In doing so, the book attempts to explain the puzzle of policy change that led member countries to move away from the post-Mexican policies aimed at fostering global financial stability through a concentration of powers in the IMF to the post-Asian policies that endorsed a decentralized system of governance where market actors played a crucial role. In the aftermath of the subprime crisis, the international policies designed to govern the risks associated with growing financial integration seem to have shifted again towards a form of centralization with a revival of the role of the Fund in crisis prevention and management.

Exploring such institutional variation, the book shows that the Fund's policies have been driven by competing policy ideas about what international financial liberalization entails and how its risks should be governed – the policy ideas of *orderly* and *market-led liberalization* that came to define the intellectual consensus inside and outside the Fund in the early and in the late 1990s. Specifically, the book argues that the ideational shift from *orderly* to *market-led liberalization* prompted a concurrent shift away from previously agreed policy choices, with the attendant redefinition of the Fund's reform agenda. The contestation of the policy idea of *market-led liberalization*, which followed the subprime crisis, has once again opened the way for a further policy shift in the policies governing international finance. Before moving on to clarify the mechanisms through which *a* policy idea becomes *the* consensual

1

idea around which policy is organized, it is first necessary to provide an overview of the changes that this book intends to analyze.

At the beginning of the 1990s, several emerging market countries, following the lead of industrial countries, started opening their economies to foreign capital flows – what is known as the process of international financial liberalization or capital account liberalization (Chwieroth, 2009).[1] In light of the growing integration of world capital markets, member countries and IMF officials started discussing a series of institutional reforms to adapt the international financial architecture to the new economic environment, in particular to encourage countries to embrace financial liberalization while minimizing the risks of liberalization. These reforms included the proposals to strengthen IMF surveillance and to increase IMF financial resources to make the organization able to help member countries cope with large and volatile capital flows. Furthermore, a proposal was made to expand the Fund's legal jurisdiction to the promotion of capital liberalization by amending the IMF's Articles of Agreement. Varied as they were, these proposals nonetheless shared an important point: governing risk in the international financial system required strengthening the traditional forms of interstate cooperation as embodied in the workings of the IMF.

At the end of the 1990s, however, member countries endorsed a new set of policies that attributed an increasingly important role to the private sector in ensuring international financial stability.[2] In contrast, the role of governments and intergovernmental organizations, such as the IMF, was downsized. In the area of crisis prevention, for instance, market actors were recognized as taking a primary role in the diffusion and enforcement of international financial standards across national authorities. In the area of crisis management, new policies were proposed based on the principle of the private sector's involvement with crisis financing. The proposal to amend the Articles was dropped and new international bodies, such as the G20 and the Financial Stability Board (FSB), were created with the aim of contributing to the governance of the international financial system. In short, there has been a shift from the view that governing risk in the international financial system requires a concentration of powers in the IMF to the view that global financial stability requires a decentralized system of governance where supervisory and regulatory powers are diffused among states and market actors.

In the aftermath of the subprime crisis, a new set of policies has again been proposed. In the area of crisis prevention, for instance, several policy makers have called for the tightening of international financial regulation of the banking and derivative industry. The IMF has been called on to take new responsibilities in macro-prudential supervision along with the FSB. In the area of crisis management, world leaders have pledged to increase IMF resources to allow the organization to effectively discharge its traditional mandate of financial assistance. In short, the international community seems supportive of a series of reforms staked on the premise that the decentralized approach of the 1990s is no longer valid. Whereas it was believed that market actors could look after themselves and contribute to international financial stability, the predominant view today is that markets require strong regulatory mechanisms to function effectively.

The variety of the policies pursued within the framework of the efforts to ensure international financial stability is the puzzle addressed in this book. Specifically, I will investigate this institutional variation by tracing the history of the IMF from the early 1990s to the present, focusing on the Mexican, the Asian and the subprime crisis, and on the institutional responses to these financial crises. This comparative historical study is meant to dispute materialist explanations of institutional variation that have long dominated the field of international and comparative political economy (Gilpin, 1981; Gourevitch, 1986). In particular, the book contends that an exogenous shock such as an economic crisis and the attendant reconfiguration of interests are not in and of themselves the explanatory variables of specific institutional choices. Since actors need to make sense of what an economic crisis is and how to work it out, explaining institutional choices requires coming to terms with the economic ideas that help social-political actors to make sense of reality and to devise solutions to existing problems (Hay, 1999; Widmaier, et al., 2007).

Building on this observation, the book develops an agent-centered constructivist framework that starts by identifying the actors that articulate policy ideas on international financial governance, and then moves on to specify the mechanisms through which those ideas become consensual allowing for their institutionalization into policy choices. In other words, the book suggests a theoretical framework based on the continuous interaction between each period's policy ideas on international financial integration and the socio-political validation that these ideas are granted by the actors – states and non-state actors – that form the Fund's social constituencies for legitimation (Seabrooke, 2007b) or the organization's 'authorizing and task environments' (Weaver, 2008a). Combining the role played by economic ideas with that played by the actors that may legitimate or resist policy developments, the book moves from existing constructivist explanations of IMF policies according to which those policies are shaped mostly by IMF staff members acting on the organization's bureaucratic culture (Barnett and Finnemore, 2004; Chwieroth, 2007; Leiteritz, 2005; Momani, 2007). This bureaucratic explanation has merits but also limitations. In particular, by focusing only on one set of agents (IMF staff), this explanation discounts the importance to the IMF of those agents (such as member countries, academic economists, and private-sector actors) whose actions are crucial for the implementation and thereby persistence of specific policies. Absent such an endorsement, policies are more likely to be replaced. Hence, we need a theoretical framework that is able to take into account the feedback coming from those actors. It is the aim of the evolutionary framework proposed in this book.

1.1   International financial integration and the IMF

Why is it important to study the IMF's policies aimed at fostering international financial stability? Although issues of financial stability may appear as technical matters that are far away from citizens' most pressing concerns, a stable international financial system is critical to domestic well-being. Indeed, episodes of financial distress, including those that arise from poor domestic policies or financial excesses, may destroy the capacity of the domestic financial sector to generate credit for activities such as consumption and investment. The resulting impact on the real economy, in terms of output loss and unemployment, can be severe and long lasting, as the crises analyzed in this book attest. In sum, international finance may well provide a platform for economic growth by boosting investment and consumption but its volatility may also cause immense disruptions. Considering the integration of today's world financial markets and the tendency of financial turmoil to spillover across border, studying the mechanisms that are of help in providing and maintaining international financial stability appears to be the most important.

The IMF has been at the forefront of the debate on international financial liberalization and stability, particularly because of its distinctive organizational mandate and features. For one thing, the IMF has the responsibility to oversee the international monetary and financial system. The Fund accomplishes this task by monitoring member countries' economic policies through its Article IV surveillance reports and by monitoring developments in the global financial system through the analyses conducted in its flagship publications – the World Economic

Outlook (WEO) and the Global Financial Stability Report (GFSR).[3] For another, the Fund possesses its own in-house research capacity. As an institution primarily staffed with PhD economists, the IMF is well-placed for elaborating and disseminating theoretical and empirical studies on topics relevant to its activities, including financial liberalization.[4]

The history of the Fund also shows how the organization has been closely associated with the debate on the merits of international financial integration and on the mechanisms that govern it. At the time of the Fund creation, the prevalent question among policy makers and economists was whether to allow the free movement of capital flows.[5] Drawing on the disastrous experience of the 1929 Great Depression, the conclusion that emerged from the Bretton Woods negotiations was that the costs associated with the free movement of capital flows significantly outweighed the benefits. Specifically, the view that 'speculative' capital flows posed a serious threat to the stability of the international financial system, as was most famously put by the UK negotiator John Maynard Keynes, and shared by his US counterpart Harry Dexter White (Boughton, 2002; 2006), substantially shaped the features of the post-World War II international financial regime. As a result, the Bretton Woods agreement created a system of international financial governance, which is also known as the regime of 'embedded liberalism' (Ruggie, 1982), characterized by fixed exchange rates and liberal trade but also by controls on capital flows. By controlling international capital, so the argument went, member countries would have retained domestic monetary authority that would have been used to sustain expansionary policies and full employment. Nowhere are the features of the Bretton Woods system more evident than in the institutional design of the IMF. Indeed, according to its Articles of Agreement, the IMF was assigned the responsibility of presiding over a system of fixed exchange rates and of promoting the liberalization of international trade. At the same time, the IMF was expressively assigned no responsibility to promote the liberalization of capital flows (De Vries, 1969, p. 224). Rather, its Articles of Agreement granted member countries the right to introduce capital controls.

The agreement reached in Bretton Woods on the risks entailed in the liberalization process and on the limited role of the IMF in the governance of international capital flows remained intact until the beginning of the 1990s, in spite of the major changes that had taken place since 1945. The progressive resurgence of private capital flows certainly stands as one of those changes. Indeed, after having virtually disappeared in the aftermath of World War II, international capital flows grew steadily, leading, among other consequences, to the demise of the fixed exchange rate system in the early 1970s.[6] Although IMF membership had already explored ways to adapt the organization to the challenge posed by the increasing volume of international capital flows,[7] until the late 1980s, the prevalent position was that the IMF should not be involved with the process of global financial integration.

By the beginning of the 1990s, however, IMF staff started moving away from the thinking that had marked the creation of the IMF. Concomitant at the debate on the Washington consensus that granted the liberalization of capital flows pride of place in the list of desirable policies to achieve economic development,[8] the debate within the IMF led the organization to embrace a favorable view of international financial liberalization (Abdelal, 2007; Chwieroth, 2007; IEO, 2005; Leiteritz, 2005). The public stance of the IMF in the early 1990s leaves few doubts that seen from 19th Street in Washington the benefits associated with the liberalization of capital flows were substantial. 'The globalization of financial markets is a very positive development,' former Managing Director Michel Camdessus (1995e) forcefully and repeatedly argued, depicting capital flows as 'one of the driving forces of global growth in recent years.' The IMF's policies became also progressively informed on the principle of capital mobility. For instance, until the late 1990s, 'the Fund...tended...to welcome members' actions taken to liberalize capital account transactions,' while it 'generally discouraged' the tightening of capital controls.[9]

This is not to say that IMF staff did not recognize the risks entailed in the liberalization process. Rather, in order to govern its risks, it was suggested that the role of the IMF be strengthened by revising its original mandate. That is to say, IMF staff members proposed to expand the mandate and jurisdiction of the Fund to give the organization the powers to promote liberalization and the responsibilities to oversee an integrated global financial system. The Mexican crisis, which vividly showed both the benefits of liberalization and its risks, marked the moment of acceptance of the ideas positing the positive effects of financial integration when carried out under the Fund's surveillance. Indeed, in the aftermath of the crisis, these ideas were institutionalized in the decision to strengthen the powers of the Fund in the liberalization and in the supervision of global capital flows.

Nevertheless, the Asian crisis, which started in Thailand in 1997 and rapidly spread to several emerging market economies both within and beyond Asia, reopened the debate on the merits of international financial liberalization and on the role of the IMF to govern its risks. In light of the disruption caused by the sharp reversal of capital flows in the crisis-hit countries, numerous observers noted that the benefits of international financial liberalization were in need of recalculation, either for not having the costs of financial crises adequately factored in or because the gains in terms of economic growth have been exaggerated (Bhagwati, 1998; Williamson and Mahar, 1998).

Furthermore, the Asian crisis sparked a vigorous contestation of the role of the Fund as the guarantor of global financial stability. Since IMF's intervention in the crisis-hit countries was unable to restore confidence and was even disruptive of domestic prosperity, the IMF was progressively marginalized in the international financial architecture debate that followed the crisis. The clearest sign of the Fund's marginalization was the creation of the G20 and the Financial Stability Board (FSB), which were two bodies tasked with the responsibility of ensuring global financial stability. Furthermore, a new consensus started emerging about the positive effects of market discipline, self- and light-touch regulation to global financial stability. That is to say, the governance of the international financial system became increasingly informed on the activities of the markets.

Nevertheless, the burst of the subprime crisis has once again opened the debate on financial integration and on the mechanisms to govern its risks. In particular, the crisis has called into question the principles of market discipline, self- and light-touch regulation that have underpinned the governance of the system since the late 1990s. At the same time, there seems to be a backlash against the view positing the irrelevance of the Fund in the management of the international financial system.

As this brief historical overview reveals, the international community has long faced the problem of how to promote an open financial system while reducing the risks associated with such an openness. In particular, over time there have been different ideas about financial integration and about the role of the IMF in ensuring global financial stability. Hence, we need a theoretical framework that is able to explain how specific policy ideas became dominant and were institutionalized into international supervisory and regulatory policies. Specifically, the trajectory of the policy ideas about how to govern the international financial system – from those positing a strengthened role for the IMF in the early 1990s to those arguing for the IMF's disempowerment in the late 1990s – raises some important questions. What are the actors and the mechanisms through which a policy idea emerges and becomes prevalent? How is consensus around an idea formed? When is consensus contested? When are ideas institutionalized? What are the factors that might discard prevalent ideas to the point of their replacement? In answering these questions, I will draw attention to the interaction of policy ideas with the historical-economic context in which they are floated. Specifically, I will examine how economic ideas interacted with the needs and expectations of a number of actors that form the Fund's constituencies for legitimation.

1.2 Policy ideas and policy change

Although the importance of economic ideas have long been discounted in the analyses of the workings of the IMF as compared to variables such as the economic interests of IMF members (Pauly, 1997; Swedberg, 1986), extant literature implicitly suggests two competing hypotheses on the mechanisms through which ideas influence policy outcomes – the external sponsorship and bureaucratic culture hypotheses.

The first hypothesis draws from the argument that economic ideas are consequential when powerful advocates sponsor them (Goldstein, 1993), the corollary hypothesis being that they fail when the sponsors withdraw their support. Applied to the case under investigation, for instance, it could be argued that, in the first half of the 1990s, the IMF was empowered with the task of promoting financial liberalization and governing its risks because the IMF's role was backed from the outside by the powerful US Treasury-Wall Street complex (Bhagwati, 1998; Wade and Veneroso, 1998). As a result, the IMF was ultimately disempowered when the political sponsorship vanished.

The second hypothesis builds on the literature on epistemic communities, thereby emphasizing factors such as organizational culture and access of experts to the decision-making process (Barnett and Finnemore, 2004; Momani, 2005a). For instance, it has been argued that the ideas in favor of liberalization gained political influence from the inside because of the common professional background of IMF staff members (Chwieroth, 2007) and because some of its most outspoken advocates held key posts in the Fund's bureaucracy (Abdelal, 2007, ch. 6). The implicit conclusion here is that ideas lose their influence when the policy entrepreneurs who promoted them are no longer in power.

While each set of hypotheses discloses important insights, archival research and interviews with key staff officials lend only limited support to the argument that external sponsorship and bureaucratic culture are the crucial mechanisms to account for the influence of policy ideas over time. The first hypothesis, for instance, has difficulty in explaining member countries' convergence around specific policies. The second hypothesis, in turn, sits uncomfortably with the timing of policy change. Take the proposal to amend the IMF's Articles of Agreement as an example. True, the US supported the economic ideas in favor of liberalization but there is no significant evidence that it actively pushed other countries to accept the amendment. This is not to deny the influence of the US, but to warn against attributing to it too much causal weight as the mechanism through which ideas 'walk their way' inside the Fund. The bureaucratic culture hypothesis, in contrast, has difficulty in explaining the failure of the amendment. There was no change of mind in the advocates of the amendment inside the Fund and no significant turnover of IMF staff when the amendment was finally abandoned.

This book argues that the limited explanatory power of extant hypotheses derives from their one-dimensional focus on one set of variables over the other – be it the economic interests of powerful members or the technical expertise of IMF staff. Rather, explaining the variation in the influence of economic ideas over time requires understanding their co-evolution with the economic environment in which they are floated. Specifically, the argument is that a full understanding of the variation in the influence of ideas over time requires an evolutionary approach that conceives of the influence of ideas as a fluid process that takes place within a dynamic historical context where ideas and interests are not 'independent' but 'interdependent' variables (Adler 1991; Blyth 2002, p. 18; Steinmo 2003, p. 229). Hence, we can simultaneously explain the persistence and change of policies that govern the risks of financial integration by analyzing the historical evolution of the interaction between ideas and the context in which they are debated.[10]

The book therefore examines *how* the idea of *orderly liberalization*, which was developed inside the IMF within an economic context characterized by a dramatic increase in the size of cross-border capital flows, influenced the policy reforms for the world's financial stability in 1995; and *how* changes in the historical/economic context influenced the successive process of policy change in 1997. In particular, the empirical analysis traces the emergence of *orderly liberalization* within the Fund against the changes in the global economy in the early 1990s. With an increasing number of developing countries accessing and benefiting from global financial integration, the idea of *orderly liberalization* became persuasive among the Fund's membership and the private sector. Not even the 1994 Mexican financial crisis undermined the emerging consensus. Rather, the fact that capital flows to developing countries quickly returned to record levels and that the consequences of the crisis were contained led policy makers to institutionalize the idea of *orderly liberalization* by agreeing on the amendment to the Fund's Articles. When the global economy changed in 1997, however, following the Asian financial crisis, the persuasiveness of *orderly liberalization* declined. Liberalizing capital flows no longer proved beneficial and rewarding for member countries' economies, leading policy makers to back step on the amendment. In the changed economic environment, then, policy makers started regarding the IMF as a weak instrument to ensure global financial stability, favoring an approach based on the involvement of private-sector actors. A new intellectual consensus then emerged around the idea of *market-led liberalization* that posited that market actors could effectively contribute to the mitigation of risks related to the integration of world's financial markets. Similarly to what had happened after the Asian crisis, however, the new consensus unraveled following the subprime crisis, when policy makers around the world stopped supporting the view that markets are self-stabilizing forces and that existing policies based on the principles of market discipline, self- and light-touch regulation are able to ensure global financial stability.

Despite the focus on the interaction between ideas and the environment in which they are floated, this book offers more than a story about experiential learning. Indeed, the influence of the idea of *orderly liberalization* was not dissipated in light of accumulated knowledge and policy failure that led to falsification of theory within a community of experts. For instance, although the Mexican crisis revealed the risks of global financial integration, it was not interpreted as a policy failure that marked a reassessment of previously held ideas. Rather, the idea of *orderly liberalization* survived the crisis almost unscathed. The process of policy change is therefore more than the result of a process of knowledge accumulation governed by experts. It is the result of the interaction between technical as well as political actors.

What this book shows, therefore, is how important it is that policy ideas gain policy makers' acceptance about what works and what does not in economic policy. In other words, this book draws attention to *legitimacy feedbacks* as a mechanism through which ideas are influential over time. Indeed, what ultimately mattered for the ratification of the amendment in 1995 or for the adoption of the international financial standard initiative in 1998 was not that these reforms were in line with the economic interests of powerful members or with the accumulated knowledge of the IMF expert community. Rather, what mattered was that the policy ideas of *orderly* and *market-led liberalization* resonated with the larger political environment made up of member countries, the private sector and the community of academic economists that constitute the Fund's social constituencies for legitimation at the elite level (Seabrooke, 2007b). The *feedback* coming from these actors, expressed in the form of consent and opposition, was pivotal in shaping the trajectory of the reforms to the international financial architecture and of the role of the IMF in it. Until member countries, market actors, and academic economists legitimated the idea of *orderly* and *market-led liberalization* by publicly supporting the policies adopted on the basis of those ideas, policy change did not occur. When those actors, however, questioned the tenets of the idea of *orderly liberalization*, in the aftermath of the Asian crisis, and of the idea of *market-led liberalization*, in the aftermath of the subprime crisis, existing policies were rejected.

1.3   Why the evolutionary approach?

What are the advantages of reading the policies of the IMF in ensuring global financial stability through an evolutionary approach? The book aims to contribute to the international political economy (IPE) literature on policy change and on the inner workings of international organizations in three respects: (1) by specifying the influence of economic ideas at bringing about institutional change; (2) by specifying the mechanisms through which the ideas sponsored by IMF staff 'walk their way' into the IMF Executive Board; (3) by analyzing the changes in the international financial system. In what follows I elaborate on each point in turn.

First, the book investigates the trajectory of policy ideas with the aim of specifying the conditions under which those ideas are transformed into policies. In this connection, the book shifts attention away from the supply of ideas to their acceptance as the primary mechanism through which ideas can effectively be instantiated into policies. Furthermore, the case under investigation is interesting because it can be read as an example of failure of economic ideas at bringing about institutional change. Indeed, both the idea of *orderly* and *market-led liberalization* at a certain point stopped being influential. While the literature on policy change in international political economy has gone a long way towards specifying the actors and the mechanisms through which ideas successfully bring about institutional change (Berman, 1998; Blyth, 2002; Parsons, 2003; Seabrooke, 2007a), we still do not have a full picture of the conditions that allow ideas to be influential. Hence, investigating cases of ideational failures, such as the ones offered by the trajectories of the idea of *orderly* or *market-led liberalization*, may help specify what factors nullify the power of economic ideas and, vice versa, magnify it. Furthermore, by explicitly investigating a case of ideational failure, this study intends to address the criticism according to which the literature on norms is baised because of it has solely focused on successful case studies, i.e. on studies where ideas have'worked' (Legro, 1997, p. 34).

Along with the exploration of the influence of economic ideas and lack thereof, the book also engages with the evolution of ideas over time. In other words, the book investigates the two processes of policy and ideational change, attempting to fill in a gap in the literature that has been primarily concerned with proving the independent influence that ideas exert upon policy choices rather than with explaining how and why ideas evolve.[11] In particular, the book shows a pattern of ideational change, as exemplified by the shift from *orderly* to *market-led liberalization*, which does not fit with the acceptance-displacement pattern that many scholars employ to explain how ideas diffuse over time.[12] Indeed, this book shows that the idea of *market-led liberalization* that gained prominence in the late 1990s did not displace the previous idea of *orderly liberalization*. Rather, it developed from the previous one. That is to say, in evolutionary terms, each idea is the result of the institutionalization of a previous idea. So, the message that markets are stabilizing forces would not have got through without the policies giving the IMF the responsibility to govern the risks deriving from the free movement of private capital flows. As the shortcomings of an IMF-led system became increasingly apparent, they became a valuable reference point for a variety of actors to show that this type of international governance did not work. This paved the way for the emergence of a policy idea based on a different mechanism of stabilization than the one provided by the Fund: market discipline, self- and light-regulation.

The process of policy change within the IMF is also relevant to the literature on the influence of economic ideas because it investigates an arena – the one offered by the politics of an international organization – that has received comparatively less attention than other arenas. Indeed, while for the most part, IR (International Relations) and IPE scholarly works have investigated how ideas drive the process of policy change at the domestic (Berman, 1998; Blyth, 2002; Sikkink, 1991) and at the regional levels (McNamara, 1998), only recently have scholars turned their attention to IOs (International organizations) to study the influence of economic ideas on organizational behavior (Broome and Seabrooke, 2007,; Chwieroth, 2007; Park, 2005; Vetterlein, 2007; Weaver, 2008a).

Second, the book contributes to the literature on the inner workings of IOs by investigating the process of policy-making within the IMF. In particular, the book attempts to specify the mechanisms through which the ideas supplied by IMF staff 'walk their way' into the Executive Board thereby gaining a deeper understanding of IMF policy-making. In this respect, the book advances research on international organizations in general and on the IMF in particular by unveiling how staff's use of ambiguity may facilitate the formation of consensus among member countries. Indeed, while at the beginning of the 1990s IMF staff members displayed few doubts about the inevitability and desirability of liberalization, numerous ambiguities bedeviled the IMF-sponsored idea of *orderly liberalization*. For instance, despite the Fund's general advice to remove capital controls, the conditions for removal-reintroduction of capital controls were not clearly specified. Still, for all the talks about 'sound' macroeconomic policies that needed to be implemented before opening the capital account, the IMF provided members only with minimal operational guidance on the sequencing of policies. Finally, although the voice coming from the Fund preached the extension of the Fund's jurisdiction over capital flows, the implications of such an extension for the use of IMF resources were discussed without any definitive conclusion.

Rather than weakening IMF staff's favorable approach to capital account liberalization, the ambiguities in the IMF economic thinking were pivotal in forging consensus within the IMF membership. Specifically, these ambiguities played a constructive role in accommodating the different interests represented in the IMF Executive Board.[13] By bracketing the most contentious issues, the ambiguities in the idea of *orderly liberalization* made it respond to two sets of concerns. On the one hand, it spoke to the concerns of industrial countries, which wanted to consolidate and expand globalization across the globe. On the other, it resonated with the needs of developing countries, and in particular what came to be known as emerging market countries, which aspired to the levels of income and stability achieved by advanced economies. In other words, the ambiguities of the idea of *orderly liberalization* secured broad state support for the principle of the freedom of capital flows.[14]

Seen from this perspective, the ambiguities in the IMF's thinking are not theoretical anomalies but part and parcel of the process of consensus-building inside the IMF. Hence, the book contributes to the literature on IOs, drawing attention to the role that ambiguity plays as a source of the Fund's influence over its members. Not only does the IMF influence its members by providing knowledge that is technical and specialized (Barnett and Finnemore, 2004), IMF staff also strategically use ambiguous knowledge to facilitate coalitional alignment within the IMF Board, thereby influencing the policy decisions that Executive Directors take.

Finally, the last contribution of this book relates to debate on the reform to the international financial architecture. In other words, I use the IMF as a laboratory to get at some bigger questions on the changes that have taken place in the supervisory and regulatory management of the global financial system. Specifically, the book traces the evolution of the main challenges that the international community has confronted since the early 1990s with the progressive integration of the world's capital markets. In doing so, the book shows that whereas in the first half of the 1990s the main problem was that of locking in the process of financial integration, in the second half of the 1990s the focus shifted to the mechanisms of financial stability. This is not to say that ensuring financial stability was not a policy concern in the first half of the 1990s. Rather, the policies that strengthened the powers of the IMF were a direct response to those concerns. The point, however, is that in the reform efforts prior to the end of the 1990s, the international community tended to emphasize the benefits of greater access to international capital flows and to pay comparatively less attention to the potential risks of financial integration.

Furthermore, as the empirical sections will show, the reforms to the international financial architecture adopted since the early 1990s have never really questioned the assumption on the benefits of global financial integration. That is to say, the contestation to the idea of *orderly liberalization* and to the policies deriving from its application was mainly directed at the role of the IMF rather than at the benefits of financial integration. Finally, the book looks to the future, analyzing the impact of the 2007–8 crisis on the design of the international financial architecture. Specifically, the book attempts to assess whether the old intellectual consensus on how to govern the risks of a globalized financial system still holds or whether a new consensus is somehow emerging.

1.4   Structure of the book

The book is organized as follows. Chapter 2 begins by disputing existing explanations of IMF policies, developing the theoretical framework that guides the analysis. Specifically, I move beyond existing constructivist explanations that attribute the content of IMF policies to the policy ideas developed by its staff. I thereby develop the evolutionary framework, identifying the mechanisms through which policy ideas interact with the historical-economic context – i.e. legitimacy feedbacks – and through which the emergence of consensus within the IMF Board is facilitated – i.e. the use of ambiguity.

The central propositions of my theoretical model are tested from Chapter 3 to Chapter 6. Chapter 3 examines the idea of *orderly liberalization* that gained the interpretative upper hand within the IMF in the period from 1992 to 1997. Specifically, this chapter singles out the actors that sponsored the idea within the IMF and the idea's normative and procedural dimension. At the same time, the chapter shows how the idea of *orderly liberalization* was in line with the climate of economic opinion that prevailed among member countries, within the economics profession and the private sector.

Chapter 4 starts by describing the Mexican crisis that provided a crucial test for the emerging consensus around the policy idea of *orderly liberalization*. It then continues by detailing how IMF staff interpreted the crisis, supplying member countries a specific set of ideas to make sense of the Mexican events and to avoid future capital account crises. Reviewing the debate among Executive Directors through archival documents, this chapter traces how the mechanism of legitimation and the use of ambiguity helped the idea of *orderly liberalization* to be institutionalized into the IMF's policies. In this connection, the chapter reviews the policies pursued after the Mexican crisis to reform the IFA (International Financial Architecture) explaining them in light of the then-predominant set of ideas – i.e. *orderly liberalization* – and the acceptance of those ideas across the Fund's social constituencies for legitimation. In particular, the chapter explores the proposal to strengthen Fund surveillance, to increase its financial resources, and to amend the Articles of Agreement to grant the IMF mandate and jurisdiction over capital transactions.

Chapter 5 investigates the process through which the consensus around the idea of *orderly liberalization* unraveled. The focus is on the Asian crisis and on the contestation to the IMF that sparked in the aftermath of the crisis. Following the method used in Chapter 4, Chapter 5 starts by describing the crisis and the IMF's interpretation of it. The chapter continues by tracing the lack of positive feedback to the IMF-sponsored ideas as attested by the criticisms leveled at the IMF and at the idea of *orderly liberalization* in 1997–98. The chapter trace how the contestation across the Fund's social constituencies for legitimation led to the reversal of previously agreed policies, including the proposal to amend the Articles.

Chapter 6 shows how a new policy consensus developed from the experience of the Asian crisis. In particular, the chapter identifies the tenets of the policy idea of *market-led liberalization* and analyzes its institutionalization into the policies adopted in the late 1990s and early 2000s. The chapter also describes the progressive marginalization of the Fund in the international financial architecture and the creation of new international bodies (i.e. the G20 and the FSB) to supervise the risks of a global economy. The chapter then introduces the subprime crisis and the policy debate that followed it. Similarly to what had happened after the Asian crisis, the subprime crisis sparked a vigorous contestation of erstwhile policy ideas. The principles of market discipline and self- and light-regulation, which underlined the idea of *market-led liberalization*, were particularly contested, calling into question markets' ability to foster international financial stability. By reviewing the major long-term policies adopted in response to the crisis, the chapter traces the signs of a renewed positive feedback for the IMF. Specifically, the same actors that had discredited the role of the IMF in the aftermath of the crisis are now advocating for a strengthened role for the organization in the governance of the international financial system.

In the Conclusions, I elaborate on the findings of the book, bringing together the questions that guide this study. In particular, I explore the implications of my findings as far as concerns the influence of ideas on the policies meant to ensure global financial stability, the relationship between the IMF and member countries, and the role of the IMF in an era of globalized finance.

2
Evolutionary Policies: Economic Ideas and Legitimacy Feedback

This chapter develops the theoretical framework applied in the empirical analysis to explain the trajectory of the policies adopted to ensure global financial stability and, in particular, the policies that the IMF followed since the first half of the 1990s to the present. In brief, the theoretical framework attributes primary explanatory power to policy ideas in order to explain the content of the IMF's policies. An ideational explanation, however, requires specifying the mechanisms through which *a* policy idea becomes *the* idea – that is, it becomes the consensus around which policies are organized and are thereby maintained over time. Before identifying those mechanisms, however, it is important to confront an alternative explanation of IMF policies: the materialist explanation. According to this explanation, which comes in a structural- and in an agent-centered variant, the policies that the IMF pursues reflect the features of the international economic system and the attendant configuration of states' interests. Specifically, the materialist explanation predicts the content of IMF policies by mapping the changes in the global economy and by pointing to the interests of those countries that since the end of World War II have enjoyed the greatest economic power in the international economic system.

This chapter is organized as follows. In the next section, I critically review the materialist explanation in both its structural- and agent-centered variant. The second section turns to constructivist explanations of IMF policies. In particular, the section reviews the constructivist explanation according to which IMF policies reflect the intersubjective understandings developed within the Fund by IMF bureaucrats. After having identified the limitations of this second explanation, the chapter proceeds by delineating the tenets of my theoretical argument in the third section. In this section, I specify the terms of the evolutionary framework and the logics of the functioning of the legitimacy feedback mechanism. The next section focuses on the inner workings of the Fund and on the importance of ambiguity as a mechanism to facilitate the formation of consensus within the IMF Board. The final section provides an overview of the main documents used to carry out the empirical analysis.

2.1   The materialist explanation: Explaining IMF policies from the outside

The materialist explanation of the IMF's policies comes in two variants. The first focuses on the structural changes that take place in the international economic system, including changes such as the growing integration of world capital markets or the dislocations caused by financial crises. The second variant focuses on agents; specifically, it focuses on the configuration of economic interests among states. Despite their differences, both variants share a common point: the assumption that Fund policies are forced upon the organization 'from the outside.'

To start with, consider the structural materialist explanation. Following this explanation, we could explain the variation in IMF policies as a function of the different conditions that characterized the world economy during the 1990s and the early 2000s. An example of the application of the structural explanation can be found in the report prepared by the Independent Evaluation Office (IEO) that investigates the IMF's approach to capital account liberalization in the 1990s. Indeed, the IEO explains the rise-and-fall of the proposal to amend the Articles of Agreement as a function of the conditions of the global economy during the decade (IEO, 2005, pp. 24, 29).[15] The amendment was shaped by the structural changes in the international financial system that were taking place in the early 1990s, including financial innovation and deregulation in the industrial world and the renewed access to international capital markets for developing countries and transition economies. The severity of the Asian financial crisis and the following economic downturn, however, combined to undermine the IMF Board's support for the amendment in the second half of the 1990s. Following a similar line of reasoning, we could argue that the benign economic outlook of the early 2000s, characterized by sustained growth and low inflation, determined the marginalization of the role of the IMF as a guarantor of global financial stability.

This explanation has definitive value, but it also leaves many questions unresolved. Focusing on macro-changes in the global financial system, for instance, may be of help to infer the direction of policy change but it is indeterminate in terms of what policy actually gets through. In other words, growing financial integration certainly posed the question of how to update the Fund's responsibility over capital flows. However, specific choices, such as the decision to amend the Articles or the creation of new lending facilities, cannot be deduced from the integration of world financial markets. Policy makers could well have chosen other courses of action to make the IMF able to govern the risks posed by international capital flows – such as simply strengthening Fund surveillance. Similarly, economic shocks per se cannot account for the policy variation in the 1990s. The Asian crisis certainly hindered the proposal to amend the Articles; but it was a financial crisis, the Mexican crisis, which provided the backdrop to the amendment. Hence, although economic crises punctuated both the first and the second half of the decade, the result in terms of policies was different. If similar shocks produced such an institutional variation, the importance of interpreting material changes becomes all the more evident (Hay, 2001; Widmaier, et al., 2007). Reality does not speak for itself, but it is interpreted by human agency and sustained through interaction. Hence, we cannot say that it was the Mexican, the Asian, or the subprime crisis that caused the reform policies to the international financial architecture. It was what was perceived as the causes of the Mexican, the Asian, and the subprime crisis that caused a particular set of reforms aiming at avoiding future capital account crises.

Recognizing the indeterminacy of structural explanations, materialist scholarship has turned to a more agent-centered explanation. This explanation, which traces back to pluralist theories, conceives of policies as shaped by the competition that takes place among political groups with competing interests. The outcome of the decision-making process is here influenced by the distribution of resources among the competing groups. Hence, the policies that are more likely to be followed through are those supported by the most powerful groups – the more powerful the sponsor the more powerful the policy proposal.[16] For instance, explaining the expansion of the Fund's mandate to industrial and competition policies, Louis Pauly (1999) ascribes this mission expansion to the IMF's leading members and societies – where 'leading' stands for the US, the other industrialized countries and their corporations. In a similar vein, qualitative and quantitative studies have attempted to demonstrate that the content of the IMF's lending programs are significantly shaped by the United States' interests (Momani, 2004; Thacker, 1998). As Joseph Stiglitz (2002a, p. 24) has succinctly put it, 'IMF programs are typically dictated from Washington.' Applied to the case under investigation, the argument would be that the preferences of the US government determined the trajectory of the Fund's policies, from those that empowered the IMF in the first half of the 1990s to those that disempowered it in the late 1990s and to the policies that strengthened again the Fund's powers in the aftermath of the subprime crisis. An example of such an interest-driven argument is well-illustrated by the studies that have investigated the proposed amendment to the IMF's Articles to give the Fund mandate and jurisdiction over the liberalization of international capital flows.

Indeed, the hypothesis that underlines this materialist agent-centered explanation is that the amendment got through to the extent that it was backed from the outside by the powerful US Treasury-Wall Street complex (Bhagwati, 1998; Wade and Veneroso, 1998) and was ultimately dropped when the political sponsorship vanished. That is to say, the amendment was debated because the objective of international financial liberalization was 'high on the agenda of the United States' (Woods, 2006, p. 136).

At first glance, there seems to be much merit in this explanation. The proposal to amend the Articles, which would have empowered the IMF to ask member countries to remove capital controls, was supported by virtually all industrialized countries in general and the United States in particular. However, contrary to the expectations of the materialist explanation, the historical record does not lend significant support to the hypothesis that the US actively pushed for the amendment within the IMF Board. Rawi Abdelal (2007, ch. 6), for instance, has provided significant empirical evidence to dispute the argument that the initiative to amend the IMF's Articles was a US-led initiative. Rather, the amendment was an IMF management-led initiative. At the same time, the amendment was dropped although international capital mobility remained high on the agenda of industrial countries. Interestingly, then, the decision to amend the Articles was not openly opposed by developing countries. Rather, as the empirical analysis will show, there was a substantial convergence of views among the Executive Directors of both industrial and developing countries on the need to strengthen the powers of the IMF under conditions of financial globalization. It was only after 1997 that the representatives of developing countries manifested an interest in reducing the power of the IMF over capital flows.

These insights suggest that interests of the agents involved in the IMF's policy-making cannot be taken for granted. For instance, developing countries' interest in the amendment in the first half of the 1990s is puzzling if the interests of developing countries are assumed to be exogenous to the context of political interaction. Similarly, we cannot assume that the economic interest of the United States in the early 1990s was to forge a global norm of capital mobility via the IMF only because the United States enjoys considerable power in the international financial system and in the IMF Board through the weighted voting system. In general terms, the 'place where an agent sits' in the international system does not automatically tell us about its interests. As Wesley Widmaier (2007) has shown, for instance, independent central banks contribute to lowering inflation only if bankers define their interests in those terms. Hence, we need to unveil how agents define their interests in specific ways and not in others. In this respect, ideas play a pivotal role in helping agents define their interests, interpreting material events and suggesting specific institutional solutions (Blyth, 2002; Wendt, 1999).

In sum, structural explanations discount the power of human agency in interpreting the material world and disregard the question of how economic interests are defined. In doing so, these explanations offer at best an indeterminate account of the policies that the IMF followed from the early 1990s to the present with the aim of governing the risks of global financial integration. Specifically, these explanations may suggest the direction of policy change but they cannot explain why specific institutional choices are taken over others. Without specifying the ideas through which material conditions are interpreted and interests are defined, our understanding of institutional variation is much the poorer. The following section reviews the scholarship that has attempted such a specification.

2.2 The constructivist explanation: Explaining IMF policies from within

While materialist explanations explain IMF policies as being shaped 'from the outside,' constructivist explanations explain those policies 'from within.' Specifically, constructivist scholars attribute the content of the policies of an IO, including the IMF, to the ideas developed within the organization by its bureaucracy. Drawing on the epistemic community scholarship (Adler, 1992; Haas, 1992b), constructivists thereby argue that the staff's 'expert authority' influences the policies and activities of an IO. Michael Barnett and Martha Finnemore (2004, p. 47), for instance, have disputed the argument that the activities of an IO systematically reflect the preferences of its principals. Rather, their empirical analysis shows that there are 'many instances in which IOs develop their own ideas and pursue their own agenda.' While it is unlikely that the IMF initiates policies against the will of powerful member states, demonstrating that IMF staff possess some agency in shaping the content of the IMF's policies has been pivotal in further research on the policies that international organizations design and follow.

Building on these insights, scholars of all strands have attempted to trace the independent effect of the ideas developed inside an IO on the policies and activities that such an IO pursues. Combining principal-agent theory with constructivist insights, Daniel Nielson, Michael Tierney, and Catherine Weaver (2006), for instance, show that policy change within the World Bank is more likely to take place when it 'fits' with the existing organizational culture – i.e. when the ideas that are used to motivate policy change are 'adjacent' to the ideas already circulating within the IO. From a more constructivist vantage, André Broome and Leonard Seabrooke (2007) have shown that what the 'IMF sees' as the functioning of the economy shapes its advice for institutional change to member countries.

Applying these insights to the case under investigation, the argument would be that the policies that member countries adopted in the aftermath of the Mexican crisis, the Asian crisis, as well as the policies that are emerging in the aftermath of the subprime crisis, resulted from the ideas developed by IMF economists about how to promote financial liberalization while ensuring systemic stability. In other words, explaining the reforms to the international financial architecture requires tracing the development of the economic ideas developed by staff members. Several studies on the proposed amendment to the IMF's Articles have used this staff-centered explanation.

For instance, some scholars have noted that the amendment to the IMF's Articles of Agreement reflected the ideas held by a group of IMF officials that took on the mission to promote capital account liberalization even in the absence of a clear mandate from its principals. The Managing Director Michel Camdessus and his close associates, including the First Deputy Managing Director Stanley Fischer, were pivotal agents in putting the IMF front and center in the management of global capital flows (Abdelal, 2007, ch. 6). Using quantitative methods to demonstrate the power of ideas in prompting change inside the Fund, Jeffrey Chwieroth (2007) has demonstrated that the massive recruitment of IMF staff trained in 'neoliberal' departments during the 1980s provided the basis for the IMF staff to advance the proposal to amend the Articles. Indeed, individuals trained in those departments held key positions in the IMF bureaucracy.

Although this bureaucratic explanation deserves credit for having unveiled the role of agency in shaping policy outcomes within the IMF, it still does not provide a satisfactory explanation of the variation in the IMF's policies. Consider, for instance, the failure of the initiative to amend the Articles of Agreement. When the amendment was finally abandoned, there was no change of mind in the advocates of the amendment inside the Fund – Camdessus and Fischer, among others – and no significant turnover of IMF staff when the amendment was finally abandoned. Still, the opinion of IMF staff was probably influential in the aftermath of the Mexican crisis but it was marginalized after Asian crisis.

Furthermore, this bureaucratic explanation seems at pains to explain how the ideas advocated by the staff are embraced by the Executive Directors sitting in the Executive Board. That is to say, the focus on the Fund's bureaucratic culture offers a limited account of the IMF's policy-making process because it does not cast light on the ways through which experts' ideas 'make the trip...to the minds of political actors' (Haas, 1990, p. 20). This lacuna has sometimes been presented as a deliberate research goal with some constructivist scholars claiming to be solely interested in the Fund's 'informal' approach to capital account liberalization, that is, in 'the ideas the IMF staff share,' rather than in 'the official policies or rules governing the IMF' (Chwieroth, 2007, p. 14).

Rather than a deliberate research goal, however, a bureaucratic explanation that solely focuses on a single community of actors (IMF staff) as the only relevant agent that shapes the IMF's policies does not do justice to the way in which the IMF actually works. In other words, the bureaucratic explanation seems largely ignorant of the fact that the IMF is an intergovernmental organization, that is, an organization made by states to solve states' economic problems and which draws its legitimacy from states. It seems that this explanation has underestimated the role of Fund's membership in shaping and constraining the content of the IMF's policies. Without membership sanction and validation of its activities, the IMF could hardly be the influential organization that it has become over the decades. The Fund's advice on fiscal or structural adjustment, for instance, could hardly have been influential on member countries' economic policy choices had members not recognized the Fund's rightness and responsibility in promoting 'sound' policies. In what follows, I thereby suggest an evolutionary approach that brings to the surface the thus far neglected element of social legitimation.

2.3 An evolutionary theoretical framework for the IMF's policies

The theoretical framework developed here builds from the bureaucratic explanation because it takes as its starting point the ideas developed by IMF staff. However, the framework departs from the bureaucratic explanation because of its dynamic perspective and its focus on the actors that accept rather than supply economic ideas. Specifically, the theoretical framework developed here builds on two assumptions. The first builds on the view that ideas are 'contested and contingent' (Katzenstein, 1996, p. 3). The second assumption draws on the argument that the influence of an economic idea is inherently relational.

The first assumption suggests that ideas do not appear in a vacuum but are embedded in a political-economic environment in which they are debated and checked against existing empirical evidence. As a result, ideas are neither fixed nor fully formed but subject to evolution. Since the 'ecology' where ideas are floated changes over time, old ideas have to be adapted to continue influencing policy. In this connection, the policy ideas that are the primary object of this book's analysis can be conceived as 'problem solutions,' that is to say, 'a kind of rational probabilistic calculation linking problems with potential solutions' (Steinmo, 2003, p. 229). In other words, ideas evolve by best guesses and by trial and error. If one economic strategy fails, policy makers try another. If it works, policy makers stick with it. Take, for instance, the ideas on economic development embodied in the Washington consensus. Indeed, following major changes in the global economy and in light of several failures in the development doctrine, these ideas have evolved over time from a narrow conception of economic development to a broader notion of development that includes social and institutional factors (Park and Vetterlein, forthcoming).[17]

Given the possibility of ideational evolution, it is necessary to recognize that even the sponsors of an idea can change over time. For instance, IMF staff members were the sponsors of the idea of *orderly liberalization* in the first half of the 1990s. As the idea was transformed into that of *market-led liberalization*, however, sponsorship shifted to regulatory and private-sector circles

The second assumption suggests that the influence of ideas does not only vary over time but also across actors. As Peter Hall (1989, pp. 369–70) put it, 'the persuasiveness of economic ideas depends, in part at least, on the way those ideas relate to the economic and political problems of the day.' This is not to say that existing interests instruct policy makers about what ideas can be accepted. Indeed, once an idea has been accepted and thereby it is institutionalized into specific policies, the idea in question changes the institutional setting in which policy is made, forcing actors to confront it. Hence, ideas persist over time and are thereby influential to the extent that they are endorsed by the actors whose everyday practices help legitimate or discard existing institutions. In other words, the collective views that actors hold about the IMF itself are central to the activities of the Fund (Broome, 2008, forthcoming).

Ideas thereby persist over time and influence policy to the extent that the actors affected by them recognize their legitimacy by providing support. It is therefore necessary to define the concept of legitimacy and the identity of the actors whose support is necessary for legitimacy to be in place.

Legitimacy feedback

The concept of legitimacy used here differs from the traditional concept of legitimacy used in political science to identify the 'Westminster model' of democracy. Specifically, I am not going to use the notion of legitimacy to provide insights into the democratic credentials of the IMF addressing questions of representation, political involvement, and participation in the decision-making process.[18] If the traditional notion of legitimacy may be defined as institutional legitimacy, the concept of legitimacy used here may be better defined as relational legitimacy. That is to say, legitimacy is not a property of the IMF political system that can be gained through institutional reforms, such as decision-making and governance reforms. Rather, legitimacy is an intersubjective belief in the validity of an idea (Weber, 1978) and it is thereby 'dependent on a collective audience' (Suchman, 1995, p. 594). It follows that legitimacy is actively given by public support that derives from how the actors affected by IMF policies evaluate them. The output of the evaluation of IMF policies, then, is not simply the result of a calculation of interests – where actors support IMF policies because the latter accrue actors' interests. The relationship between the IMF and the actors that grant it legitimacy is more profound. Not only is support based on the evaluation of whether the policy benefits an actor but also on the judgment of whether the policy is the right and appropriate thing to do. Indeed, actors rarely follow policies that they do not believe in themselves.

These observations lead us to investigate the identity of the actors that grant legitimacy to the IMF and that can initiate and stop the process of policy change. For the purpose of this book, the relevant actors that form the Fund's social constituencies for legitimation, or the organization's 'authorizing and task environments' (Weaver 2008a), include state representatives, economists, and private actors such as international investors. In other words, although the Fund's constituencies may well include non-elite actors such as citizens affected by IMF policies (Edwards, 2009; Seabrooke, 2007b; Thirkell-White, 2004), the focus of this study is narrowed down to elites. Specifically, I identify three constituencies that can legitimate the Fund's policies to ensure international financial stability: the legal, the technical, and the operational constituencies.

The first constituency is made up of member states and is defined as legal to indicate the formal relationship between the organization and its principals as defined in the Articles of Agreement. Indeed, although the IMF enjoys a high degree of autonomy in its day-to-day operations, ultimately it is an intergovernmental organization. That is to say, the role that the IMF plays in the international financial system depends on member countries' willingness to delegate specific powers to the Fund. Consider the proposal to amend the Articles to give the Fund the powers to promote liberalization while overseeing systemic risks. Indeed, extending Fund jurisdiction to capital movements entailed a new obligation for member states. Whereas under the present Articles, member countries have the right to introduce controls at their will, an amended Article VIII would have imposed an obligation on each member to remove controls. Hence, absent member countries' willingness to accept the Fund's jurisdiction, the extension of the Fund's powers to the realm of financial liberalization would have been unlikely. In other words, countries' resistance to the IMF's activities, in the form of both formal opposition during the negotiations or refusal to accept the IMF's approach in the conduct of domestic monetary policy, would have undermined the process of policy change.

The second constituency is made up of academic economists and the economics profession at large. This constituency is particularly relevant to the IMF's activities because of the close links between IMF staff members and the profession. As has been widely recognized, IMF staff members are primarily recruited from the economics profession and their educational background significantly shapes the organization's policies (Barnett and Finnemore, 2004, ch. 3; Momani, 2005b). For instance, it has been noted that the common background of IMF staff members shapes the Fund's bureaucratic culture that, in turn, influences how the Fund builds its relationship with borrowing countries (Momani, 2007). Furthermore, several studies have shown that the IMF is more inclined to accept the criticisms 'framed' in the language of economics than to accept the criticisms that are not presented with an economic logic (Moschella and Seabrooke, 2008; Vetterlein, 2008). In other words, IMF economists seem to crave the technical legitimacy that derives from the respect that the economics profession attributes to the Fund. Hence, it is plausible to expect that the acceptance/resistance of the economics profession to what the IMF does in the area of financial integration and its governance strongly reverberates around the debate about what policies the IMF can effectively carry through.

Finally, the operational constituency is made up of private-market actors. These actors are relevant to what the IMF does to the extent that they can amplify or undermine the Fund's efforts. For instance, it is widely recognized that market actors endorse IMF activities when they acknowledge that the Fund's financial assistance to a member country is of help in restoring the conditions for fruitful investments. In this event, the IMF is regarded as playing a signaling effect to private actors catalyzing private investments (Marchesi and Thomas, 1999; Tirole, 2002). At the same time, however, market actors may also nullify the effectiveness of the IMF's policies. For instance, Layna Mosley (2003) has shown that the limited involvement of private actors with the IMF-sponsored Special Data Dissemination Standard (SDDS) has undermined the success of the process of international data standardization. Hence, similarly to what has been argued for the other two constituencies, it is plausible to expect that the private sector's support/opposition to the IMF's policies influence the likelihood of the persistence of those policies.

Building on the importance of social acceptance to the persistence of the policies that the IMF pursues, the change in the IMF's policies can be conceived as the result of the interruption of such an acceptance. That is to say, policy change is correlated with the size of the gap between the institutionalization of specific economic ideas into the Fund's policies and the acceptance of those policies by the actors of its social constituencies for legitimation (Seabrooke, 2007b, p. 258). Whereas during the first half of the 1990s, the IMF's policies were largely accepted by member countries, academic economists, and the private sector, at the end of 1997 acceptance gave way to contestation and to a crisis of legitimacy for the IMF. Arising from this, new ideas about the governance of the international financial system gained dominance across the Fund's constituencies, influencing the economic reforms of the late 1990s and early 2000s. The eruption of the subprime crisis has once again reopened the gap between existing ideas and their acceptance leading to a thorough debate on policy change in the international financial architecture.

In spite of the close relationship between ideas and their acceptance by particular social groups, what this book argues and illustrates, however, is that economic ideas are influential beyond their ability to relate to the interests of the time. Specifically, the ideas are influential in that they raise new expectations that provide the foundations for old ideas to be dismissed and for its sponsor to be trapped into its own rhetoric when expectations are disappointed. That is to say, ideas alter the environment in which policy is made, forcing the actors involved in the policy-making to confront those ideas. For instance, the idea of *orderly liberalization* raised expectations across the Fund's constituencies about the positive effects of the free movement of international capital flows on domestic economic growth and about the role of the IMF in ensuring that liberalization was not disruptive of domestic prosperity. Likewise, the idea of *market-led liberalization* set a new standard against which to assess reality, by raising the expectation that market discipline could provide global financial stability. These expectations, however, were severely disappointed in the aftermath of the Asian crisis and the subprime crisis. For one thing, the policies that had empowered the IMF in 1995 suddenly looked unable to preserve stability in light of the dislocations caused by the 1997 Asian crisis. For another, the early 2000s policies that gave market actors a primary role in ensuring stability looked to be a one-off success in the aftermath of the subprime crisis. Building on the disappointment of expectations in 1997–98 as well as in 2007–8, contestation was sparked, setting the stage for future policy developments.

In sum, different policy ideas about how to govern the risks of financial integration were institutionalized and thereby persisted over time not because they were supported by the most powerful countries or backed by a unified epistemic community like the one made up of IMF economists. It is one thing to have a strong ideational consensus within a group of countries (such as the G7) or within a technical community (such as the IMF staff community); it is another to get others to buy into it. Therefore, theoretical considerations should be given to the actors whose actions and agreement are crucial for the persistence of existing policies. Ideas were consequential because the policies that they suggested were accepted in the political environment in which they were floated. In other words, member countries, academic economists, and private actors provided a legitimacy feedback to existing policies that, in turn, embodied 'an ideational consensus about the shared goals and values that are to be promoted' (Cottrell, 2009, p. 242).

The comparison between the Mexican and the Asian crisis well illustrates the importance of feedback from member countries, academic economists, and the private sector in shaping IMF policies. Indeed, although the Mexican crisis was a crisis characterized by a sharp reversal of international capital flows, it did not unleash a backlash against the idea of *orderly liberalization* neither within nor outside the Fund. The evidence drawn from the crisis probably falsified the theory in favor of global capital integration as some economists pointed out (Krugman, 1995), but it did not discard its social legitimacy. After the Asian crisis, however, the idea of *orderly liberalization* was profoundly challenged outside the Fund. While IMF economists continued to interpret the crisis as a traditional currency crisis, the IMF faced a variety of criticisms for its management of what came to be identified as a capital crisis. In an attempt to respond to the criticisms coming from member countries, academic economists, and the private sector, the Executive Board started reconsidering the IMF's position on capital account liberalization. In other words, in contrast to the Mexican crisis, the Asian crisis did not simply falsify the theory of *orderly liberalization*. It also triggered a crisis of legitimacy that undermined the consensus around the idea of *orderly liberalization*. Likewise, the subprime crisis can be considered to be a crisis of legitimacy. Other crises have preceded it, such as the one in Argentina or in Turkey, but they did not unleash any calls for change in the policies for crisis prevention and management. What changed in 2007–8, however, was the emergence of a public disappointment for the role of markets as a mechanism to govern financial risk.

2.4 Beyond the legitimacy feedback: Ambiguity and the inner workings of the Fund

Although the main theoretical argument of this book relates to the relationship between economic ideas and the policies to ensure global financial stability, the book also advances some suggestions about the inner workings of the IMF. That is to say, the book investigates the policy-making within the Fund by identifying the mechanisms that facilitate the formation of consensus among member states. Specifically, the book draws attention to the role that ambiguity plays as a means of influence that IMF staff members use over member countries in the decision-making process.

Indeed, although it is usually claimed that the IMF's policies are 'dictated from Washington' (Stiglitz, 2002a, p. 24), historical evidence and empirical studies reveal that the pressures of powerful countries are not always critical in shaping what the IMF does. Rather, member countries often rely on IMF staff expertise and advice. Barnett and Finnemore (2004, p. 47), for instance, found that 'the creation of most...forms of conditionality can be traced to the IMF staff and the intellectual equipment they use,' rather than to the pressures of powerful states. Similarly, Catherine Weaver (2008b) has shown that the introduction of gender issues in the development agenda of the World Bank is largely attributed to internal advocates rather than to preferences of member states.

Hence, IMF staff are policy entrepreneurs that elaborate new ideas and promote their ideas, trying to shape other actors' interests in ways that reflect their normative commitments (Finnemore and Sikkink, 1998, p. 910). As Jack Levy (1994, pp. 283–84) has pointed out, policy entrepreneurs actively interact with the ideas they hold in three respects. First, they use their ideas to 'interpret historical experience.' Second, they 'test' their ideas, through 'experimentation.' Finally, policy entrepreneurs 'make great efforts to influence how others interpret experience.' As a result, policy entrepreneurs 'promote their ideas and try to build internal coalitions around them, and through their statements and actions they try to influence how they are perceived by external adversaries.' In other words, policy-advocates engage in persuasive battles (Finnemore and Sikkink, 1998, pp. 895–97; Widmaier, et al., 2007) during which they frame their ideas in such a way to win support. The opportunity for policy entrepreneurs to engage in such persuasive battles increases under conditions of uncertainty, such as the ones following an economic crisis (Blyth, 2002; Campbell, 2004; Culpepper, 2008).

As several studies have shown, IMF staff and management have often played the role of policy entrepreneurs within the IMF by supplying distinct set of ideas on how the economy works to member countries (Abdelal, 2007, Chwieroth, 2007, Leiteritz, 2005).[19] As an epistemic community, IMF staff and management have contributed to the Fund's policy-making, 'articulating the cause-and-effect relationships of complex problems, helping states identify their interests, framing the issues for collective debate, proposing specific policies, and identifying salient points for negotiation' (Haas, 1992a, p. 2). In the case under investigation, for instance, IMF staff supplied the idea of *orderly liberalization* that articulated the positive relationship between capital liberalization and economic growth and between the role of the IMF and the process of liberalization. Drawing on their analytical assumptions, IMF staff also proposed a specific set of policies to cope with the problem of financial integration, including strengthening the powers of the IMF through an amendment to its Articles of Agreement.

Furthermore, given the IMF's heterogeneous membership, composed of industrial and developing countries, the way in which policy entrepreneurs communicate their ideas, or 'speak to power' (Weaver, 2008b), is critical to explain the outcome of the IMF decision-making process. Specifically, the way in which staff members frame the problem at stake and its solution may well affect the negotiations by helping member countries overcome their conflicting interests.

In this connection, ambiguity plays a crucial role. Indeed, ambiguity helps evacuate political conflict from the negotiations by deferring the decision on the most controversial issues to an undefined stage of the negotiations thereby helping member countries converge around general principles. Specifically, policy entrepreneurs exploit the ideational ambiguities embedded in their ideas to defer the debate on the most controversial issues, thereby avoiding exacerbating the divide among competing interests. That is to say, leaving important questions ambiguous, policy entrepreneurs, such as IMF staff members, neutralize political divisions, casting the debate in a win-win fashion for the actors involved. Hence, ideas are cast with a 'crossover appeal' to the negotiating parties (Culpepper, 2008). In the case under investigation, IMF staff championed the idea of *orderly liberalization*, battling for its institutionalization in an amendment to the IMF's Articles of Agreement. This institutional solution, however, remained ambiguous in its operational implications for member countries. In particular, IMF staff did not specify what would have happened had the Fund helped a member face large capital flight. Similarly, it was not specified what criteria the Fund would have applied to approve the use of capital controls had the amendment won support within the Board.

Interestingly, however, the ambiguities in the Fund thinking did not undermine but strengthened the influence of the staff over the negotiations to amend the Articles. Leaving important questions unresolved, IMF staff neutralized the political implications of the decision to institutionalize the principle of capital mobility in the Fund's Articles. Without resolving its ambiguities, the idea of *orderly liberalization* thereby seemed to benefit different interests at the same time. In contrast, when the Board asked the staff to clarify those ambiguities in the aftermath of the Asian crisis, the political cleavages between industrial and developing countries was brought to the surface, making consensus hard to reach. Borrowing from Jacqueline Best's (2005, p. 3) typology of ambiguity in global finance, it is possible to say that the ambiguity in the IMF's thinking is not simply the product of insufficient empirical evidence, that is, an ambiguity produced by 'problems of information.' Rather, ambiguity in the IMF is deeply rooted in the organization's political economy. It is inherently political and plays a constructive role in helping to forge consensus within the IMF Board.

In sum, the book will show that the consensus within the Board in the first half of the 1990s was reached through successful persuasive struggles rather than powerful interests. The consensus within the Board around specific policies was the product of an active agent-driven process shaped by the actors through which and on which ideas operate (Berman, 1998, p. 22). Agents frame and manipulate their ideas to mobilize support around them and to facilitate coalitional alignments (Blyth, 2002; Weir, 1992). Hence, whereas several studies on the IMF and its approach to capital account liberalization have already brought to the surface the distinct role played by IMF staff and management in elaborating the IMF's 1990s policies (Abdelal, 2007; Chwieroth, 2007; Leiteritz, 2005), this book contributes to the literature on the Fund's inner workings by specifying the mechanism through which IMF staff make their preferred ideas acceptable to Executive Directors.

Indeed, the book builds on the assumption that when we talk about 'the IMF's policies' the appropriate empirical reference is not the position of individual staff members, no matter how influential they are. The policies of the IMF are the outcome of the meetings of the Executive Board. Without specifying the mechanisms through which Executive Directors adopt the ideas advocated by the staff, our understanding of the inner workings of the Fund is much the poorer.

2.5   Methodological notes

In order to ascertain the influence of economic ideas on the policies adopted to ensure global financial stability, and in order to trace the impact that ambiguity exerted on the Fund's decision-making process, data are drawn from different sources. These include IMF archival and public documents, interviews with relevant participants in IMF policy-making, and secondary sources such as official communiqués and private-sector reports.

First, the empirical analysis largely relies on sources available in the IMF archives.[20] Some documents – the minutes of the Executive Board (EBM) and the staff memoranda (SM) – are particularly relevant to this study. The minutes of the Executive Board, for instance, help cast light on the position of individual IMF members. Indeed, EBMs provide the statements delivered by each Executive Director during internal consultations and negotiations. The analysis chiefly focuses on particular meetings of the Executive Board, that is to say, those meetings convened to discuss the implications of global financial integration for global stability. In this connection, the book devotes attention to the analysis of the Board meetings during which issues related to the international financial system at large were discussed – including the EBMs during which the World Economic Outlook (WEO) and the Global Financial Stability Report (GFSR) were discussed.[21] Still, the analysis is built on the analysis of the Executive Board meetings during which specific policies to govern the risks of global financial integration were assessed, including the meetings convened to discuss the amendment to the Articles of Agreement from 1995 to 1998.

Staff memoranda (SM) are another important set of archival documents on which I concentrated. These documents are staff papers prepared as background material to the Executive Board meetings. Given their content, the analysis of staff memoranda helps trace the features of IMF staff economic thinking on specific issues. Staff memoranda are also an important source of information because they help detail what John Maynard Keyes would have called the 'climate of economic opinion' prevalent among economists. Indeed, these documents usually include a literature review of the main academic theoretical and empirical studies on the problem under discussion within the Board. Still, an important set of empirical data comes from IMF public documents, which are usually available on the IMF website. These documents include IMF Working Papers, Staff Papers, Occasional Papers, and the speeches of IMF staff members. It is worth noting some differences among these documents. IMF Working Papers are technical papers produced by IMF staff members and visiting scholars. According to their usual disclaimer, the views expressed in these Working Papers are those of the author(s) and do not necessarily represent those of the IMF or IMF policy. Occasional Papers, in contrast, are more department-driven and may well be considered as a valid indicator of the IMF prevalent stance on a specific economic issue. Staff papers, then, are usually written by senior staff officials thereby offering interesting insights on the organization's thinking over a medium-term period.

Second, to track the evolution of IMF ideas on international financial liberalization and their influence on policy outcomes, I conducted interviews with key IMF staff officials, Executive Directors, economists, and people operating in the private sector (a list of interviewees is provided in the Annex). Individual in-depth interviews were carried out between 2006 and 2007, in Washington, DC.

Finally, secondary sources are also used to corroborate the findings. For instance, I undertook a broad search of the major financial newspapers from 1992 to 2002.[22] The analysis of the G7-G24-G20 communiqué as well as the reports prepared by the global association of international banks (the Institute of International Finance, IIF) also contribute to the narrative developed in the following chapters.

Building on these resources, in what follows, the book traces the process through which IMF staff elaborated a specific set of ideas on what international financial liberalization is and on what policies should be pursued to govern its risks. It is then showed how IMF staff, acting on those ideas, engaged in a persuasive battle to redefine the interests of member countries sitting in the Executive Board, thereby leading them to adopt certain institutional solutions and not others. Finally, the analysis shows how the staff lost the persuasive battle, setting the stage for the ideational shift to occur and for the attendant transformation of the policies to ensure global financial stability.

3
The 1990s Consensus on International Financial Integration

This chapter traces the emergence of the idea of *orderly liberalization* inside the International Monetary Fund. Specifically, the chapter is organized as follows. The first section reviews the material and ideational changes that were taking place in the early 1990s in the global financial system. The increasing volume of international capital flows and the emergence of the Washington consensus are the two changes upon which the analysis chiefly focuses. The second section looks within the IMF, identifying the tenets of the idea of *orderly liberalization* and the actors that helped to forge it. The third section moves the focus outside the IMF to the Fund's social constituencies for legitimation, bringing to the surface the expectations of industrial, developing countries, and private-sector actors on capital account liberalization. The fourth section reviews one of the first debates to reform the international financial architecture, namely the one that took place in 1994 within the framework of the fiftieth anniversary of the Bretton Woods institutions. This section shows how IMF management and staff started engaging in a persuasive battle to win the support of IMF state representatives thereby transforming their ideas into a specific agenda of reforms for the IMF – an agenda that included an amendment to the IMF's Articles of Agreement. In other words, the ideas supplied by IMF staff set the boundaries on the institutional choices that member countries could pursue to manage the risks deriving from the increasing volume of cross-border capital flows.

3.1 The international economic system in the early 1990s

During the first half of the 1990s, both economic and political events in developing countries defied all expectations. Nations that most thought would not regain access to world financial markets for a generation abruptly became favorites of private investors, who plied them with capital inflows on a scale not seen since before World War I. Governments that had spent half a century pursuing statist, protectionist policies suddenly got free market religion. It was, it seemed to many observers, the dawn of a new golden age for global capitalism. (Krugman, 1995, p. 28)

In this short observation, Paul Krugman nicely captures the most distinctive features of the international economic system in the early 1990s: the revival of substantial capital flows to developing countries, which had suffered a severe blow from the 1980 debt crisis, and the intellectual climate favoring global economic integration. The material and ideational dimension of the phenomenon of financial globalization were shaping the world of the 1990s.[23] These changes appeared the most remarkable when viewed in comparison with prior trends. While during the 1970s the system witnessed a revival of global financial integration, the 1980s, in contrast, marked a serious setback in the process of further integration.

During the period 1973–82, the liquidity generated by highoil prices, so-called petrodollars, pushed capital to flow downhill from capital-rich creditors, such as the oil-exporting countries, into capital-scarce borrowers – Latin American countries in particular. Largely intermediated by the activities of commercial banks, these flows linked together many countries across the globe. Low global interest rates and the belief that 'governments never go bust,' as Citibank's CEO Walter Wriston is reputed having said, initiated the spiral of developing countries' indebtedness and international banks' exposure to financial risks.[24]

In 1982, Mexican default on its sovereign debt nonetheless highlighted the fragility of global financial integration. The rise of global interest rates, accompanied by poor domestic macroeconomic management, severely strained Mexico's capacity to service its foreign debt.[25] Unable to meet its international obligations, national authorities declared default. For their part, international banks, in particular US banks, quickly reassessed their portfolios, refusing to roll over outstanding loans to Mexico and to many other developing countries, causing massive capital flight and a string of bankruptcies that put the entire global financial system at risk. Indeed, the events in Mexico initiated an escalating crisis that deeply affected Latin America, and many other developing countries, for almost a decade. One of the hallmarks of the crisis was the rapid turnaround of capital flows. Average annual net capital inflows to developing countries as a group fell sharply from around $30 billion in the period 1977–82 to less than $9 billion in 1983–89 (IMF, 1994b, p. 48) wiping out the extent of financial integration achieved previously. In the group of developing countries, Latin American countries experienced the sharpest shift in market sentiment: flows turned negative and their composition changed dramatically with official flows replacing private flows.[26] At the beginning of the 1990s, however, the signs of major changes in international capital markets began to surface.

New patterns in international capital markets

When the decade began, important economic developments in both industrial and developing countries provided the conditions for a revival of global financial integration. Across the industrialized world, developments in domestic financial markets boosted the trend toward globalization. Financial deregulation and the removal of capital controls on cross-border capital transactions, measures that had been adopted in virtually all industrial countries, resulted in greater competition and increased capital mobility.[27] Sluggish rates of growth and low interest rates significantly influenced the direction of capital flows, which returned to developing countries.[28] Low interest rates, which diminish the attractiveness of investing at home, pushed investors to put their money into high-yielding assets, such as developing countries' securities. Emerging markets rapidly became a 'respectable asset class' (IMF, 1995a, p. 4).

Across the developing world, the economic performance of these countries was as much a crucial factor as the level of interest rates to appreciate the new patterns in international capital markets. For instance, the success of macroeconomic stabilization and structural adjustment programs was of utmost importance.[29] With inflation under control and with trade and financial liberalization well under way, developing countries created an investor-prone environment that increased opportunities for investments and lowered the perception of country risk. Considerable progress in reducing external debt burdens also contributed to the revival of large capital inflows to numerous developing countries.

Against this background, the renewed confidence of international investors in the economic outlook for many developing countries translated into a dramatic increase in private capital flows. As a result, while in 1983–89 the total net capital flows to developing countries as a group was less than $9 billion, in 1990–94 capital flows rocketed to around $105 billion, with a peak of $155 billion in 1993 – a nearly fourfold increase over the previous five-year period (IMF, 1995a, pp. 33–4). Disaggregating the data, both foreign direct investments and portfolio investments grew sharply during the period 1990–94, with a marked increase for the latter.[30]

Focusing on the experience of specific regions, Latin America attracted record foreign inflows, shifting from a cumulative net capital *outflow* of $116 during 1983–89 to a cumulative net *inflow* of $200 billion during 1990–94.[31] According to the IMF International Capital Markets Report (IMF, 1995a, pp. 2, 36), 'the most surprising turnaround was in Mexico,' which quickly became the 'benchmark' for other middle-income countries' performance.[32] In a single year, 1993, Mexico received $31 billion of capital inflows, which amounted to 45 percent of the total inflows to Latin America, 8 percent of its GDP. Mexico was followed suit by Argentina, Brazil, and Chile. Outside the Western hemisphere, Korea, Malaysia, the Philippines, Thailand, and Turkey also recorded capital inflows well above the 1983–89 averages (IMF, 1995a, pp. 110–11).

High-capital-inflow countries experienced a rate of growth remarkably high for most of the period from 1990 to 1994. Of course, there were marked differences across groups of countries and among countries. With regard to largest recipient regions, in Asia, the rate of growth was sustained at over 5 percent of GDP.[33] Domestic investments were relatively high, as reflected in the increasing ratio of private investment to GDP. Korea approached full employment in 1994. Strong growth was also projected in the Philippines, Indonesia, and Thailand. Growth, in contrast, was somehow moderated in the group of Latin American countries, indicating that a large part of capital inflows was absorbed in consumption rather than in investments.[34] Nevertheless, investment ratios in Argentina, Chile, and Mexico, the largest recipients of capital inflows in Latin America, rose consistently during the period (IMF, 1994b, pp. 24–5, 57–61).

The increased size of cross-border capital flows to developing countries was accompanied by a change in their composition. According to the data of the World Economic Outlook (IMF, 1994b, pp. 48–61), the 1990–94 flows differed markedly from the 1977–82 flows in that they had been in the form of non-debt-creating flows, such as foreign direct investment and acquisition of equity in emerging stock markets. In particular, although international bond issues became the main source of external funding for developing countries, rocketing from $6.3 billion in 1990 to around $59 billion in 1993 (IMF, 1995a, p. 35), international equities by developing-country companies and direct purchases of securities in developing-country domestic markets provided a substantial source of funding (IMF, 1995a, pp. 37–40). 'Not since the opening decades of the twentieth century have private portfolio capital inflows been such a significant source of financing for developing countries,' Michel Camdessus (1995e), IMF Managing Director, emphatically commented. As a growing amount of funds were placed in the bonds and stocks of developing countries, the new term *emerging markets* entered the lexicon of global investors (IMF, 1995a, p. 33).

The identity of global investors, in turn, underwent a profound change, following a process known as *disintermediation* that led institutional investors to contend banks' primary role in international financial markets. That is to say, pension funds, hedge funds, and insurance companies challenged banks' primacy in their domestic and international activities. As of 1994, for instance, mutual funds administered by institutional investors contained $2 trillion in assets – an amount not much less than the $2.7 trillion held in US bank deposits.[35] Institutional investors also started expanding on a global scale. Mutual funds dedicated to investment in developing countries' securities, for instance, grew rapidly. In an attempt to diversify their portfolio and to raise their profits, institutional investors placed their money in those countries that had just liberalized their economies, opened to foreign investors and offered high interest rates, thereby making investments the most appealing. US and UK institutional investors led the process, showing interest in the securities of developing countries in Asia and in Latin America through the use of 'emerging markets mutual funds'[36] (IMF, 1995a, p. 41).

As of 1994, investors made a strong commitment to international diversification. Financial experts recommended allocating a significant amount of investments in foreign assets, which appeared particularly profitable. 'It's been stupendous,' John Collins, a spokesman for the Investment Company Institute, the mutual fund trade association, said in 1993. 'International funds grew twice as fast as all funds.'[37] The concentration of individual investment decisions in the hands of a small number of institutional investors made money managers important players in international capital markets. In particular, it made their decisions relevant to an increasing number of developing countries that relied on them to finance domestic investments. Industrial countries tested the growing influence of these new actors too. The image of George Soros, one of the world's most influential money managers, betting billions of dollars against the British pound in 1992, with the British government eventually forced to devalue its currency, came to epitomize the power of individual global investors.[38]

The Washington consensus

It is commonly claimed that since the 1980s a new intellectual wave had swept the world. As a result, Keynesian economic ideas had been replaced by ideas based on monetarist, supply-side and rational expectations assumptions.[39] The governments of Ronald Reagan in the US and of Margaret Thatcher in the UK, as well as the election of US trained political elites around the developing world, were instrumental in the diffusion of those ideas.[40] At the beginning of the 1990s, then, the Washington consensus gave neoliberal ideas new prominence in academic and public debates.[41]

The intellectual foundations of the Washington consensus as a recipe for economic development were formalized by a group of economists working at the Institute of International Economics (IIE) based in Washington, DC. After having long explored the causes and consequences of the debt crisis in Latin America in the 1980s,[42] these economists expanded their focus to the set of policies that were the key to successful and sustainable economic development. As the Director of the Institute, Fred C. Berger (2003, p. vii), recalls, 'In the mid-1980s, we began to look "beyond the debt crisis" in an effort to chart a path for restoring sustained prosperity in the region.' In 1986, a study titled *Toward Renewed Economic Growth in Latin America*, edited by Bela Balassa, with contributions by a number of Latin American economists such as Gerardo Bueno (Mexico), Pedro-Pablo Kuczynski (Peru), and Mario Enrique Simonsen (Brazil), started to draft a comprehensive set of development proposals. The book was swiftly followed by John Williamson's essay 'The Progress of Policy Reform in Latin America' (1990) where the editor sketched one of the most well-known set of development policies, grouped under the label of the Washington consensus.[43]

Ten different aspects of economic policy, which were deemed crucial in the first stage of policy reform, made up the Washington consensus. Specifically, Williamson (1990b, p. 7) identified ten 'policy instruments,' including fiscal discipline (small balance budget deficits to be financed without recourse to the inflation tax), competitive exchange rate, financial and trade liberalization, with emphasis on the elimination of barriers to entry to foreign firms, privatization, and deregulation. As far as concerns capital account liberalization, the merits of this policy as a 'policy instrument' to achieve economic development have been controversial even at the height of the Washington consensus in the early 1990s. As John Williamson (1994b, p. 17) himself concedes, the prescription to liberalize the financial system was far more controversial than policies such as low budget deficits and inflation, privatization and deregulation. However, as Williamson (2003, p. 49) also notes, at that time, 'official opinion (perhaps especially in Washington) seemed incapable of entertaining the thought that faster financial globalisation might not necessarily be better.' That is to say, the official opinion shared by the US government and by the economists working at the IMF and World Bank and in the numerous think tanks and multilateral banks headquartered in the city was that capital account liberalization deserved pride of place in the list of reforms to achieve economic development. How exactly the IMF came to see international financial liberalization as a desirable economic policy is the question that the following sections address.

3.2 The consensus on 19th street: The idea of orderly liberalization

At the beginning of the decade, the IMF was an important laboratory for the articulation of policy principles in the area of capital market liberalization as attested by the explosion of theoretical and empirical studies on the topic. Among other aspects, particular attention was devoted to the determinants of capital flows (Goldstein, et al., 1991), and to the implications of those flows for domestic macroeconomic management (Goldstein, et al., 1993; Schadler, et al., 1993) and international stability (Goldstein and Folkerts-Landau, 1993; Quirk, et al., 1995). These studies were certainly highly influential inside the organization. Nevertheless, an account of how globalized finance became a top issue in the IMF agenda would hardly be complete without bringing into relief the role that the Managing Director, Michel Camdessus, and his close associates, played during their term in office.

Appointed in 1987, Camdessus is widely regarded, both within and without the IMF, as a 'regal' Managing Director (*The Economist*, 2000b), that is, a strong leader, with 'boundless energy, firm convictions, and securely grounded optimism' (IMF, 2000). Just one year after his appointment, Camdessus revealed his strong personality by refusing to yield to a direct appeal from the US Treasury Secretary James Baker to approve a new loan for Argentina.[44] *The Wall Street Journal* reported 'a furious behind-the-scenes quarrel between the US and ... Camdessus' (as quoted in Boughton 2001, p. 524, fn. 126).

Both his strong personality and the rapid economic developments of his time helped Camdessus impress a distinctive mark on the organization. As the IMF official historian put it, 'The story of Michel Camdessus's long tenure as the seventh Managing Director of the IMF and Chairman of its Executive Board is nothing less than the history of the institution over those 13 years' (Boughton, 2000). With important economic changes unfolding all over the world, Camdessus's main concern was to put the IMF front and center in dealing with the most important economic issues of his time.[45] Assuring the IMF a primary international standing in dealing with the debt problem and with the transition to the market economy of the former communist countries was one of the main challenges Camdessus set forth the IMF since his appointment.

Since the early 1990s, Camdessus put his political weight behind a substantial involvement of the IMF with the process of international financial integration. He tenaciously championed an increased role for the Fund in globalized finance, 'as its promoter, its crisis manager, and as an agent for its humanization' (IMF, 2000). Camdessus did strongly believe that the IMF had both the mandate and the instruments to cope with the new challenges. 'Our globalized world economy has opened up new opportunities and increased the scope for economic progress in the world. ... But it has also brought increased risks ... The IMF is well aware of its increased responsibilities in this environment, and you can count on the Fund to make every effort to fulfill them' (Camdessus, 1995h). Even in the aftermath of the Asian countries, Camdessus still forcefully argued that 'the liberalization of capital movements is now an extremely important issue for the Fund, and it is a challenge we must face head on.'[46]

The leadership and vision of the Managing Director were strengthened by the personal relationship between Camdessus and his first Deputy Managing Director Stanley Fischer, who was appointed to the post in September 1994. Fischer arrived at the IMF with an enviable reputation for being a 'brilliant economist but also a crystal-clear articulator of policies' (*The Economist*, 2000a). Professor and Head of the Department of Economics at MIT (Massachusetts Institute of Technology), Fischer also served as Chief Economist at the World Bank (1988–90) before joining the Fund in 1994. Not only did Camdessus and Fischer work well with each other, they complemented each other extraordinarily well. Whereas the Managing Director had a natural instinct for politics, his Deputy provided him with well-respected intellectual support. As the Director of the Policy Development and Review Department (PDR), Jack Boorman (2006) recalls, 'Camdessus was a strong and passionate leader with a hard-nose for politics. He was a master in playing Executive Directors against each other. Fischer, however, provided the bulk of intellectual support.'

The issue of the liberalization of capital movements provides a noticeable example of the Camdessus-Fischer working relationship. Camdessus's support for increased IMF involvement with capital liberalization was complemented by Fischer's economic analyses on the benefits and costs of the free movement of capital flows. 'I believe,' Fischer (1995a) said, 'that the increasing integration of capital markets... brings potentially massive benefits' even though he conceded that these benefits are 'more controversial' than the ones resulting from trade integration. Without dismissing the risks that liberalization entails, Fischer (1998b) has repeatedly pointed to the opportunities that free international capital movements provide and to the importance of the IMF's jurisdiction over those movements.

Among the other authoritative voices inside the Fund, which helped shape the IMF's agenda on capital liberalization, the voices of the Directors of the Policy Development and Review Department, Jack Boorman, and of the Monetary Affairs and Exchange Department (MAE), Manuel Guitián, were particularly influential. Head of one of the most powerful IMF departments,[47] Boorman forcefully drew attention to the benefits of global financial integration and to the importance of the IMF's involvement in the process of liberalization to minimize its risks – beliefs still present in his most recent remarks (Boorman, 2003; 2004). On his part, Guitián (1992, p. 45) was an early advocate of the removal of restrictions 'regardless of the nature of the transaction,' including capital transactions. A long-standing member of the IMF, where he served as staff member from 1970 onwards, and one of the main architects of the design of macro-adjustment programs during the 1980s, Guitián, in the words of Camdessus (2000), 'strongly held the view that the Fund was entrusted with an important and distinctive role' in the promotion of capital liberalization as well as in the governance of its risks.

Along with the personal beliefs of management and prominent staff officials, the analysis of IMF documents of the early 1990s reveals a broad convergence of views even among Executive Directors on the issue of liberalization. The terms of the emerging consensus inside the Fund revolved around the idea of *orderly liberalization*, the word *orderly* being carefully chosen here. Indeed, *orderly liberalization* was generally understood to distinguish such liberalization from 'an unwise and hasty rush to eliminate capital controls' and, at the same time, to convey the message of progressive liberalization.[48] Specifically, the emerging consensus revolved around two dimensions, which formed the tenets of the idea of *orderly liberalization*. First, there was a *normative* dimension that defined liberalization as both an inevitable and desirable course of economic policy. As technological advances progressed, and as countries increasingly recognized the beneficial effects of liberalization in terms of economic growth and market discipline, the push towards further integration would have been irresistible. Second, there was a *procedural* dimension that laid down the policies that member countries were expected to pursue to attain the benefits of liberalization. In this connection, particular attention was devoted to policies that could be of help to manage large capital flows, including the use of capital controls, macro and structural policies as preconditions for liberalization, and international cooperation under the aegis of the IMF. In what follows, I analyze each dimension in turn.

The normative dimension of orderly liberalization

> Globalization is something we must embrace
> (Camdessus, 1995h)

The normative dimension of the idea of *orderly liberalization* revolved around the notion that the liberalization of capital markets is an inevitable and desirable course of economic policy. Drawing on the experience of industrial countries, which by the mid-1990 had all liberalized their capital accounts, IMF officials drew the conclusion that it was logical to assume that developing countries would and should liberalize their capital account at some stage in the course of their development (Quirk, 1994). The progressive pattern of removal of capital controls in developing countries corroborated this point. Indeed, from 1991 to 1997, developing countries progressively removed barriers to capital flows. The speed of information technology advances and the associated decrease in transaction costs also lent significant support to the presumption that the integration of capital markets was unlikely to be reversed. In addition, the collapse of the planned economies at the end of the 1980s and progress in international trade talks, with the conclusion of the Uruguay round and the creation of the World Trade Organization (WTO) in 1995, accelerated the momentum behind the view of an ever-expanding global integration.

The perception that liberalization would have proceeded apace was further re-enforced by pointing to the still unrealized potential of global financial integration. 'Since international portfolio diversification is far from complete, the scale of international financial flows is bound to continue increasing for some time,' Stanley Fischer (1997b) noted. This statement reflected the awareness that information about investment opportunities in developing-country markets and international diversification of portfolios in industrialized countries had still not reached their full potential. Hence, from the IMF's perspective, it was logical to assume that as soon as information and diversification expanded so would financial integration. Furthermore, the ineffectiveness of capital controls in retaining domestic savings, reflected in residents' ability to circumvent existing controls, contributed to the perception that financial integration could not be prevented from further expansion (Goldstein, et al., 1991, p. 38).

Not only was liberalization seen as inevitable; it was also conceived as desirable because of its impact on member countries' economic prospects. Specifically, IMF staff maintained that liberalization was beneficial as a mechanism of economic growth (welfare-enhancing argument) and as a mechanism to enforce sustainable economic policies (discipline argument). In other words, IMF staff identified a clear, positive causal relationship between liberalization and economic growth.

Seen from 19th Street, there were few doubts that the benefits of liberalization were substantial. 'The globalization of financial markets is a very positive development,' Camdessus (1995e) forcefully and repeatedly commented, depicting capital flows as 'one of the driving forces of global growth in recent years' (see also Camdessus, 1995h). With hindsight, Boorman (2003) notes that the 'IMF has long been a proponent of the benefits of open capital markets. These include faster growth and rising standards of living; higher returns and better portfolio diversification for investors.'

Furthermore, strong views were expressed that the opening of the capital account might increase the efficiency of the domestic financial system by introducing competition from abroad and stimulating innovation (Fischer, 1997a; see also Guitián, 1996). While it was recognized that international financial liberalization can increase domestic financial sector risks absent critical supporting reforms, the dominant view favored the notion of 'interactive liberalization,' that is, the presumption that international and domestic financial liberalization are mutually reinforcing, in that the former helps to develop deeper and more competitive financial markets. This understanding had important implications for the sequencing of liberalization. Indeed, the standard argument is that strengthening regulation and supervision of domestic financial markets and institutions are crucial prerequisites to successful liberalization. Nevertheless, the strong presumption that domestic and international financial systems were 'interactive' lent support to the view that they should proceed simultaneously rather than being sequenced over time. International liberalization was conceived of as an inducement to improve domestic-sector regulations and supervision.

The experience of developing countries and transition economies, then, provided an immediate image of the positive effects of global financial integration. The rate of growth of the high-inflows countries in Latin American and Asia, for instance, fueled the presumption of the link between global financial integration and economic growth. Excluding Brazil, Latin America's average rate of growth rose from 1 percent per year in 1985–89 to about 4 percent per year in 1990–94 (Camdessus, 1996a). Similarly, East Asian economies, which were the largest recipients of foreign direct investments, were growing at an average rate of 7 percent a year (IMF, 1994b, pp. 6–8, 22–7, 57–61).[49] Even when the crisis hit Mexico, the Managing Director kept on making the argument that 'the recent problems in Latin America...can be understood only in the context of the region's economic progress of the past decade' (Camdessus, 1995a). Likewise, when the Asian crisis began bubbling, Fischer (1997a) still posited that the 'benefits' that these countries 'have derived from capital inflows also remind us that no country can afford to cut itself off from the international capital markets.' In other words, there was a strong presumption that capital inflows were an important feature in the economic growth of developing countries. Not only was financial globalization a product of the economic progress achieved in many developing countries; it was also 'a contributor to the economic progress of our time' (Camdessus, 1995a). Providing additional sources to finance domestic investments, foreign capital would contribute to domestic growth.

The agreement on the benefits of financial liberalization did not remain at the conceptual level but translated into the IMF's actual advice to member countries. Indeed, the IMF had few doubts about the compelling need for member countries to integrate with global financial markets. As the Managing Director Michel Camdessus (1997e) put it, member countries faced a 'stark choice' under conditions of globalization. They can 'either...integrate themselves into the international economy or...become marginalized from it and thus fall farther and farther behind in terms of growth and development.' Hence, as the internal assessments of the Fund's surveillance reveal, until late 1997, 'the Fund has tended...to welcome members' actions taken to liberalize capital account transactions.' Specifically, with regard to inflows, 'the tightening of controls...was generally discouraged' and the staff has generally conveyed to national authorities of both industrial and developing countries a sense of 'general distaste' for the imposition of controls on outflows, even as a way of addressing balance of payments difficulties.[50] Similarly, as Fischer (1998d) recalls, in the years before 1997 the IMF had advocated capital liberalization as 'very naturally something in which the Fund should be concerned, and something that...we have pushed in the context of programs.'

From the Fund's perspective, another factor made the liberalization of international capital flows beneficial for member countries' economic growth: market discipline. Along with the provision of extra funding for domestic investments, increased global financial integration would accrue to the domestic welfare by narrowing the scope for economic mismanagement. 'Normally, when the market's judgment is right,' Fischer (1997a) noted, 'this discipline is a valuable one, which improves overall economic performance by rewarding good policies and penalizing bad.'

Again, the empirical record of the early 1990s provided supporting evidence. In general, markets appeared able to discriminate among countries, as reflected in the patterns of capital flows. In the words of the World Economic Outlook (IMF 1994b, p. 6), 'most of the beneficiaries of capital inflows have been those countries where growth has been strong or where growth is expected to strengthen because of the pursuit of appropriate macroeconomic, trade, and exchange-rate policies.'

This is not to say that markets were considered to 'get it right' in any circumstance. Fischer (1997a), for instance, made this point clearly, recognizing that market discipline 'may sometimes go too far'. Nor was the beneficial argument in general used to dismiss the risks inherent in the globalization of the world's financial markets. Rather, it was forcefully argued that, in an era of globalized finance, risks are magnified. 'The globalization of financial markets, for all the benefits it brings, also transmits the effects of weak policies among economies faster than ever before' (Camdessus, 1994). 'Notwithstanding the benefits of capital movements,' IMF staff commented, 'the potential volatility and volume of these flows can also occasionally undermine the "orderly underlying conditions" that are necessary for the stability of the international monetary system.'[51] Reasoning along these lines, the elaboration of a mechanism to secure progressive liberalization while minimizing the risks for domestic and financial stability became a central policy concern. This brings us to the procedural dimension of the consensus developed inside the Fund.

The procedural dimension of orderly liberalization

Not only did the voice coming from the Fund posit the inevitability and the desirability of capital account liberalization; it also identified the policy measures that members were required to adopt in order to reap the benefits of global financial integration. That is to say, IMF staff members suggested a number of policies that would have helped member countries ensure domestic and international financial stability in spite of the opening to international capital flows.

Indeed, the process of international financial liberalization poses significant risks to the stability of both the domestic and the international financial system. At the domestic level, capital inflows may lead to inflationary pressures, loss of competitiveness induced by exchange-rate appreciation, and increased vulnerability to crisis caused by sudden shifts in market sentiment. At the international level, the process of financial integration increases the risk of spill-over effects from market to market and from country to country. In light of these risks, the debate within the Fund chiefly concentrated on three measures with which to govern the process of global financial integration: capital controls, macro and structural preconditions, and the role of the IMF.

On the first issue, the voice coming from the Fund systematically argued that capital controls were no longer an effective tool for policy makers to avoid overheating and vulnerability to crises because of their increasing costs and ineffectiveness. For one thing, in an environment in which the liberalization of current account transactions was a reality, the opportunity to circumvent controls abounded,[52] thereby raising the costs of administering and enforcing those controls. For the other, numerous theoretical studies and empirical observations lent substantial support to the hypothesis that capital controls were becoming increasingly ineffective, especially in the long run. For instance, drawing on the data of a large panel of developing countries' experience with capital account liberalization, staff documented that capital flight is likely to occur, the introduction of capital controls notwithstanding.[53] The experience of those countries that resorted to controls during the 1993 Exchange Rate Mechanism (ERM) crisis is illustrative here. Indeed, from the Fund's perspective, the temporary controls imposed by Ireland and Portugal on short-term capital flows during the crisis proved ineffective in reducing the speculative pressures on their currencies (Quirk, et al., 1995, p. 12).

Not only were capital controls 'ineffective.' From the Fund's perspective, they were also viewed as damaging in that 'they may discourage longer-term portfolio and direct investment flows' and spill-over to other countries.[54] In the words of the staff, 'controls imposed by one country typically affect others adversely (for example, by delaying necessary exchange-rate adjustments, or limiting the repatriation of invested capital or financial market access) and can, therefore, be destructive of international prosperity.'[55] In essence, the mainstream view inside the Fund conceived of liberalization as the 'first best' solution. 'The rapid integration of capital markets has shifted the balance of costs and benefits away from the controls.'[56]

The second set of policies upon which IMF staff focused as a means to manage the process of international financial liberalization pertained to the macroeconomic and structural policies deemed necessary in the sequence of liberalization. Looking within the IMF's general call for 'sound' macroeconomic policies, the voice coming from the IMF tended to emphasize certain policies over others. Specifically, the IMF showed some preference for fiscal policy over monetary and exchange-rate policy as an instrument to stem the demand pressure arising from the decision to open the domestic economy to international capital flows (Camdessus, 1996b; IMF, 1996b, pp. 62–4). As far as concerns structural policies, then, IMF staff and management repeatedly emphasized the importance of an efficient domestic financial system for a member country to integrate with the international financial system. As Michel Camdessus (1996d) repeatedly put it, 'we [at the IMF] believe banking systems [can] be strengthened.'

Finally, IMF management and staff focused on the role of the IMF, suggesting that members strengthen the powers of the Fund in order to manage the challenges posed by growing financial integration. Specifically, by strengthening the Fund's powers over capital account liberalization, member countries would have enjoyed Fund advice and financial assistance to cope with the risks of global financial integration. Seen from the IMF's perspective,

> The IMF, with its mandate over the smooth functioning of the international monetary system, has a keen interest in ensuring that the process of capital account liberalization is carried forward in an orderly way. Moreover, with its nearly universal membership, the Fund is well-placed to distil and disseminate the lessons of experience from our 182 member countries.[57]

Furthermore, the fact that the Fund may be called upon to finance balance of payments problems associated with the capital account provided another compelling reason for the IMF to help countries to manage the challenge of globalized finance. Drawing on this line of reasoning, IMF management and staff forcefully advocated an amendment to the IMF's Articles of Agreement that would have extended the Fund's jurisdiction to the promotion of capital account liberalization. Specifically, amending the wording of Article I and VI, the IMF would have allowed the Fund to lead member countries towards liberalization by sanctioning the use of capital controls while providing financial assistance in the event of balance of payments disequilibria caused by capital flight. For instance, in an influential pamphlet, the Director of the MAE Manuel Guitián (1992, p. 43) called 'for updating the code of conduct' of the IMF to make it respondent to the 'profound change' in the international economic system. As a later staff memorandum put it, 'it may...now be an appropriate time to review the practical implications of the Fund's remaining jurisdictional responsibilities...the Fund's jurisdictional responsibilities should be extended to include payments and transfers...related to international capital movements.'[58]

In sum, amending the Articles of Agreement was IMF management and staff's preferred institutional solution. More than a bureaucratic impulse to expand the scope of action of their organization, IMF management and staff were acting on their ideas on the benefits of capital account liberalization. Emblematic of this ideational impulse was the politically demanding requirements for the amendment to be adopted, prescribing the support of three-fifths of members, having 85 percent of the total voting power. Indeed, had the IMF management and staff simply wanted to enhance their bureaucratic power they could have opted for less demanding policies, such as strengthened surveillance. IMF management and staff, however, were not simply campaigning for an increased involvement by the IMF in capital issues. They were advocating the case for *orderly liberalization*. In this respect, the amendment appeared as the only 'appropriate' policy choice, in the sense that it would have secured the case for *orderly liberalization*.

The discussion led thus far is not meant to suggest the existence of an unambiguous consensus inside the Fund. Rather, there were several unresolved questions relating to the use of capital controls, the sequence of liberalization, and the role of the IMF.

For instance, the consensus on the principle against the use of capital controls was purchased at the cost of specificity. Specifically, IMF staff did not disaggregate the notion of capital controls. In other words, limited attention was devoted to the assessment of the effectiveness and costs of different types of controls, including reserve requirements on foreign deposits, quantitative controls, controls on inflows or outflows. As late as September 1997, for instance, Fischer (1997a) noted that the Fund still had 'to develop its analysis and evaluation of different types of capital controls, to advise countries on which types of controls are most likely to help them attain their goals, and on optimal methods of liberalization.' Furthermore, there was an issue as to how flexible the criteria for approving capital controls should be had the IMF expanded its jurisdiction to capital flows through an amendment. The amendment, indeed, would have given the IMF the powers to approve capital controls akin to the existing powers over controls on current account transactions. However, until late in 1997, IMF staff did not provide a preview of the operational criteria that would be applied to temporary and non-temporary restrictions.[59] Likewise, IMF staff failed to specify to what extent controls introduced for balance of payments purposes would be justified. Indeed, in the case of capital flows, the logic of controls for balance of payments purposes may easily apply to capital outflows – i.e. if a member faces a large capital outflow it may invoke the balance of payments purpose to introduce controls. In principle, however, members could invoke the same clause as applied to capital inflows – i.e. a member facing excessive capital inflows can impose controls to prevent overheating the national economy. Hence, as IMF staff conceded, 'the criterion of "balance of payments purposes" would require elaboration in the case of inflows.'[60]

Ambiguity also colored the IMF's discourse on 'sound' macroeconomic and structural policies as preconditions to liberalization. For all the emphasis on the importance of fiscal restraint over alternative macroeconomic tools, the IMF did not specify the exact policy mix. For instance, it is hard to find prescriptions on how much fiscal adjustment was in order as compared to monetary tightening or the interaction between monetary and exchange-rate choices. Interestingly, as late as 1995, the choice of the exchange rate was not considered 'a critical factor in successfully moving to capital account convertibility.'[61] Furthermore, in spite of the discourse on the importance of an efficient domestic financial system, IMF staff did not articulate specific guidelines on banking regulation, supervision, and transparency to assess member countries' performance.[62] The Independent Evaluation Office report on the IMF approach to capital account liberalization makes the point that the broad range of prudential regulations and requirements to strengthen the domestic financial sector 'largely remained at the conceptual level and did not lead to operational advice' to member countries (IEO 2005, pp. 4, 29, 57).

Finally, the implications of the extension of the Fund jurisdiction to the promotion of capital liberalization in terms of the use of its financial resources were left ambiguous. In particular, it was not clear whether the IMF would have had sufficient resources to go to the rescue of a country suffering a crisis in its capital account and whether, even if granted such resources, the IMF would have actually used them to go to the rescue. For instance, at certain points, staff memoranda excluded the possibility that the IMF would use its financial resources to help a country facing capital flight had the amendment won support. IMF staff motivated this position by appealing to moral hazard concerns – the implicit assurance that the IMF would go to the rescue raised the probability of capital flight by inducing investors and policy makers to take on risky behavior.[63] At other points, however, IMF staff and management suggested that the IMF would have not let a member face a crisis on its own. In his speeches, the Managing Director, for instance, repeatedly emphasized that one of the main functions performed by the IMF over time had been the provision of timely and adequate financial assistance to its members – implying that members could expect the same treatment in the foreseeable future (for instance, Camdessus, 1994, 1996c). For instance, asserting the central role played by the IMF in assisting Mexico in 1995, Camdessus (1995e) concluded that one of the lessons to be drawn from that financial crisis was 'the importance of the IMF's role in giving confidence to members.'

In sum, in the first half of the 1990s, within the IMF there was a strong presumption on the positive effects of capital flows on member countries' economic performance. Similarly, strong views were expressed about the ineffectiveness of capital controls as a means to manage capital inflows, about the importance of appropriate preconditions and sequencing, and about the role of the IMF to govern the risks of financial liberalization. Behind these apparent strong views, however, the IMF had yet to specify many implications of member countries' movement to capital convertibility. As Stanley Fischer (1997a) noted, the IMF 'can envisage members eventually accepting the obligation to liberalize the capital account fully.' Nevertheless, 'what precisely that means will have to be worked out.'

3.3   The Fund's social constituencies for legitimation

The ideas articulated by the IMF management and staff did not appear in a vacuum. The policy consensus developed inside the Fund needs to be 'embedded' in the historical context of the 1990s. Specifically, it needs to be understood against member countries' choice to advance the cause of international financial integration, assigning priority to capital mobility in their economic policy. For industrial countries, that choice signified to consolidate and expand global integration. For developing countries, it promised to bring about the level of income achieved by the advanced economies. Following this orientation in favor of capital mobility, by the mid-1990s, authorities in both industrial and developing countries were opening their markets or were advocating it. In this atmosphere, industrial countries' calls 'to remove obstacles to foreign direct investment' (G7, 1994) were echoed by developing countries' explicit recognition of the positive influence of greater financial integration (G24, 1993).

The industrial World

Among the G7 countries, the Clinton administration played a paramount role in encouraging market integration, a corollary to its domestic economic policy. In his first State of the Union address, the newly elected President Bill Clinton clearly argued that, among 'all the many tasks that require…attention,' making sure that the US 'economy thrives once again' stood high on his political agenda. Nevertheless, as the President emphasized, the government alone could not achieve this goal. 'The private sector is the engine of economic growth in America' (Clinton, 1993b).

The faith in the private sector, a faith larger 'than had been true of previous twentieth century Democratic administrations' (Delong and Eichengreen, 2004, p. 195), was translated in the economic strategy of the *investment-led growth*. As Clinton summarized the strategy,

> The heart of our plan deals with the long term. It has an investment program designed to increase public and private investment in areas critical to our economic future. And it has a deficit reduction program that will increase savings available for private sector investment, lower interest rates [and] decrease the percentage of the federal budget claimed by interest payments. (Clinton, 1993b)

The key here is the emphasis placed on low interest rates on long-term securities. By reducing debt-servicing costs and stimulating private investments, low interest rates were deemed crucial for the US to achieve deficit reduction and to boost productivity. This domestic economy strategy, then, had an international counterpart. Indeed, an increase in US productivity required a strong global demand and open markets to be sustained. Fostering open markets abroad became the crucial corollary to Clinton's domestic economic policy and the bulk of its foreign economic strategy. As Jeffrey Garten, Undersecretary of Commerce, aptly put it in March 1995, 'our exports and jobs are dependent on gaining a larger market share in the big emerging markets. No US firm will be a world-class company without substantial involvement in the big emerging markets' (as quoted in Krugman, 1995, p. 29).

Building on the foreign economic policy pursued by his predecessors, Clinton magnified the strategy of promoting US exports and investments abroad. 'I think that more and more the job of the modern president will involve relating with the rest of the world because we are in an interdependent world,' Clinton said. 'Whether we like it or not, money and management and technology are mobile and the world is interdependent.'[64] Recognizing the challenges and opportunities that a global economy entailed for the United States, Clinton was an early advocate of market integration. During his 1991 electoral campaign, for instance, he met with top Democratic executives on Wall Street, 'impressing the executives with his willingness to embrace free trade and free markets.'[65] His belief in the opportunities that a global economy may offer to the US also made their way into the Presidential Inaugural address. Clinton (1993a) emphasized that in the post-cold war world the separation between 'what is foreign and what is domestic' no longer existed. Rather, 'profound and powerful forces are shaking and remaking [the] world' requiring the US to overhaul its foreign policy priorities.

Convincing other countries of the benefits of global integration, thereby opening their markets, became one of the priorities of the administration's foreign policy agenda. 'We pushed full steam ahead on all areas of liberalization, including financial,' Jeffrey E. Garten, Undersecretary of Commerce, is reported having said. 'I never went on a trip when my brief didn't include either advice or congratulations on liberalization.'[66]

Symbolic of the importance devoted to international economic issues was the creation of the National Economic Council (NEC). Mirroring the activities of the National Security Council, the NEC was created for advising the President on matters related to US and global economic policy.[67] The President's choice of Robert Rubin as head of the NEC in 1992 and as Treasury secretary in 1995 further revealed the administration's stance on foreign economic matters. Indeed, Rubin came to the White House directly from Wall Street.

One of the senior partners in Goldman Sachs & Co, the preeminent New York investment bank, where he had spent his previous twenty-six years, Rubin can be credited as a fine interpreter of Wall Street interests inside the administration. On several occasions, Rubin helped the administration to package its economic policies in appealing terms for the private sector. For instance, it is on public record that Rubin 'pushed to make the administration's health initiatives business-friendly and counseled the president against "tax the rich" rhetoric.'[68] Furthermore, Rubin was a vocal supporter of the US strategy of fostering global economic integration. When Mexico got into trouble in 1994–95, for instance, Rubin made a strong case for extending US financial support on the grounds that Mexico's collapse would have set back the clock for trade and financial market liberalization worldwide (Rubin and Weisberg, 2003, p. 12).

At the US Treasury, Rubin's support for international trade and financial integration was shared and amplified by his Deputy, Lawrence Summers (1995–2001). Son of two PhD economists, and nephew of two Nobel Prize winners in economics, Summers was himself a distinguished academic economist. One of the youngest professors ever to receive tenure at Harvard, where he got his PhD in 1982, Summers was, in the words of Rubin (Rubin and Weisberg 2003, p. 8), 'a forceful, self-assured theoretical economist with a good feel for the practical, both in politics and in markets.' A former Chief Economist at the World Bank (1991–93), Summers was Under Secretary of the Treasury for International Affairs since 1995. In that position, he had broad responsibility assisting the Secretary of the Treasury in the formulation and execution of international economic policies and served as the American deputy in the G7 international economic cooperation process.

A strong believer in the benefits of financial liberalization, Summers persistently argued that increased openness to capital flows had generally proved essential for countries seeking to rise from lower- to middle-income status and that it had strengthened stability among industrial countries. 'When history books are written 200 years from now about the last two decades of the twentieth century,' the *New York Times* reported Summers saying, 'I am convinced that the end of the cold war will be the second story. The first story will be about the appearance of emerging markets – about the fact that developing countries where more than three billion people live have moved toward the market and seen rapid growth in incomes.'[69] Even in the aftermath of the Asian crisis, and the global financial turmoil, Summers (1998) argued that the 'right responses to these experiences is much less to slow the pace of capital account liberalization than to accelerate the pace of creating an environment in which capital will flow to its highest return use.'

With the case for liberalization firmly entrenched in both the Treasury and the White House, because of the professional and academic biographies of the top Treasury officials, the US international foreign economic policy of the first half of the 1990s moved securely towards preaching global integration. 'Financial liberalization, both domestically and internationally, is a critical part of the US agenda,' Lawrence Summers commented.[70] Referring to Rubin, and to the two Commerce Secretaries Kantor and Ron Brown, Garten commented that 'There wasn't a fiber in those three – bodies or in mine – that didn't want to press as a matter of policy for more open markets wherever you could make it happen.'[71]

Intellectual support aside, the push was in part motivated by domestic reasons. 'Our financial services industry wanted into these [emerging] markets,' Laura D'Andrea Tyson, Rubin's successor at the National Economic Council, commented.[72] Promoting capital account liberalization, so the argument went, would be of help in removing restrictions in those financial markets, such as the Asian ones, where high barriers to entry were still in place and where the US financial industry had the greatest interest.[73] Indeed, restrictions on foreign ownership of companies and on the holding of overseas assets by pension and insurance funds were widely spread across the Asian countries. According to the data of the US Trade Representative Report (USTR, 1996), as of 1996, Korea still maintained a 'tightly controlled financial sector' in some important service sectors relevant to the US economy – such as insurance and brokerage – to an extent that impeded US and foreign banks and securities firms' operations.[74] The situation for the US banking industry in Malaysia was even worse. As of 1996, the Malaysian Central Bank did not permit the opening of new banks and did not allow existing foreign banks to open additional branch offices. In other words, the US private industry faced significant barriers to their investments in a number of key emerging market economies – that is, those economies that Clinton once characterized as having shifted from 'dominoes to dynamos.'[75]

In their global search for access to emerging countries' markets, the US industry forcefully supported the Multilateral Agreement on Investment (MAI).[76] In May 1995, the OECD had formally launched the beginning of negotiations for a treaty whose aim was to provide 'a broad multilateral framework for international investment with high standards for the liberalization of the investment regimes and investment protection and with effective dispute settlement procedures' (OECD, 1995). The MAI would have forbidden discrimination between domestic and international investors, in both short- and long-term investments, providing global investors with the right to sue governments in the event of non-compliance with OECD norms.[77]

In broad terms, the US business community firmly supported the MAI. Specifically, the service firms, grouped into the Coalition of Service Industries (CSI) and the Security Industry Association (SIA), pushed the most to include both portfolio and foreign direct investments (FDI) within the scope of the MAI. Although less active than the service sector in their support to the MAI, the commercial banking industry and the manufacturing sector endorsed a supportive stance –with individual banks such as Citicorp and the National Association of Manufacturers (NAM) particularly eager to push the agreement through.

The MAI treaty was open 'to accession by non-OECD Member countries' (OECD, 1995), reflecting the interest of the industrial world in access to emerging market countries, which were not yet OECD members.[78] Specifically, Argentina, Brazil, Chile, and Hong Kong, China early participated as an observer to the MAI negotiations. Estonia, Latvia, Lithuania, and the Slovak Republic were later also invited.[79]

The OECD treaty aside, the euphoria for the prospects of emerging markets may further be gleaned from the comments of global investors at the time. In August 1994, Barton M. Biggs, the chief global investment strategist for Morgan Stanley, with quite a reputation among investment fund managers for his brilliant and funny reports, boldly declared, 'I'm bullish on the Asian market.'[80] The smaller Asian markets, Thailand, Indonesia and Hong Kong, were considered 'the best place in the world to be for the next five years.'[81] Similarly, Gunter Ecklebe, director of International Asset Consulting at Frank Russell Company, publicly commented that 'Southeast Asia is just a great market. It has low wages, a good educational background and great economic potential. It produces goods cheaply and of high quality, and that makes it a formidable competitor. And these markets are fairly priced.'[82]

Not only did markets reward the Asian countries which received cumulative capital inflows of $261 billion during 1990–94, with FDI accounting for 45 percent of these flows (IMF, 1995a, p. 2); Latin America also became one of the most prominent areas to allocate overseas investments and Mexico was one of the preferred areas. 'We really like Mexico,' Lincoln F. Anderson, director of global research at Fidelity Investments [US], was reported saying. 'The Mexican stock market is moving ahead strongly, and there are a lot of investment opportunities

even at current prices.'[83] As a result of such a favorable market sentiment, 'Latin American stock markets became stars in the international
financial firmament. Each year between 1989 and 1994, one or more
Latin American stock markets ranked among the world's best perform-
ers' (Naim, 1995, p. 50). As Feinberg (1992, p. 2) put it, Latin America
was 'back on the screen.' Market euphoria was so widespread that the
overall sentiment among investors was 'not whether optimistic expectations about growth in the big emerging markets would be fulfilled,'
Paul Krugman (1995, p. 29) aptly observed. Rather, 'it was whether
advanced countries would be able to cope with the new competition
and take advantage of the opportunities this growth now offered.'

The emerging and developing World

Despite such an enthusiasm, Washington and Wall Street were not forcing financial liberalization down unwilling throats. 'The United States
pressed for capital liberalization, recalled a former top Thai official, but
he added that it was like pushing on an open door.'[84] Along the same
lines, one of the findings of the Independent Evaluation Office's Report
(IEO, 2005, pp. 4, 5, 59) on the Fund's approach to capital account liberalization is that 'in all the countries that liberalized the capital account,
partially or almost fully, the process was for the most part driven by the
country authorities' own economic and political agendas.'[85]

Indeed, the view that the liberalization was a desirable and appropriate course of economic policy was widespread among emerging market
elites. In the early 1990s these political elites, which have been defined
as 'technopols' (Feinberg, 1992) to indicate the considerable number of
US trained economists in key government positions, significantly contributed to forge national economic policies that aimed at integrating
their countries into global commodity and financial markets.

Latin America provided the most visible indicator of the changes
that were taking place across the emerging markets world. 'Things have
changed,' the *Financial Times* empathically commented in mid-1994.
'For those that think of Latin America in terms of generals, jungles,
and sackfuls of worthless currency, it may be a time to overhaul some
myth....South America's soldiers have long since goose-stepped back
to the barracks, their power usurped by squadrons of technocrats
and battalions of economic miracle-makers.'[86] Well-known examples
of the members of these new battalions were President Carlos Salinas
de Gortari and his Finance Minister Pedro Aspe in Mexico, Minister
Domingo Cavallo in Argentina, and Finance Minister Alejandro Foxley
in Chile.

The influence of the 'technocrats' was in turn reinforced by those capital flows that the new investor-prone policies attempted to attract. As the former Venezuelan Minister of Industry Moises Naim (1995, pp. 50–1) explains, the political support to the reform agenda of the new political elites was due to the fact that large capital inflows 'greatly helped governments by lowering the political costs of implementing the reforms' – at least in the short run. Absent these flows, the costs of reforms would have been higher, speeding up popular protests and opposition.

With large capital inflows financing domestic investments and consumption, and contributing to economic growth, emerging markets authorities were all so enthralled by the economic success that ideas contrary to the choice of advancing global financial integration were virtually absent or weak. 'We were convinced we were moving with the stream,' Garten said, 'and that our job was to make the stream move faster.'[87] In this atmosphere, representatives of developing countries looked favorably at achieving 'a greater measure of integration, through trade and financial flows, with the industrial country economies' (G24, 1993).[88]

In conclusion, in the first years of the 1990s, the support for global financial integration cut across the traditional developed-developing countries divide. This is not to say that emerging and developing countries uncritically accepted the push to open their markets to foreign capital or that there were no points of controversy between developed and developing countries. What is striking, however, is the extent to which the ideas favoring global integration were embraced and the lack of alternative views. Even among those personalities, who were about to become the most vocal against global financial integration, criticism was still confined. The Malaysian Prime Minister Mahathir Mohamad is a telling example here. In front of the attempt to remove barriers to trade and investments among the countries of the Asia-Pacific Economic Cooperation (APEC), an attempt that met the reservations of many of the East Asian countries because of the competition of the APEC most advanced countries' firms, 'even Mahathir did not try to break the consensus … by dissenting outright.'[89]

3.4   Redesigning the IMF in an era of globalized finance

Aware of the profound changes that were unfolding under their eyes, IMF member countries started discussing the implication of globalized finance for both domestic and international financial stability. In this connection, they turned to the international financial institutions for guidance, as attested by the debate that took place for the fiftieth anniversary of the Bretton Woods system, which was held in Madrid in September 1994. Specifically, the conference gave IMF staff members the possibility to bring to public attention the connection between financial globalization and the role that the IMF could play in governing its risks. In other words, IMF staff engaged in a persuasive battle to win member countries' support around the idea of *orderly liberalization*.

Anniversaries are likely occasions to reflect on achievements and failures. The fiftieth anniversary of the Bretton Woods institutions, the World Bank, and the IMF, was no exception. The conference held in Madrid provided a venue to celebrate the creation of the international post-World War II economic order, regarded as a 'symbol of international economic cooperation and stability' (Boughton and Lateef, 1995, p. 1). The Madrid conference also provided a venue to reflect on the achievements of the Bretton Woods institutions and on the challenges of the 1990s to which the organizations were expected to respond. As the IMF Managing Director, Michel Camdessus, and the World Bank President, Lewis T. Preston, put it in their opening statement to the conference, the fiftieth anniversary was 'an opportunity for reflection and for reassessing the roles of our institutions as we approach the twenty first century.' The conference brought together policy makers, academic economists, representatives of non-governmental organizations, and private-sector representatives. Therefore, it provided the first occasion to test the consensus developed inside the Fund against the Fund's social constituencies for legitimation.

Among the several issues addressed, some issues occupied center stage during the discussions. A prominent theme at the 1994 conference was that the globalization of financial markets had substantially changed the international architecture as designed at Bretton Woods. That 'the world had changed beyond recognition,' as emphatically put by Manmohan Singh, the Finance Minister of India (Boughton and Lateef, 1995, p. 35) became the leitmotiv of the conference. The increasing integration of international capital markets was generally welcomed as a positive development. Saifur Rahman, the Minister of Finance of Bangladesh and Chairman of the Boards of Governors of the Fund and the World Bank, summarized the prevalent mood across the membership, industrial and developing countries alike, observing that 'the great expansion of private equity flows to a number of developing countries in recent years can also be seen as the eventual realization of a dream our founders had half a century ago' (Boughton and Lateef, 1995, p. 22).

Virtually all participants pointed to the expansion in membership, which resulted from the collapse of communism and the admission of former planned economies into the Fund, and to the integration of global economy to corroborate the sense of historical watershed.[90]

Camdessus used the public stage provided by the fiftieth anniversary to engage economists and policy makers in the articulation of a new role for the IMF in an era of globalized finance. He directly addressed the international community, testing whether consensus existed on the overall objective the IMF had to pursue – encouraging the process of international financial liberalization while governing its risks. Specifically, Camdessus (1995d, p. 25), a strong advocate of the ongoing relevance of the IMF in the global economic system, took his view directly to the conference, arguing that,

> Over the past 50 years, the IMF's role and activities have grown and changed dramatically. This is not because its purposes have changed: its statutory purposes, set out in the Articles, are the same as when they were formulated 50 years ago. ... They remain equally valid today, and in fact they have become even more relevant as growing economic interdependence among nations has increased the need for international cooperation on economic and monetary issues.

Despite the faith in the still relevant IMF mandate, the Managing Director conceded that important changes in the global economy system required the IMF to reform itself. 'For the fulfillment of [its] purposes,' Camdessus (1995d, p. 25) added, 'the IMF has had to adapt its operations to a changing world economy,' which, among other challenges, was characterized by the growing importance of global private capital markets. In line with his personal convictions about making the IMF actively involved in capital issues, Camdessus suggested a number of policy proposals to adapt the Fund to the circumstances of the global economy. They ranged from strengthening its surveillance activity to the creation of a 'a fast-disbursing, very short-term financing mechanism that could help cushion the reserves of countries experiencing short-term balance of payments pressures' (Camdessus, 1995b, p. 274).

Even though Camdessus did not bring up the proposal to amend the Articles, which was formally circulated to the IMF Board later in November, the proposal had already been informally floated, as the remarks by Gerald K. Helleiner (Camdessus 1995a, p. 77), research coordinator of the G24. Helleiner, indeed, took issue with Camdessus's suggestions. He dismissed the proposal to include capital liberalization within the purposes of the Fund as 'inappropriate' and the proposal for the fast-disbursing financing facility as 'unworkable,' given the large sums required to stem capital flight. Nevertheless, Helleiner did not dismiss out of hand an enhanced role for the Fund in ensuring global financial stability, arguing, in contrast, that 'the role and responsibilities of the IMF in international financial markets need to be clarified, and almost certainly strengthened.'

In light of the political support that emerged in Madrid, IMF management and staff' calls for reforming the Fund's policies in capital issues gained strength. In the immediate aftermath of the Madrid conference, the Interim Committee endorsed the 'Declaration on Cooperation to Strengthen Global Expansion' in which Governors encouraged the IMF 'to continue its work on capital issues' (Interim Committee, 1994). The Executive Board explicitly discussed the possibility to overhaul the Fund's jurisdiction in the area of capital account convertibility and several Directors advocated a new role for the Fund in 'monitoring capital account restrictions and encouraging capital account liberalization.'[91] With the support of both industrial and developing countries, the issue of reforming the IMF's policies to govern the risks of financial integration was officially on the international political agenda.

3.5 Conclusion

When the decade began, major changes were taking place in international capital markets, which were becoming larger, more complex, and more integrated than they had been during previous decades. These developments were not confined to the industrial world. Recovering from the 1980s debt crisis, numerous developing countries gradually regained access to international capital markets. Along with these changes to the size, composition, and actors involved in cross-border capital transactions, no new doctrine seemed to rival 'the ideological wave' that had swept the world since the end of the 1980s (Frieden, 2006, p. 398). Neoliberalism, in its popular and global version of the Washington consensus, established itself as the 'intellectual zeitgeist' of the time (Krugman, 1995, p. 28), incorporating calls for the removal of barriers to the free movement of capital flows.

Inside the IMF, the consensus on the issue of the liberalization of international capital movements was shaped around the idea of *orderly liberalization*. The advocates of the idea – the IMF management and staff – presented the removal of capital restrictions as an inevitable and desirable course of economic policy. While the adjective *orderly* served as a reminder of the risks that liberalization entailed, the emphasis was laid on the beneficial effects of liberalization in terms of its ability to foster economic growth and to impose macroeconomic discipline. The benefits of liberalization outweighed its risks, and the costs of maintaining capital controls appeared to be increasing. Outside the IMF, the policy choices of industrial and developing countries were in line with IMF-sponsored ideas. Specifically, the idea of *orderly liberalization* seemed to respond to two sets of concerns. On the one hand, it spoke to the concerns of industrial countries and private-sector actors, which wanted to consolidate and expand globalization across the globe. On the other, it resonated with the needs of what came to be known as emerging market countries, which aspired to the levels of income and stability achieved by advanced economies.

In such a permissive global environment, the ideas of *orderly liberalization* informed the IMF's policies and practices. They also led to the questioning of existing institutional financial order as embodied in the IMF's Articles of Agreement that, reflecting the 1944 Bretton Woods compromise, still legitimized the use of capital controls. At its fiftieth anniversary, several proposals to reform the institutional design of the Fund were spelled out, ranging from improving the quality and focus of the Fund's surveillance to amending its Articles of Agreement. These early proposals were going to prove highly influential in future months. Their influence should be judged not by whether they produced definitive answers but by IMF management and staff having helped set the agenda for the debate. Framing the debate around the idea of *orderly liberalization*, IMF management and staff set the broad parameters around which an agreement on the reform of the Fund could be struck among its members. Such an agreement, however, was quickly called into question by the eruption of the crisis in Mexico.

4
The Mexican Crisis:
Testing the Consensus

This chapter traces the influence of the idea of *orderly liberalization* on the policies pursued by the IMF after the Mexican crisis. Specifically, the chapter is organized as follows. The first section describes the events that led to the crisis and the unfolding of the financial crisis. The second section shows how the IMF interpreted the Mexican crisis, that is, it shows how the idea of *orderly liberalization* set the boundaries on the interpretation of the crisis and on the policies to pursue in its aftermath in order to reform the international financial architecture. The third section goes on to show how the idea of *orderly liberalization* went unscathed in the aftermath of the crisis across the Fund's social constituencies for legitimation. After the crisis, the faith in the benefits of capital account liberalization and in the role of the IMF as a promoter and a manager of the risks of liberalization remained largely intact among member countries, academic economists, and private-sector actors.

The fourth section reviews the policies pursued in the aftermath of the crisis in the area of crisis prevention and crisis management. In particular, this section extensively focuses on the negotiations of the IMF Board and on the outcomes of those negotiations, bringing to the surface the process through which the ideas supplied by IMF staff came to be endorsed by the Executive Directors sitting on the Board. Specifically, it is shown how IMF management and staff engaged in a persuasive battle to win Executive Directors' support around their preferred institutional choices thereby encouraging Executive Directors to strengthen IMF surveillance, increase IMF financial resources, and amend the Article of Agreements to give the IMF mandate and jurisdiction over capital transactions. Using the minutes of the Executive Board meetings, for instance, the fourth section shows how IMF staff members depoliticized the debate on the amendment by exploiting ambiguous economic ideas. The section also shows how Executive Directors were sensitive to the signals coming from the outside, that is, from the Fund's social constituencies for legitimation. The combination of IMF staff's use of ambiguity and the perception that the Fund's authorizing environment favored an extension of the role of the IMF in the management of globalized finance eventually led Executive Directors to agree on the reforms that IMF staff had suggested, acting on the idea of *orderly liberalization*.

4.1   The Mexican crisis

Analyzing the state of the Mexican economy from the perspective of the early 1990s, it was hardly disputable that the country had embarked on a significant 'transformation' process, as was put by its MIT-trained Secretary of Finance Pedro Aspe Armella (1995, p. 127). By this time, indeed, Mexico had reduced its inflation to the lowest rate in 21 years and recorded GDP growth at an average rate of around 2.5 percent in real terms from 1989 to 1994. The public-sector deficit had been also significantly curtailed (IMF, 1995b, p. 92) and major structural reforms were carried out, including a tax reform, the freeing of interest rates, the elimination of credit controls, the privatization of a number of commercial banks and important public-sector enterprises, and central bank independence. Mexico's strengthened economic position proceeded with an outward-looking orientation based on financial and trade liberalization. From 1990 onwards, for instance, foreigners were allowed to hold government bonds and to buy (non-voting) shares in almost all sectors of the economy. Following the signing of the North America Free Trade Agreement (NAFTA) in January 1994, which created a free-market area between Canada, Mexico, and the US, the Mexican stock market boomed, reflecting the markets' perception that the agreement would improve corporate performance in the country and that Mexico's macroeconomic policies and outward orientation were unlikely to be reversed.

Stabilization and structural reforms, combined with a widespread perception that Mexico was a valuable example of successful market-oriented reform, unleashed large capital inflows. In the period 1990–93, the Mexican economy attracted substantial capital inflows, accounting for over 40 percent of total flows to all Latin American countries. Jumping from cumulative net *outflows* of about $15 billion during 1983–89, Mexico received $31 billion of capital inflows in 1993 alone, which amounted to 8 percent of Mexican GDP (IMF, 1995a, pp. 2 and 53; IMF, 1995b, p. 43). As Armella (1995, p. 131) put it,

> Mexico has shifted from a situation of transferring considerable amounts of resources to the rest of the world to being a net recipient of foreign capital.

As a result of these large capital inflows, foreign exchange reserves increased sharply, from a level of $6.3 billion at the end of 1989 to $25.1 billion at the end of 1993 (IMF, 1994b, 1995a).

Mexico quickly became a role model for the international community. Visiting Mexico City in February 1994, US Treasury Secretary, Lloyd Bentsen, was reported as having said that Mexico's policies are 'an example for all of Latin America.'[92] Mexico's success was crowned in May 1994 when the country joined the Organization for Economic Cooperation and Development (OECD), that is, the organization of the most advanced economies in the world. Becoming a member, Mexico accepted, among others, the obligation to implement the Codes for the Liberalization of Capital Movements.[93]

Inside the IMF and the economics profession, there was a widespread view that Mexico's economic progress was a 'remarkable success on many fronts...an inspiration for many countries' (Camdessus, 1995c). In the words of two economists, 'before December 1994, Mexico was hailed as the prime example of success of market-oriented reforms. It was widely believed that...the country was poised for ascending to a sustainable high-growth, low-inflation equilibrium....the strength of the country's fundamentals was rarely questioned' (Calvo and Mendoza, 1996, p. 170).

In spite of these positive developments and assessments, Mexico's economic fundamentals was suffering from major pitfalls. From the beginning of the 1990s, the Mexican current account deficit deteriorated sharply, widening from about 5 percent of GDP during the period 1990–93 to more than 8 percent in 1994.[94] The deficit was further complicated by the overvaluation of the Mexican peso, with the real exchange-rate appreciating by 35 percent from 1990 to February 1994 (IMF, 1995a, p. 54). In addition, GDP growth slowed, recording a disappointing 0.6 percent in 1993 (IMF, 1995b, p. 92). Before March 1994, however, the current account deficit and the peso overvaluation did not spark public concern.[95] The deficit was securely financed by large capital inflows and the interest rate required by foreign investors on Mexican securities was relatively low – especially in the immediate aftermath of the signing of NAFTA.

In a replication of the 1980s script, however, both external and internal shocks severely stressed Mexico's economic fundamentals. On the external front, the rise in US interest rates had important repercussions on the Mexican economy. On 4 February 1994, the Federal Reserve raised the federal funds rate by 25 basis points after having left the rate at 3 percent since September 1992. During 1994, US official interest rates were raised five times, with the Federal funds rate reaching 5.5 percent by end of November (IMF, 1995b, p. 54).[96] High US interest rates made borrowing from international capital markets more expensive, exacerbating the current account deficit.

On the internal front, a series of political shocks raised concerns among market participants about the country's political stability and economic commitments. The first domestic shock that upset financial markets occurred in January 1994, when insurgents in the region of Chiapas demanded independence from the central government. These uprisings were followed by the assassination of the then-ruling Institutional Revolutionary Party (PRI) presidential candidate Louis Donaldo Colosio. Short-term peso interest rates rose significantly and the Mexican stock and bond markets came under selling pressures. The interest rate spread between Mexican bonds and US Treasury bills, a common indicator of a country's creditworthiness, began to widen – reflecting investors' expectation that the exchange-rate policy would likely be abandoned. The first speculative attack against the peso took place on 23 March 1994. The exchange rate experienced a nominal devaluation of around 10 percent and interest rates increased by 7 percentage points. The devaluation and the increased interest rate, however, did not stop the capital hemorrhage. Government sales of bonds proceeded apace.

The government reaction was first and foremost a public pledge not to devalue. It was the stated objective of the authorities to maintain the value of the peso within the exchange-rate band since doing otherwise could seriously impair the country's credibility vis-à-vis financial markets.[97] Despite the commitment to defend the value of the peso, the public authorities' response was not a conventional policy of high interest rates to repel the speculative attack against the currency. Instead, the central bank kept interest rates down by expanding domestic credit – primarily providing credit to the banking sector and purchasing government securities held by private sector. Domestic factors certainly account for the rejection of a policy of high interest rates. On the one hand, the fragility of the Mexican banking sector discouraged the central bank from tightening interest rates. In its 1995 Monetary Program, for instance, the Banco de Mexico justified its policy of keeping interest rates down on the basis that doing otherwise would have pushed interest rates to 'exorbitant levels, which would have affected debtors, including financial intermediaries, in a highly unfavorable way,' that is, causing banking bankruptcies and failures (as quoted in Sachs, et al., 1996, p. 35). On the other hand, presidential elections were scheduled in August, making the adoption of an unpopular policy such as high interest rates the most difficult.

Given the choice not to raise interest rates, Mexican public commitment to maintain the value of the peso took the form of an offer to exchange short-term (Cetes) and long-term peso-denominated bonds with short-term dollar-denominated bonds (Tesobonos).[98] The problem was that if the country had come under selling pressure, the central bank could not resort to printing money to meet government obligations and even devaluation would not have helped. With debt denominated in foreign currency a reduction on the value of the national currency is no relief on its external debt – at least, in the short term.

The transformation of government debt into foreign currency-denominated debt met with the enthusiasm of financial markets. Since the government was committing itself to repay in foreign currency, it was unlikely that it would renege on its promises.[99] As a result, the stock of *tesobonos* grew rapidly, pushing down foreign exchange reserves and building up a threatening short-term foreign-denominated government debt. Specifically, the stock of outstanding *tesobonos*, that is, the stock of government debt, grew tenfold between February and November 1994 pushing down the stock of foreign exchange reserves.[100]

After the August presidential election, which brought the PRI candidate Ernesto Zedillo to the presidency, there was a temporary recovery. Reserves stopped falling and remained constant until October. During the fall, however, outflows resumed again on the heels of another domestic political shock. Deputy Attorney General Mario Ruiz Massieu resigned, denouncing the government for an attempt to block the investigations on the assassination of his brother, Ruiz Massieu. Political instability fuelled a second attack against the peso.

With an increasing stock of *tesobonos* falling due, the gap between government foreign-denominated liabilities and foreign reserves grew large. In the three-month period of September through November the net outflow amounted to $744 million and the stock of reserves depleted to around $13 billion by the end of November 1994 – almost half the stock of reserves recorded at the end of 1993. By mid December, rumors surrounding Mexico's imminent devaluation gained strength, pushing reserves further down. 'What looked like a huge cushion of international reserves in February–March 1994 ($29 billion) was nearly depleted (80 percent, down to $6 billion) only nine months later' (Goldstein and Calvo, 1996, p. 248).

Mexico was forced to devalue on 20 December 1994 – by widening the exchange-rate band by 15 percent. During the course of the trading day on 20 December, the peso lost an immediate 3 percent of its value and short-term interest rates rose. Two days later, Stanley Fischer, IMF Deputy Managing Director, commented that 'the exchange-rate adjustments...will help reinforce the economic recovery that has been evident since early 1994 and secure the viability of Mexico's external position' (IMF, 1994a). Despite the Fund's support, continuous selling pressures and a loss of confidence led Mexican authorities to float the currency. From December 1994 to March 1995, the peso declined 32 percent against the dollar eventually stabilizing at about 7.5 pesos per dollar – a fall of more than 50 percent since the beginning of the crisis. According to the data the IMF relied on, during December, there was a net outflow in the form of foreign holdings of Mexican government securities (including Cetes and Tesobonos) of about $790 million and a further decline of $6.6 billion in foreign reserves (IMF, 1995a, p. 60). With the government unable to roll over its short-term debt, Mexico's access to international capital markets was sharply curtailed. 'After the devaluation,' Guillermo Ortiz, the new Mexican Finance Minister, commented, 'financial markets for Mexico virtually disappeared, and there was a true stampede, in which all Mexican public and private debt instruments were literally thrown out' (as quoted in Calvo and Mendoza, 1996, p. 173).

Under exchange market pressures, interest rates rocketed, reaching levels as high as 80 percent in the first quarter of 1995, threatening the stability of the Mexican banking system. Indeed, as of December 1994, a third of the total loans made by Mexican banks were denominated in foreign currency. Devaluation and tightened monetary policy increased the number of non-performing loans, thereby aggravating the banks' dollar liquidity position.

The 'remarkable progress' (Camdessus, 1995f) the Mexican economy had achieved during the past five years were rapidly wiped out. The crisis, which forced the country to tighten interest rates and cut expenditures, caused a major contraction in output and employment. The entire Mexican economy was at risk and with it the economic prospects of many emerging markets. As already pointed out, Mexico, which had been the first debt-restructuring country to re-establish access to international financial markets, provided a 'baseline for emerging markets' measuring the riskiness of sovereign debt issues (IMF, 1995a, p. 64). Consequently, the events in Mexico in December 1994 prompted a broad sell-off of developing countries' securities by foreign investors. The bulk of market pressures was concentrated in Western Hemisphere markets, where 'the rebalancing of institutional portfolios seemed to fall hardest on Argentina (where stock and bond prices fell on the order of 50 percent in the first trimester following Mexico), and next hardest on Brazil' (Goldstein and Calvo, 1996, p. 268). Nevertheless, with global investors restructuring their international portfolio investments, the 'tequila effects' were felt worldwide, so that Asian countries – Thailand, the Philippines, and Hong Kong – experienced financial pressures as well, even if relatively less so by way of comparison with Latin America (IMF, 1995a, pp. 67–9).

The (short-term) response to the crisis

The IMF arrangement with Mexico was the largest ever approved for a member country, both in the absolute amount and in relation to the country's quota in the Fund.[101] On 1 February 1995, the Executive Board of the IMF approved a $17.8 billion stand-by loan (around seven times the Mexico's IMF quota) by invoking the 'exceptional circumstances' clause. The United States contributed an additional $20 billion to the rescue package and the Bank for International Settlement (BIS) and commercial banks extended $10 and $3 billion respectively. Both the IMF and the Clinton administration were harshly criticized for the support provided to Mexico, and both made a staunch defense of this decision. It is therefore interesting to explore the reasons that led to what some commentators have defined as an 'extraordinary' rescue package (Sachs, et al., 1996, p. 48). The way in which the reasons to help Mexico were packaged provide interesting insights into the predominant understanding on both capital account liberalization and the role of the IMF in an era of globalized finance.

The Clinton administration had high political stakes in Mexico's economic prospects. Despite the fact that the NAFTA agreement was initially negotiated in 1992 by the Bush administration, the agreement was amended and implemented by the Salinas and Clinton administrations in 1993. Clinton, not Bush, is the President's name that is most closely associated with NAFTA. Winning Congressional approval for the agreement turned out to be more difficult than expected (Delong and Eichengreen, 2004, p. 204), thus becoming one of the first political battles the new administration was to fight with a fierce and inward-looking Congress. Therefore, when Mexico found itself on the brink of default in December 1994, it could hardly have been possible for the Clinton administration to be a passive spectator in what appeared to be a major economic breakdown.

The case for intervening in the Mexican crisis was strongly advocated in the US Treasury. Appointed in January 1995, the new Treasury Secretary Robert Rubin immediately became active in managing the crisis. According to the US Treasury Secretary, two main reasons justified US intervention in Mexico. First, as Rubin and Weisberg (2003, p. 4) put it in his memoirs, 'We weren't proposing intervention for the sake of Mexico...but to protect ourselves.' Simply put, American interests were at stake. Specifically, Mexico being the US's third-largest trading partner, it was feared that a peso collapse, with the associated inflationary and recessionary pressures, would have affected the US economy through two channels. On the one hand, with Mexico in recession, the demand for US goods would be curtailed – hurting US workers and firms. This was an especially threatening scenario considering the prospect of contagion to Latin America and other emerging market countries. 'According to an estimate made by the Federal Reserve Board, a Mexican default and the consequent "contagion" that was possible could, in a worst-case scenario, reduce growth in the United States by ½ to 1 percent' (Rubin and Weisberg, 2003, p. 4). On the other, a deep economic crisis triggering political instability was likely to cause massive waves of illegal immigration to the United States – a point the White House and State Department strongly emphasized. For instance, National Security Adviser Anthony Lake was among those arguing that the crisis in Mexico 'pos[ed] the risk of political instability and economic decline that could undercut US exports and boost illegal immigration.'[102]

The second reason justifying US intervention was that Mexican collapse would have set back the clock for trade and financial market liberalization. This line of reasoning reveals an important aspect of Clinton's foreign economic policy agenda: its focus on prying open markets, both commercial and financial. Rubin and Weisberg (2003, p. 12) makes this point quite bluntly in his memoirs,

> We also worried that the Mexican crisis could affect the global movement towards trade and capital market liberalization and market-based economic reforms. ... If Mexico went into default ..., in part for failure to properly manage the influx of foreign capital,

the case for further reform might be set back in the United States and abroad.

To put it differently, the failure of a country that had been hailed 'as a role model for developing countries pursuing economic reform ... could deal an enormous setback to the spread of market-based economic reforms and globalization.' Rubin's view was strongly supported by his Deputy. 'Letting Mexico go,' Larry Summers argued, 'would send a discouraging signal to other developing nations – such as Russia, China, Poland, Brazil, and South Africa – that had been moving forward with market-oriented reforms' (Rubin and Weisberg 2003, pp. 5, 12). In the words of the *New York Times*, 'A generation ago, the fear was over Vietnam and whether its fall to Communism would inevitably take Thailand or Malaysia or Indonesia with it. The Vietnam of the economic age is Mexico.'[103]

Having made the case for the United States to intervene in Mexico, the administration forcefully fought within the US Congress and within the IMF Board to put together a support package for Mexico.[104] Within the IMF, the administration ensured a larger financing than the one originally committed. Hence, a $10 billion Stand-by Program, on top of the already $7.8 billion given on 26 January, was approved by the IMF Executive Board on 1 February 1995. The approval of the loan package, however, proved difficult, because of the criticism of a number of European Executive Directors.

The US Treasury Secretary Robert Rubin and Weisberg (2003, p. 24) recalls, for instance, that the G7 allies were 'furious' at Camdessus and 'upset' with the US. Publicly committing the IMF to provide a promised $10 billion on top of the $7.8 billion already committed before approval from the Executive Board raised concerns on IMF financial exposure and on the use of IMF resources to finance capital flight.[105] Marc-Antoine Autheman, the French representative on the Board, for instance, was quite explicit in charging the Mexican authorities with using Fund resources to finance capital outflows – in clear contravention of the IMF's Articles of Agreement, according to which Fund resources cannot be used to face 'large or sustained' capital outflows.[106] Jon Shields, Gerrit Hendrik Huisman, and Willy Kiekens, UK, Dutch, and Belgian representatives respectively, voiced similar concerns.[107] Kiekens was particularly vocal in questioning the role of the IMF in Mexico and asking whether the use of Fund resources for finance capital flows was compatible with the Articles of Agreement. In his words,

The purposes of the Fund as conceived at Bretton Woods and since then broadly maintained is not to guarantee free capital movements... In cases of large or sustained net capital outflows, in other words, outflows that cannot be offset by new international credit.[108]

It took considerable US diplomacy to calm European resistance and no less than arm-twisting on IMF management to secure Fund financing, which was nonetheless approved in February and disbursed (Rubin and Weinsberg 2003, pp. 24, 30–1).[109]

4.2 The IMF interprets the crisis

In the words of an economist, 'when a new crisis hits, the previous generation of models is judged to have been inadequate' (Rodrik, 1998, p. 58). And, indeed, the Mexican crisis was no exception, by putting the Washington consensus on trial. Economists and policy makers concentrated on the questions of what the crisis signified, and what its lessons were in both economic and political terms. The focus on fundamentals and on the overvaluation of real exchange rate, combined with the emphasis on better provision of information to the markets, became the main factors used to explain the peso crisis and on which to concentrate to reduce the probability of future crises. The crisis also offered a conspicuous example of the speed with which financial risks spread across the globe. Showing the risks of a globalized economy, where 'Mexico's financial problems mean trouble for Malaysia,'[110] the crisis injected a sense of urgency in the search for political responses to the governance of financial globalization.

Within the IMF, the 'in-house reflection' (Camdessus, 1995g) sparked by the Mexican crisis provided an opportunity to reflect on the process of international financial integration and on the policies that needed to be adopted at the domestic and international level to avoid episodes of financial instability. In interpreting the crisis, however, the IMF did not appreciably call into question the policy idea of *orderly liberalization*. Indeed, from the Fund's perspective, the crisis did not negate the presumption of the benefits deriving from global financial integration. At the same time, the imposition of capital controls continued largely to be seen as an inappropriate policy choice because of the ineffectiveness and costs of these controls.

In the aftermath of the crisis, Camdessus (1995h) summarized the policy consensus of the time, reaffirming the faith in the 'increasing openness to trade and financial flows' as 'an essential and reliable basis of economic progress.' The quick pace of recovery from the crisis, both in Mexico and Latin American, seemed to lend significant support to this presumption. Furthermore, Camdessus (1995a) pointed out that 'reverting to closed economic systems with exchange controls and less open markets ... would be to turn the clock back and forego the benefits of globalization.' Rather than 'to fall back on restrictions because of financial market reactions to policy inadequacies,' Camdessus (1995h) forcefully argued, 'It is policy inadequacies that have to be addressed.'

Pointing to 'policy inadequacies' as the main culprit of the crisis, the IMF provided an interpretation of the 1994–95 events consistent with the logic of currency crises, which points to the collision between domestic goals and an unsustainable exchange rate to explain sudden and massive reversals of capital flows. 'What happened in Mexico was the typical crisis of an overvalued currency,' magnified by the speed of capital outflows typical of an era of globalized finance (Fischer 1995b). 'Data on the key economic and financial variables,' the IMF staff noted in its 1995 International Capital Markets Report (IMF, 1995a, p. 70), 'suggest that developments in Mexico surrounding the devaluation were consistent with the classic properties of a speculative attack.'

In other words, the sharp reversal of capital flows that Mexico experienced was attributed to its weak fundamentals – both internal and external imbalances. As stressed by Camdessus (1995a; 1995h), Mexico suffered from severe 'shortcomings' that can 'be traced in large part to the widening of its external current account deficit (to 8 percent in 1994) – which was related to a low and declining private saving rate and the appreciation of its real exchange rate – and also to an insufficiently tight domestic monetary policy.' Hence, the incompatibility between domestic macroeconomic policies and exchange-rate policy drove investors to think, with some reason, that the peso might be devalued thereby making them unwilling to hold Mexican financial assets.

Conceived in these terms, the peso crisis was not interpreted as an instance of market *pathology* or speculative bubble. The voice coming from the IMF lent support to the view that the Mexican crisis may well be considered as an instance of the market *rational* response to perceived inconsistencies in economic policies (IMF, 1995a, p. 70). Increasingly, investors came to believe that the fixed exchange-rate policy would eventually be abandoned. In an attempt to anticipate profits and losses, market investors reacted by restructuring their portfolios, a move that ultimately speeded up the collapse of the peso exchange rate. In short, the prevalent view was that 'Markets are not always right, but they are often appropriately discriminating' (Camdessus, 1995a). As Stanley Fischer (1997a) emphasized, 'While I believe we sometimes see examples of market overreactions and unjustified contagion effects,

I also believe that capital movements are mostly appropriate: currency crises do not blow up out of a clear blue sky, but rather start as rational reactions to policy mistakes or external shocks.' Mexico provided an apt example, thereby reinforcing the prior consensus on the benefits of financial globalization.

Hence, from the Fund's perspective, the peso crisis clearly indicated that the key to crisis prevention lies in sound monetary and fiscal policies and in a strengthened role for the IMF in the governance of the international financial system.

The importance of sound domestic policies to withstand the risks of global financial integration was corroborated by way of comparison with the economic performance of those countries that suffered from the tequila effects. According to the IMF staff World Economic Outlook (IMF, 1995b, p. 6), 'Countries with a stronger saving performance and greater success in managing the surge in capital inflows are generally less vulnerable to shifts in market sentiment, although they have not been immune to contagion effects from the crisis in Mexico.' This interpretation found further supporting argument in the successful experience of the 'dynamic Asian economies,' where 'sound macroeconomic policies' combined with measures 'to open up their economies' and 'to remove structural impediments to economic efficiency' had not been reversed in the wake of the Mexican crisis, sustaining a strong economic growth rate (IMF, 1995a, p. 34). The Argentinean reaction to the crisis, then, provided one of the most valuable examples at which the IMF could point to prove its interpretation right.

Argentina was the first country to experience financial market pressures in the wake of the Mexican crisis in early 1995. The Argentine stock market fell by 14 percent in dollar terms in less than ten days (19–27 December 1994), as a result of sizeable private short-term capital outflows, forcing down its foreign exchange reserves. Specifically, from the last week of December to March, Argentina sold more than one-third of its reserves, putting its entire banking system under strain and undermining market confidence in the Convertibility Plan – the fixed exchange-rate regime that linked the Argentinean peso to the US dollar at one-to-one parity (IMF, 1995a, p. 64).

The authorities' response to the crisis was aimed at preserving the credibility of the Convertibility Plan, a goal that was fully supported by the IMF staff, as an internal evaluation reveals.[111] In line with the IMF's financial orthodoxy, Argentina avoided recourse to capital controls on capital outflows but tightened its fiscal policy, cutting government expenditure.[112] It also privatized provincial banks and provided liquidity support for the banking system.

Argentine's response proved successful, as attested by the relatively small fall in its GDP and exchange rate, the recovery in the prices of stocks and bonds, and the stabilization of the banking system. The lack of contagion and the positive reaction of capital markets also lent support to the predominant view that markets discriminate on the basis of fundamentals rewarding sound policies, the discipline argument. 'By transforming the crisis into an opportunity to address in depth the worrying signs of weakness in its provincial banks,' Camdessus (1995c) emphatically commented, 'Argentina, with strong support from the IDB, World Bank, and IMF, has paid a great service not only to itself but to the Americas and the world at large.' Defending the exchange rate by strengthening fiscal policy and avoiding recourse to capital controls,[113] Argentina showed that it was possible to harness the risks of global financial integration.

The comparison with Brazil is telling. The prevalent consensus against the use of capital controls, and the importance of sound domestic policies in the management of capital flows, led the IMF to criticize Brazil's use of capital in response to the crisis. For instance, the IMF staff commented that 'although [controls] can provide useful breathing room for the formulation of more fundamental measures, they create distortions and tended to lose effectiveness over time.' In contrast, IMF staff stressed the importance of 'strengthening fiscal policy to achieve a more lasting improvement in the macroeconomic environment that would be more conducive to longer-term capital inflows.' These views were fully endorsed by the Executive Directors, who called on Brazilian authorities to remove capital controls, in that their effectiveness would be eroded 'the longer they remained in effect' and in that their use would impede 'the development of the financial system.'[114] Brazil aside, in the first Board meeting on the issue of capital convertibility after the Mexican crisis, 'most Directors' continued to regard controls on both inflows and outflows as 'distortionary' and having decreasing 'ineffectiveness over time.' They also 'emphasized that...controls should not be used as a substitute for more fundamental policy adjustments.'[115] On this issue, there was unanimous support. As the Acting Chairman recorded, 'All speakers agreed that controls should not – and in fact could no longer – support inefficient policies.'[116]

In particular, then, the continued 'general distaste' for the use of capital controls to address balance of payments difficulties,[117] that is, to manage crises once they occur, may also be glimpsed from the debate on the

IMF Board pertaining to the approval of the stand-by arrangement with Mexico. As already pointed out, one of the main concerns about the loan to Mexico was that Fund resources would be used to finance capital outflows in clear contravention to its constitutional purposes. Considering these widespread concerns among Executive Directors, and considering that according to Article VI (section three) a member may exercise such controls that are deemed necessary to regulate international capital movements, a Board decision encouraging Mexico to introduce such controls would have not been implausible. Nevertheless, as the US Executive Director clearly put it, 'the Board had rejected them' with the decision to endorse the program for Mexico. Not only had the IMF rejected capital controls, but 'the Mexican authorities had also rejected those options, and the US authorities too ... [they] had deemed them too costly and too damaging, not only to Mexico's long-term interests, but also to those of the international community.'[118] Camdessus also picked out the argument, noting that controls would have been damaging for both Mexico and the international community because of the negative signal that they would have sent to market investors.[119] Controls would have dealt 'a terrible blow' for both the country's economic growth and other emerging markets' economic prospects (Camdessus, 1995e).

Finally, the Mexican crisis reinforced the policy consensus on the role of the IMF as the manager and promoter of global financial integration. Indeed, from the Fund's perspective, the crisis showcased that 'the responsibilities of the IMF, [were] now greater than ever before,' as Camdessus (1995h) emphatically commented. For one thing, the Mexican crisis showed that 'Vigilance and discipline provide the most effective deterrent and defense against financial market setbacks' (Camdessus, 1995c). As the international organization that regularly oversees the economic policies of its members thereby disciplining member countries' policies, the relevance of the IMF to the economic performance of its members was safely reasserted. For another, the crisis showed the ongoing need of Fund resources to instill confidence in the process of global integration. In assisting Mexico, the IMF had helped to avoid contagion and a rush to capital controls. Absent IMF assistance, 'A decade of unstinting international efforts to open markets and liberalize emerging economies would have been at risk' (Camdessus, 1995e).[120]

In conclusion, the Mexican crisis, which had 'certainly demonstrate[d] the power of the international capital markets' (Fischer, 1995c), left the tenets of the policy consensus on capital liberalization intact. The predominant view was still that the free movement of private capital flows should be relied on to attain economic growth and to impose macroeconomic discipline. Even though the crisis provided a powerful image of the scale and volatility of capital flows in a globalized world, the IMF did not embrace the principle of capital controls, neither for preventing nor for managing crises. The IMF was rather depicted as a useful instrument that member countries might rely upon to govern the risks deriving from the process of global financial integration. In particular, IMF advice and financial assistance appeared more salient than ever before. Nevertheless, for the IMF to perform its tasks efficiently, a reform of its activities appeared in order. Explaining the course of institutional reform initiated in the wake of the Mexican crisis, it is now timely to look at those actors who supported (or opposed) specific reform proposals, thereby validating (or questioning) the policy consensus articulated inside the IMF.

4.3   The socio-political validation of the idea of orderly liberalization

Member countries, economists, as well as private investors, extensively and substantially shared the IMF's analysis of the crisis. The active support, or the lack of opposition, that these actors displayed helped to consolidate the consensus on international financial liberalization as a policy required to achieve economic growth and on the role of the IMF as a manager of such liberalization.

In the communiqué released after the June 1995 Halifax summit, for instance, the representatives of the most industrialized economies repeated their faith in the benefits of global integration. They stressed that 'new investment and increased trade are vital to achieving our growth and employment objectives', pledging 'to work for the reduction of remaining internal and external barriers.' In this spirit, they also called on fellow countries 'to remove capital market restrictions.' The G7 countries also laid considerable emphasis on the risks of global integration. In this respect, strengthening the international financial institutions (IFIs) appeared of paramount importance in ensuring the international community remains able to manage 'the risks inherent in the growth of private capital flows' (G7, 1995).

The ideas on the benefits of capital account liberalization and on the inappropriateness of capital controls were so widespread that they were hardly questioned even among developing countries. Voices condemning global investors along with Mexican policies, for instance, or calls for resorting to capital controls were virtually absent. Not even the fact that Chile and Colombia, two countries which had continued to use controls, were among the least affected in the Western Hemisphere by the Mexican crisis helped to undermine the predominant view. The idea that controls might have been helpful in partially insulating these economies from the capital flight did not gather significant support. On the IMF Executive Board, for instance, few Directors took the view that capital controls could be used to confront major capital outflows. The majority of Directors 'supported the view that restrictions on capital controls had proven largely ineffective ... In particular, such controls were seen to be incapable of preventing the outflow of domestic savings or of delaying the need for fundamental policy adjustment.'[121] Among the Directors who did not buy into the prevalent consensus, there was the Indian representative K. P. Geethakrishnan who, pointing to the Chilean experience with capital controls, provocatively noted that 'Maybe some restrictions would ... be in order.'[122] Despite a few exceptions, however, the rejection of capital controls, in particular on outflows, still constituted the organizing principle of much of the economic debate and coalitional alignments inside the IMF Board.

Even the calls for more gradualism and sequencing in opening domestic markets to international capital flows were limited. They appeared in the analyses of a number of economists (Crockett, 1996, pp. 298–9, Sachs, et al., 1996, pp. 24–5) and in the remarks of a number of Executive Directors representing developing countries on the Board,[123] but they did not translate into specific political demands or points for coalitional alignments within the Fund. For instance, there still was no country coalition opposing the concept of 'interactive liberalization,' that is, the presumption that important policy reforms such as stabilization, trade and domestic financial liberalization could be achieved simultaneously with capital account liberalization.[124] In particular, the presumption that capital account liberalization and the development of a secure domestic banking and financial system are mutually reinforcing, thereby they should proceed in lockstep rather than being sequenced, was still strong.

The Mexican crisis did not dampen the early 1990s market euphoria for emerging markets. Skepticism about the future was limited. True, there was a pause in the investment flows to developing countries in the first half of 1995. Nevertheless, the speed of recovery was astonishing. In Mexico, for instance, economic and financial conditions started improving at the end of summer 1995 and they stabilized by the beginning of 1996. With the trade deficit turning out to be a surplus and the stock of outstanding *tesobonos* being reduced, the Mexican economy grew and attracted foreign capital again. The comparison with the 1982 crisis made the recovery the most remarkable. As the US Treasury Secretary Robert Rubin and Weisberg (2003, p. 34) noted in his memoirs,

> The 1982 crisis led to what has been called a 'lost decade' of negative growth, financial instability, and political and social unrest throughout Latin America. The 1995 crisis caused real suffering on the part of the Mexican poor and middle class – and real wages were very slow to recover – but only one year of economic growth was lost. After the 1982 crisis, Mexico took seven years to regain access to capital markets. In 1995, it took seven months.

Not only Mexico but Latin American countries on the whole quickly recovered from the crisis, with flows returning. By the end of 1995, net capital flows to developing countries exceeded their previous highs, recorded in 1993 (IMF, 1996a). As early as October 1995, the IMF staff on the World Economic Outlook enthusiastically concluded that 'the maintained market confidence and the continued solid economic performance by a large number of countries are testimony to the substantial progress throughout the developing world toward greater economic and financial stability' (IMF, 1995b, p. 8).

Indeed, the reaction of international markets to the Mexican shock was impressive. Stock markets boomed and interest rates around the world declined.[125] Institutional investment managers made clear that 'they intend[ed] to press steadily and purposefully ahead with the international diversification of their portfolios' and industry surveys suggested that the share of foreign investment going to emerging countries was unlikely to change radically in the next years (IMF, 1995a, p. 4). The head of emerging markets research at Salomon Brothers, John Purcell, publicly summarized the position of global investors, predicting that 'pension funds and mutual funds [were] going to come back to the market.'[126] In brief, Wall Street euphoric prospects for the future were robust.

Views contrary to the predominant optimism were weak or nonexistent. Voices such as those of the economist Paul Krugman (1995, p. 43), who warned that 'the 1990–95 euphoria about developing countries was so overdrawn ... [that] the huge capital gains in emerging market equities will not continue,' did not attract widespread currency.[127] Rather, countries' excesses were to be kept in check. In the words of two economists, 'The Mexican economy crisis also illustrates how easy it is for host countries to be lured into a sense of overconfidence – both about the permanence of private capital flows and about the size of the protective cushion against potential outflows' (Goldstein and Calvo, 1996, p. 246).

4.4 Institutionalizing the consensus on orderly liberalization

Having long emphasized the need to reform the IMF to meet the challenge of a global economy, IMF management and staff built on the consensus nurtured after the Mexican crisis to institutionalize their earlier reform proposals. That is to say, IMF management and staff actively advocated the adoption of new policies in an attempt to make the organization the fulcrum of international financial governance. In a famous remark, Camdessus (1995h) characterized the Mexican crisis as 'the first major crisis to have arisen in an emerging market economy in our new age of globalized financial markets.'[128] Stressing that the crisis in Mexico was the first in the twenty first century, the Managing Director nonetheless implied that it was not going to be the last – a prediction that proved unfortunately right. Hence, so the argument went, had the organization to be ready to withstand future financial crises, its policies needed to be reformed.

Building on the positive signals coming from the Fund's social constituencies for legitimation, where the G7 calls for 'strengthening' the international financial institutions to make them 'effective' and 'efficient' in an era of global capital markets (G7, 1995) were echoed by developing countries, the IMF management pushed its earlier proposals to reform the IMF on to the tables of the IMF Board. Three activities figured prominently on the institutional reform agenda: strengthening IMF surveillance, increasing IMF financial resources, and amending the IMF's Articles of Agreement to give the organization mandate and jurisdiction over capital transactions.

Crisis prevention: Reforming IMF surveillance

The first activity requiring reform related to the prevention of financial crises. 'The experience with Mexico ... demonstrated ... that prevention is better than cure' (Camdessus, 1995e). Prevention, in the IMF language, means surveillance, that is, the regular activity through which the Fund assesses the policies and performance of its member countries as mandated in Article IV.[129]

IMF staff had already circulated proposals to reform the Fund's surveillance. For instance, the Director of the Monetary Affairs and Exchange (MAE) Department, Manuel Guitián, had called for reforming the 'code of conduct' of the IMF, in order to bring the practice of the organization in line with the historical economic reality (Guitián, 1992; 1995). Similarly, Camdessus had formally exposed the suggestion to strengthen the Fund's surveillance in his public address at the fiftieth anniversary of the organization in Madrid, September 1994. On the heels of the Mexican crisis, however, these early proposals gained political salience.

Indeed, the crisis pointed to the failure of the Fund's surveillance, in the sense that the IMF failed to warn the Mexican authorities of the risks implied in their economic policy choices.[130] Seen from the perspective of IMF staff, Fund surveillance appeared to have not paid sufficient attention to the capital account (Fischer, 1995b) and to have suffered from information problems. As Fischer (1997a) recalls, 'information on reserves was provided with a long lag, and information on the structure of the external debt was not readily available.' IMF staff also found problems in statistical reporting of economic data (i.e. fiscal data – distinguishing between regular and extraordinary fiscal expenditures – and reserves and external liabilities). For instance, the decline in reserves that took place in November 1994, which forced down the stock of reserves to $12.9 billion, was not publicly announced until after the devaluation in December (IMF, 1995a, p. 56).

By bringing the shortcomings of the Fund's surveillance activity to the surface, the Mexican crisis provided the opportunity to transform the IMF management and staff's earlier proposals into policy choices. However, the reform of the Fund's surveillance was not simply the mechanical response to the technical problems that the crisis had sharply highlighted. The reform, which clearly reflected the principles of *orderly liberalization* in its attempt to further the movement of capital flows while minimizing its risks, spoke to the interests of both developed and developing countries. Indeed, strengthening IMF surveillance echoed the G7 call to create an 'early warning system' that would provide timely information of member countries' economic and financial conditions to financial markets.[131] It also met the G24 expectations on the role of the IMF to help developing countries proceed safely along the path of liberalization. In addition, the reform of surveillance was a reform with zero costs, in the sense that it did not entail any significant new obligations for member countries.

Among the reforms adopted in the area of crisis prevention, three stand out. The first policy change took place in April 1995 when the Executive Board decided to amend the 1977 decision so that the Fund should devote more attention to capital account issues in its surveillance activity. Specifically, two paragraphs were added to the 1977 decision. They specified that, in the exercise of its surveillance, the IMF staff should discuss with each member those domestic policies that provide 'abnormal encouragement or discouragement of capital flows' and should inquire into the causes of 'unsustainable flows of private capitals.'[132] Reflecting the lessons driven home from the Mexican crisis, the Fund's amended decision also clarified that 'The Fund's appraisal of a member's exchange-rate policies shall be based on an evaluation of the developments in the member's balance of payments, including the size and sustainability of capital flows, against the background of its reserve position and its external indebtedness.'[133] In short, the 1995 decision reflected the recognition that both internal and external policies contribute to the adjustment of the balance of payment.

A second and important policy change pertained to the expansion of the information that the Fund maintains on capital controls. The Fund has traditionally collected and published information on members' exchange systems in the context of the Annual Report on Exchange Arrangements and Exchange Restrictions (AREAER). Nevertheless, the AREAER traditionally focused on the regulations affecting *current* international transactions. After July 1995, however, following a mandate from the Executive Directors, staff intensified work to improve the information in the AREAER database, by filling significant gaps in the data, increasing the frequency of updates, the accessibility of the information, and upgrading information on controls on both inflows and outflows.

The development of more comprehensive information on the controls maintained by members on capital movements was complemented by the establishment of the Special Data Dissemination Standard (SDDS). Approved by the Executive Board at a meeting held on 29 March 1996, the SDDS established a 'flexible and evolutionary' system through which member countries were encouraged 'the provision to the public ofcomprehensive, timely, accessible, and reliable economic and financial statistics in a world of increasing economic and financial integration.' The SDDS logic of functioning reflected the prevalent view that '[c]omprehensive economic and financial data, disseminated on a timely basis, are essential to the transparency of macroeconomic performance and policy.'[134]

Finally, at the end of December 1995, staff received the first operational guidelines, which set 'the next steps to be followed by the staff in adapting Fund practices to elicit greater emphasis on capital account issues, and to promote more actively capital account liberalization.'[135]

These guidelines, prepared by the Monetary and Exchange Affairs (MAE) and Policy Development and Review (PDR) departments and circulated to the Area departments under a cover memorandum from the Directors Boorman and Guitián, specified a code of behavior for IMF staff involved in Article IV consultations, other missions, and technical assistance reports. Specifically, the guidelines significantly extended the range of domestic policies over which the IMF exercises surveillance. Staff missions were requested to pay due attention to 'the implications of capital movements for the balance of payments and exchange and interest rates' and to the key factors influencing private capital movements, 'including the regulatory framework,' that is banking regulation, supervision, and transparency.[136] The notes also specified that IMF staff missions were expected to provide a thorough evaluation of the system of capital controls, 'particularly in situations where capital flows are sizable and where there is scope for liberalizing capital account transactions.'

Crisis management: Reforming IMF assistance

In the aftermath of the Mexican crisis, a second area of the IMF's activities ranked high in the list of policies requiring institutional reform. It was the area related to the IMF's financing activity, hence pertaining to the area of crisis management.

Again, IMF management and staff had already circulated reforms pertaining to the IMF's financing activity in the years that preceded the Mexican crisis. On the one hand, there was a proposal to create a fast-disbursing and short-term financing mechanism to help member countries cushion against balance of payments pressures deriving from capital outflows. On the other, there was the proposal for a new round of Special Drawing Right (SDR) allocation that would increase member countries' access to IMF's financing, in particular developing and transition economies (Camdessus, 1995b, p. 274).

The Mexican crisis added to the sense of urgency to speed up these earlier proposals. The scale of capital flows, in particular, was the variable most immediately reflecting the risks of global financial linkages. As Fischer (1995c) recalls, 'It was frightening to see what a switch in sentiment on that scale could do.' Specifically, 'within a period of two and half days, capital markets turned from being willing to lend to Mexico at an annual rate of about 25 billion dollars, 8 percent of GDP, to wanting to take out not only that 25 billion dollars but also another 60 or 70 billion dollars previously invested in Mexico.' In addition, the assistance extended to Mexico brought into sharp relief the ambiguities of outstanding practices. In particular, the IMF's loan to Mexico raised two sets of concerns. The first was the moral hazard issue. The use of Fund resources to finance capital flight had shifted the burden of risk away from global investors. It has thereby created a dangerous incentive for more risk-taking in the future.[137] The second set of concerns pertained to the use of Fund resources. Indeed, the Articles of Agreement deny member countries' access to Fund resources in the event of capital flight. The fact that the IMF had nonetheless extended its financial assistance to Mexico raised new concerns on the use of Fund resources under conditions of globalization.

In this connection, IMF staff and management called for a review of IMF lending criteria and size of lending. As the IMF Deputy put it, 'if capital account liberalization increases the likelihood of larger, even if fewer, crises, it would also be appropriate to review Fund lending criteria, to ensure that Fund loans – in some cases together with supporting funding – will remain adequate to their task' (Fischer, 1997a). In the aftermath of the crisis, then, proposals to reform the IMF's financing activity gained currency. Specifically, two courses of action were launched. The first was the launch of a general quota review to double the size of IMF resources,[138] to make them in line with the volume and speed of global financial integration. The second was the proposal to have a one-time allocation of the SDRs across the membership, that is, the IMF's reverse asset that member countries are assigned on the basis of their quotas and that members can exchange for other usable currencies, thereby providing an extra cushion in the event of capital outflows. In addition, a round of SDR allocation would have made up for the fact that countries that joined the Fund subsequent to 1981 had never received an SDR allocation.[139]

The amendment to the Articles of Agreement

Despite the initiation of important reforms, IMF management and staff engaged in a persuasive battle with Executive Directors to convince them of the need to deepen the reforms to the IMF's activities. Specifically, acting on their beliefs on *orderly liberalization*, IMF management and senior staff officials strongly advocated an amendment to the IMF's Articles of Agreement. By prodding and exhortations, indeed, IMF staff ruled out the appropriateness of alternative policies to manage international capital flows on the ground that these alternative policies, including a strengthened IMF surveillance, did not guarantee the achievement of the goal of *orderly liberalization*.[140] As the IMF General Counsel Gianviti forcefully noted, 'the Fund [does] not have the means at present to achieve its mandate to oversee the proper functioning of the international monetary system; the Fund ha[s] a mandate, but it [does] not have the means to achieve it.'[141]

Indeed, under Article IV, the Fund may find that a member had recourse to restrictions on capital inflows and outflows that negatively affect the member's exchange-rate policy. Nevertheless, even if these restrictions are in place, under the present articles, the Fund is not entitled to promote liberalization of capital investment or capital transactions. Similarly, under Article VI, the Fund is not allowed to extend financing to its members in case of 'large or sustained' capital outflows. From the Fund's perspective, these provisions reduced members' confidence in likely Fund support, thereby depriving members of one of the incentives to proceed along the path of liberalization and calling into question the legitimacy of its actions.

In brief, from the IMF's perspective, strengthening surveillance did not guarantee members' compliance with the principle of liberalization, and financing capital flight under the present Articles might prove self-defeating in terms of the organization's legitimacy. The process of *orderly liberalization* – slow but sure liberalization – would not have taken place.

Drawing on these limitations, the Fund management and staff articulated a policy proposal that aimed at meeting the standard of *orderly liberalization*. Amending the Articles of Agreement to give the IMF mandate and jurisdiction over capital transactions was conceived as the most 'appropriate' response. As the First Deputy Managing Director put it, 'an amendment of the Fund's Articles of Agreement is the best way of ensuring that capital account liberalization is carried out in an orderly, non-disruptive way, that minimizes the risks that premature liberalization could pose for an economy and its policymakers' (Fischer, 1997a). The proposal suggested giving the IMF mandate and jurisdiction over capital transactions akin to the mandate and jurisdiction the IMF already exercised over the payments and transfers for current account transactions. Specifically, by assuming the mandate, the promotion of capital liberalization would be inserted into the goals that the IMF pursues (Article I). By assuming jurisdiction, member countries' resistance to capital liberalization might be sanctioned by the Fund (Article VIII).

Extending the Fund's responsibilities from the current to the capital account, however, marked a significant departure from the consensus reached at Bretton Woods and institutionalized in the Fund's Articles. Indeed, the amendment implied tearing apart the provision that left member countries the discretion to introduce capital controls, prohibiting their use. This would have involved a substantial transformation in the code of conduct governing the international monetary system in that it was 'the *opposite* of what Keynes and the other founding fathers of the IMF intended' (Kirshner, 1999, p. 316).

Given the profound change that the amendment implied, and given the politically demanding requirements for the amendment to be adopted, prescribing the support of three-fifths of members, having 85 percent of the total voting power, IMF staff had to secure the support of both industrial and developing countries. In doing that, IMF staff had to address some reservations that circulated among Executive Directors at the prospect of extending the Fund jurisdiction to capital flows through an amendment to the Article of Agreement. Among these reservations, three stood out. First, in various Board meetings, Executive Directors asked IMF staff about the conditions under which members countries would have retained their existing right to impose capital controls had the amendment won support – the so-called approval policies. For instance, it was frequently asked whether the IMF would have used greater flexibility in approving controls than under the policy presently applied to payments and transfers for current international transactions. Second, several Directors asked IMF staff to know at what point in the reform process member countries would be asked to open the capital account. Indeed, an extension of the jurisdiction over capital movements needed to provide for transitional arrangements to assure that liberalization was sequenced with macro and structural policies thereby reflecting the circumstances of individual countries. Finally, Executive Directors had reservations on the effects of capital account liberalization on the demand for Fund financing. For instance, one of the oft-repeated questions raised during Executive Board meetings was whether the IMF had sufficient financial resources to help countries face capital account crises.[142] Aware of these concerns, IMF staff largely relied on the ambiguity in the idea of *orderly liberalization* to win support within the Board.

In particular, IMF staff papers did address the issues of the conditions on the use of capital controls, the sequence of liberalization, and the size of IMF resources. Nevertheless, IMF staff addressed these issues by offering alternative options to Executive Directors and without pressing them to solve those issues in their current discussions. Rather, IMF management and staff depicted the issues of the conditions on the use of capital controls, the sequence of liberalization, and the size of IMF resources as 'technicalities' whose implications could be debated and fixed later in the negotiation process. For instance, in a number of staff memoranda prepared from 1996 through 1997, IMF staff systematically analyzed different aspects of the potential amendment. However, IMF staff also stressed that it was not feasible to consider all of the issues related to an amendment in a few documents and that the treatment of several important aspects, including the treatment of transitional arrangements, approval policies, and the financial implications of the amendment would be addressed separately.[143] In this connection, during a meeting held in April 1997, IMF management strongly invited Executive Directors to accept the amendment to the Articles in spite of the still unresolved issues, noting that 'the time it would take for members to ratify the amendment would have given members the additional time they were looking for' to clarify many of the outstanding questions on capital account liberalization.[144] That is to say, Executive Directors were encouraged to agree with the basic thrust of the approach to capital account liberalization as delineated in IMF papers.

IMF staff thereby encouraged members to concentrate on what was depicted as the substance of the debate: the benefits of liberalization and the role of the IMF in it. As a result, staff papers framed the discussion around the questions *if* capital account liberalization is good for economic growth and *if* the IMF is the right institution to help member countries move along the path of liberalization. The much more complicated questions of *how* capital account liberalization is beneficial and *how* the IMF may help member countries in the liberalization process were postponed. As a result, issues such as approval and transitional arrangements and the relationship between capital account liberalization and the Fund resources were relegated to the margins of the debate. Given the lack of specification of these important issues, it is not surprising that several Executive Directors recall the negotiations on the amendment as revolving around technicalities.[145] Some Directors even complained about the lack of clarification of important issues. For instance, in a 1998 Board meeting, the Chilean Alternate Director Nicolas Eyzaguirre retrospectively noted that 'discussions thus far have privileged the consideration of procedural and legal aspects, but some important conceptual issues remain somehow obscure.'[146]

Having cast the ambiguity surrounding the imposition of capital controls and the sequence of liberalization as technical matters that could be solved later on in the negotiations, IMF staff succeeded in diluting the political divide between industrial and developing countries. As Camdessus (1997a) captured the outcome of the negotiations within the Board that led to the decision to proceed with the amendment to the Articles, 'we will certainly have a lot of work to do to define the modalities of the process leading to this full liberalization.' However, he remarked that 'we have the unanimous support of the membership on the objective.' Indeed, if no distributional outcome was really at stake in the ongoing negotiations, industrial and developing countries could easily converge around the views that capital account liberalization is welfare-enhancing and that the IMF has the capacity to help member countries move towards such a desirable policy course.

Indeed, as the IMF archival documents reveal, Executive Directors regarded the presumption in favor of liberalization and the proposal to amend the Articles of Agreement as closely intertwined. That is to say, the opposition to an extension of the role of the IMF over capital flows was undermined by the overall presumption that capital account liberalization is beneficial. While this is not surprising for industrial countries that by and large supported the amendment, even the most critical representatives of developing countries shared the linkage between the benefits of liberalization and the role of the IMF. For instance, the Colombian Alberto Calderon, who deemed that an amendment 'does not seem appropriate', conceded that '[c]ountries should strive towards capital account convertibility.'[147] Similarly Zhang, the Chinese Executive Director, was quite skeptical on the opportunity to amend the Articles because liberalization is 'best promoted by economic necessity and on a voluntary basis', hence 'pressure and haste on the part of the Fund would be counterproductive.' Nevertheless, he recognized that liberalization, though 'arduous', had proved 'rewarding' for his country.[148]

Hence, the merits of the advocates of the amendment lay in having packaged the amendment as closely linked with the arguments in favor of capital liberalization. Having accepted the idea that 'capital account convertibility is a desirable end,' as the Saudi Director Al-Tuwaijri put it, the logical consequence was that it was 'in the interest of the membership as a whole that greater capital movement be encouraged by this institution [the IMF].'[149] As a result, by April 1997, Executive Directors went public with the proposal to amend the Articles, suggesting an extension of mandate and jurisdiction over capital transactions (IMF, 1997a, p. 39).

This is not to say that there was an undisputed consensus.[150] Whereas Directors agreed on the principle to liberalize the capital account eventually and on the importance of the role of the IMF in the process, reservations persisted on the conditions for the use of capital controls, on the timing of liberalization, and on the extent of help that could be granted by the IMF in the event of capital flight. However, the persuasive struggle conducted by IMF management proved successful to the extent that these contentious issues were deferred to an undefined stage of the negotiations thereby convincing Executive Directors to accept the amendment because those issues would be addressed later and separately. For instance, in one of the Executive Board meetings that preceded the issuance of the IMF Annual Report (1997a) where Executive Directors endorsed the proposal to amend the Articles, the UK representative Gus O'Donnell remarked, 'it is important at this stage not to be bogged down in details,' suggesting that the crucial issues at stake were recognizing the benefits of free capital flows and the importance of the role of the IMF in the international system characterized by growing capital flows.[151] Similarly, Benny Andersen, representative of the Scandinavian constituencies, noted 'there are still many operational aspects of an expanded mandate that need to be addressed.' Nevertheless, 'we can ... agree with the basic thrust of the approach ... outlined by the staff.'[152] Still, a number of representatives made clear that they could accept to move toward the amendment only with the understanding that its details would clearly be refined over a longer period of time.[153]

Along with the use of ambiguity by IMF management and staff, another factor contributed to push the amendment firmly onto the IMF's books in April 1997: the perception among Executive Directors that an extension of the Fund's mission to capital transactions was welcome across the Fund's social constituencies for legitimation. For instance, several Directors recall no opposition from developing countries as a reason that led the Board to continue along the path of an amendment.[154] As one Executive Director put it,

> The feeling within the Board was that many member countries were confronted with the challenge of globalization and that the IMF could help them confront that challenge. We felt that member countries were asking us to endow the IMF with the instruments to deal with the risks of globalization. To perform this task, however, a new legal framework was required. (Esdar, 2006)

In this perceived favorable environment, during the summer of 1997, IMF staff intensified their efforts to reach a deal on the amendment to be submitted to the Interim Committee in September, in time for the Annual meeting. Expectations were not defied. Drawing on the consensus nurtured within the Executive Board on the initiative to amend the Articles, the Interim Committee invited the IMF Board

> to complete its work on a proposed amendment of the Fund's Articles that would make the liberalization of capital movements one of the purposes of the Fund, and extend, as needed, the Fund's jurisdiction through the establishment of carefully-defined and consistently applied obligations regarding the liberalization of such movements. (Interim Committee, 1997)

4.5 Conclusions

The Mexican crisis provided a critical test for the ideas elaborated inside the Fund in earlier years. By showcasing what may happen to national economies when they do not meet the requirements of global markets, the crisis spoke directly to the idea of *orderly liberalization* as had been articulated inside the Fund. Indeed, the scale and speed of capital outflows that materialized in Mexico and other emerging market countries seemed to raise doubts on the notion of liberalization as a desirable and effective policy choice. It seemed but, in fact, it did not. Rather than questioning the policy consensus on *orderly liberalization*, the crisis reinforced it in that it provided the organizing principles through which to interpret the crisis itself. From the IMF's perspective, the crisis reaffirmed the faith in the benefits of growing financial integration and in the costs of capital controls for both individual countries and the international economy. Even accepting the argument that increased risks are intrinsic features of global capital markets, 'if properly managed, such risks need not diminish the substantial benefits that come with increased access to international capital' (IMF, 1995a, pp. 26–7). The benefits of capital liberalization were deemed to outweigh significantly its costs. The crisis did not question neither member countries' choice to embrace global financial integration nor market euphoria for emerging market countries. In other words, the actors forming the Fund's social constituencies for legitimation continued supporting the idea of *orderly liberalization*. In this atmosphere, competing ideas were weak. There were concerns about speed and sequencing of liberalization but it would take the Asian crisis to give these concerns resonance.

Building on the urgency prompted by the crisis, IMF staff engaged in a persuasive battle during which they attempted to win Executive Directors' support around a set of reforms that would have strengthened the role of the IMF in the area of capital account liberalization.

Specifically, by postponing the discussion of the most controversial issues related to the process of liberalization, IMF management and staff secured a wide convergence of views between industrial and developing countries on a specific set of reforms. The IMF thereby embarked on a process of institutional adaptation that aimed at strengthening IMF surveillance and financial assistance. Furthermore, the membership agreed to endorse a more profound institutional change: the amendment to the IMF's Articles that, expanding the Bretton Woods compromise, would have given the Fund the mandate and jurisdiction over capital transactions. Despite all this, the Asian crisis, which loomed in the background, was about to shift the path of institutional reform.

5

The Asian Crisis: Questioning the Consensus

This chapter traces the declining influence of the idea of *orderly liberalization* on the policies pursued by the IMF after the Asian crisis. Specifically, the chapter is organized as follows. The first section describes the Asian financial crisis and its effects on the stability of the global financial system. The second section reviews how the IMF interpreted the crisis using the lens provided by the idea of *orderly liberalization*. In contrast to what had happened after the Mexican crisis, after the Asian crisis the interpretation provided by the IMF was severely contested across the Fund's social constituencies for legitimation. The third section therefore reviews the criticisms leveled at the IMF. Specifically, the chapter shows that an increasing number of member countries, economists, and private investors concluded that the IMF was part of the ongoing financial turbulence rather than a contributor of its solution. In short, the IMF stopped being regarded as the appropriate mechanism to ensure global financial integration and stability.

The fourth section explains how the contestation voiced outside the IMF influenced the reforms to the international financial architecture in the areas of crisis prevention and management. In particular, this section reviews the final stages of the negotiations for amending the Articles of Agreement showing that Executive Directors became primarily concerned with the external criticisms leveled at the IMF because these criticisms posed a threat to the legitimacy of the organization. In an attempt to respond to its critics, Executive Directors also started asking IMF staff to clarify those issues that had been discussed without any definitive conclusions in previous Board meetings, including the conditions under which to (re)impose controls, the preconditions for successful liberalization, and the exact scope of the Fund's jurisdiction. Addressing the ambiguities that characterized the Fund's idea of *orderly liberalization*, however, nullified the persuasive battle conducted by IMF staff thus far, making an agreement within the Board difficult to achieve and thereby leading to the failure of the initiative to amend the Articles of Agreement.

The fifth section concludes by drawing attention to the intellectual reassessment that followed the Asian crisis. This reassessment undermined the international consensus around the idea of *orderly liberalization* setting the stage for new ideas to gain currency with the attendant redefinition of the reform agenda for the governance of the international financial system.

5.1   The Asian crisis

Few propositions about the global economy commanded as much assent in the aftermath of the Mexican crisis as the confidence in the future. Global growth, which had slowed during 1995, was projected to pick up to around 4 percent a year in 1996 and 1997 (IMF, 1996b) and 'favorable global economic conditions' were recorded in both industrial and developing countries (IMF, 1997b). In terms of global financial markets, after a brief pause in 1995, capital flows to developing markets reached a new record high with a net total of around US$235 billion, 'higher than in any previous year' (IMF, 1996a, p. 85). 'This is not a small amount,' Fischer (1997a) pointedly remarked, 'it is nearly 0.8 percent of world GDP, and well above 2 percent of developing-country GDP.'

Along with this favorable economic outlook, the IMF displayed renewed confidence in the stability of international capital markets. As staff members noted in the 1996 International Capital Markets Report, after the Mexican crisis, 'the global financial system appear[ed] to have emerged stronger and more resilient' and market participants appeared to have 'move[d] up the learning curve'. In particular (IMF, 1996a, p. 1), 'market participants, including such risk-tolerant investors as the macro-hedge funds, are more disciplined, cautious, and less likely to ignore market fundamentals in their market activities, and markets appear better able to shrug off periods of turbulence, at least for now.'

Against this background, Asia continued to stand out as one of the most remarkable examples of economic transformation among developing countries ever occurred. During 1992–95, the developing economies of Asia recorded average real GDP growth above 9 percent. 'Although double-digit growth rates in China formed the largest single component of this regional growth performance, Indonesia, Malaysia, and Thailand all experienced average growth above 7 percent in this period' (IMF, 1997c, pp. 2–3). These countries also attested to dramatic improvements in living standards – the best performance among developing countries. Between 1965 and 1995, per-capita income rose tenfold in Korea, fivefold in Thailand, and fourfold in Malaysia thereby achieving significant convergence towards industrial country living standards (IMF, 1997b, pp. 76–7). As Fischer (1998a) put it, 'This record growth and strong trade performance is unprecedented, a remarkable historical achievement.' Hence, it became commonplace to refer to the region as the 'Asian miracle.'[155]

From the IMF's perspective, the extraordinary economic performance of the Asian countries was not the result of fortuitous circumstances. Rather, it was economic growth by design. 'In my opinion,' Camdessus (1997g) remarked, 'the region's economic success over the last couple of decades can be described in many ways – as outstanding, superlative, and certainly admirable. But it was no 'miracle.' Rather, it was the result of good policies.' Although 'there has been no single blueprint for economic success,' the Managing Director also noted, some ingredients appeared the most important in explaining the Asian miracle. These included prudent macroeconomic policies, high rates of savings and investments, investment in human capital, and outward oriented policies (Camdessus, 1997b).

With notable exceptions,[156] both within and without the IMF, few observers doubted the solidity of the Asian miracle – a miracle that appeared to be confirmed in the investment decisions of emerging markets' investors and lenders. Indeed, until the crisis erupted, Asia attracted almost half of capital inflows to developing countries at an average of more than US$60 billion per annum from 1990 to 1996. Only in 1996, this amount reached almost $107 billion (IMF, 1996a). Although in most cases large foreign direct investments dominated net private inflows, as was the case in China, in other cases, short-term inflows became substantial, as was the case in Thailand (IMF, 1997c, pp. 4, 6).[157] A large proportion of short-term flows was channeled by international bank lending, with European and Japanese banks providing the bulk of credit to the Asian countries.[158]

Under these favorable circumstances, Fund surveillance was complacent. As the staff itself concedes, 'in Southeast and East Asia, the Fund's views were formulated against a background of broad agreement, even admiration for economic policies that had underpinned one of the longest periods of sustained high economic growth in history.'[159] Furthermore, the amount of capital flows allocated to the countries in the region was largely interpreted as a sign of economic success rather than a cause for concern. For instance, Camdessus (1996e) pointed to the region's share of international capital inflows – 'the largest share of private capital flows to developing countries of any region in the world' – to corroborate the hypothesis of the region's economic success. Although the Managing Director did not miss the opportunity to identify some reasons for concern, specifically growing current account deficits and the vulnerability of the banking sector, the general conclusion was that the region's economic fundamentals were 'strong', thereby providing 'a margin of comfort against possible risks' (Camdessus, 1996b).

In terms of standard indicators, there were indeed no worrying signs of macroeconomic imbalances: inflation was moderate throughout the region as were fiscal imbalances. Thailand, the country where the crisis initiated, recorded government surpluses every year between 1988 and 1996 (IMF, 1997c, p. 51). As late as 19 September 1997, Stanley Fischer (1997a) was referring to the East Asian economies as 'an astonishing record of sustained economic growth, that within less than two decades has improved the living standards of more people, more rapidly, than at any other time or place in history.' Against the background of these achievements, it is hardly surprising that 'the crisis – and particularly its depth and breadth – came as an enormous surprise,' as Fischer (1999a) himself later noted.

If Mexico was 'a stark reminder... [of] an era in which shifts in market sentiment can have sudden and destabilizing effects' (Camdessus, 1996c), Asia was a remarkable confirmation test.[160] Countries that right up to the crisis had received the largest share of capital inflows among developing countries experienced capital reversals of unprecedented scale. 'South Korea, Indonesia, Thailand, Malaysia and the Philippines received $93 billion of private capital *inflows* in 1996. In 1997 they saw an *outflow* of $12 billion.'[161] In other words, there was a reversal of about $105 billion of net capital flows, amounting to more than 10 percent of the region's GDP.

The crisis started in Thailand, and had the appearance of being a typical currency crisis. The country's current account deficit had become large, at around 8 percent of GDP, and was financed by short-term inflows. External debt, particularly private debt, had risen quickly.[162] Furthermore, by mid-1995, the Thai real exchange rate had appreciated substantially, following the appreciation of the US dollar to which the Thai baht was pegged. With the dollar appreciating against the yen, and with Japan being the largest trading partner of the East Asian countries, the change in the dollar/yen exchange rate negatively affected these countries' external competitiveness as well as their ability to service foreign debt.

The deterioration of the country's macroeconomic outlook led investors to bet against the Thai baht in an attempt to anticipate the collapse of an unsustainable exchange-rate choice. Serious pressures on the currency started in July 1996 and continued in early 1997, particularly in February when it became known that a substantial number of domestic finance companies exposed to the property sector were in default on their foreign debt payments.[163] Capital outflows continued in May when reports circulated on the decline of foreign exchange reserves among market participants, with net reserves falling from about $32 billion to $26 billion. In an attempt to respond to capital flight, national authorities introduced capital controls on 15 May.

Faced with the pressure on their currency, the Thai authorities responded to the speculative attacks as the Mexican authorities had done in 1994. Instead of raising interest rates, given concerns about financial sector fragility and a slowing economy, the central bank sold its foreign exchange reserves to defend the value of the currency. Specifically, the Bank of Thailand intervened in the spot market (selling US dollars) and simultaneously in the swap market (purchasing dollars with commitments to sell them on at a future date). About $25 billion out of $26 billion, the actual holding of foreign exchange reserves, were committed in forward liabilities.

Although market participants expected a devaluation, 'the timing,' according to IMF staff notes (IMF, 1998a, p. 46), 'took most by surprise.' The Thai baht depreciated by 8 percent on the day of its float on 2 July 1997 – a substantial fall though not as rapid as the Mexican fall in 1994–95 during which the peso lost half of its value in one week after the devaluation. Building on the comparison with Mexico, an emerging market country in which large current account deficit financed by large capital inflows laid the ground for substantial capital reversals, few observers anticipated the evolution of the Thailand currency crisis into a full-blown financial crisis of a global dimension.[164] However, as the economist Takatoshi Ito (2007, p. 26) put it, 'what followed the Thai crisis was a domino of the currencies in the region.'

In October 1997, the most severe pressures in the foreign exchange market were felt in Malaysia and the Philippines where the ringitt and the peso were floated in July. At the same time, the situation in Indonesia deteriorated sharply. As the rupiah came under increasing pressure from both domestic and foreign market participants, Bank Indonesia widened the rupiah trading band from 8 percent to 12 percent on 11 July.

The move, however, did not help restore market confidence, which further deteriorated given market perceptions of political unwillingness and inability to raise interest rates and to deal with financial sector problems. As a result, the rupiah trading band was abandoned by mid-August letting the currency depreciate.

In late October, the value of the Taiwanese dollar depreciated substantially, triggering further downward pressures in Hong Kong and Korea. In contrast to the Mexican crisis, during which the deterioration of investor sentiment towards Mexico translated into a reallocation of funds to the other emerging market countries, the shift in market sentiment towards the Asian countries spread to several other emerging market economies. The effects of the crisis were felt in Latin America where the stock markets of Brazil, Argentina, and Mexico followed the Asian markets in their decline. Following the October Hong Kong stock price decline, the crisis also spread to industrialized countries. When the crisis reached the New York Stock Exchange, which on 27 October suspended trading in advance of the closing bell, it was official: the Asian crisis was a global crisis. International credit ratings, then, confirmed what was already evident to analysts and market participants by rapidly downgrading Asian sovereign debt in the last quarter of 1997.

Even Korea fell to below investment-grade status.[165] The country that had just entered into the OECD club succumbed to the crisis at the end of October. Pressures on the Korean won had already initiated in January on the heels of a major domestic bank's bankruptcy, Hanbo Steel, which put under stress the solidity of the entire banking system, squeezing liquidity for domestic corporations. Despite the liquidity support the Bank of Korea provided to help the domestic financial and corporate sectors, important *chaebol* (industrial conglomerates) went bankrupt or came close to doing so.[166] In this atmosphere, external financing conditions for Korean financial institutions deteriorated sharply in August, with the terms of access to capital becoming increasingly costly and short-term. In addition, the depreciation of the won, concomitant to the depreciation of the other Asian currencies, further worsened domestic sector financing conditions. Highly indebted domestic corporates rushed to hedge their foreign exposure, exacerbating the downward pressure on the currency.

Along with domestic banks and corporates, foreign market participants grew increasingly nervous about the Korean economic situation, particularly about the amount of foreign exchange reserves held by the central bank. In this uncertain environment, both domestic and international investors rapidly abandoned the country. On 17 November, authorities abandoned the defense of the currency. The won depreciated by more than 50 percent in just five weeks, hitting a low of 55 percent on 23 December.

As IMF staff put it in their International Capital Market Report (1998a, p. 2), 'the extreme turbulence in emerging market currencies during the Asian crisis has been virtually without precedent. When these currencies reached their low points in January 1998, the Indonesian rupiah had fallen (relative to its July 1997 level) by 81 percent, the Malaysian ringgit by 46 percent, and the Thai baht by 55 percent.' With exchange rates plummeting across the region, high interest rates pushed the five most affected countries into deep recession. In 1998, GDP fell by 14 percent in Indonesia and by an average of more than 7 percent in Malaysia, South Korea, Thailand, and the Philippines (Brealy, 1999, p. 286). The Asian Development Bank calculates that the post-crisis average growth rates 'have slipped by an average 2.5 [percentage points] in the five countries that were most directly affected.'[167]

The (short-term) response to the crisis

Asked about where the next Mexican-style crisis would have taken place, Camdessus (1996d) thus replied, 'I don't know, but I suspect it will begin with a banking crisis. And even if such a crisis does not start in the banking sector, it will almost certainly be worsened by a banking crisis.' This prescient remark captures one of the main problems that contributed to the depth and breadth of the Asian crisis. While current account deficits and pegged exchange rates are important factors to account for the problems that some countries initially faced, weaknesses in the domestic financial sector are crucial to account for the severity of the crisis and its scale. Indeed, financial weaknesses contributed to – and amplified – the effects of the crisis.

Tax and regulatory distortions, for instance, provided substantial incentives to the private sector for short-term foreign borrowing, as illustrated by the Bangkok International Banking Facility (BIBF).[168] In addition, government guarantees and poor regulation and supervision of the domestic financial and corporate sector facilitated the build-up of foreign-denominated debt. It is on historical record that the debt of Korean corporate conglomerates (*chaebol*) was supplied by directed lending, with banks required by government to allocate loans to specific firms. Likewise, government authorities provided the *chaebols* with explicit and implicit guarantees against risk by keeping them afloat through extension of credit when corporate entities faced financial difficulties. The situation was no significantly different in Thailand or in Indonesia where, for instance, President Suharto's son reopened his bank branches under a different name only a few weeks after their closure under an IMF program.

Financial weaknesses also amplified the effects of currency devaluation and economic slowdown. Indeed, the large depreciation of Asian currencies, and the concomitant rise in interest rates, seriously impaired domestic financial institutions and corporations' ability to service their foreign debt obligations, thereby triggering a cycle of bankruptcies. Financial weaknesses also complicated the response to the crisis. On the one hand, they made the choice to raise interest rates politically difficult, given the vulnerability of domestic financial systems. On the other, they raised concerns on the scope of IMF's conditionality in that addressing those weaknesses pushed the Fund to engage decisively with sensitive domestic issues. Indeed, structural reforms became a crucial part of IMF programs to the East Asian countries.

As a study of the Policy Development and Review Department (2000, pp. 6, 9) points out, 'structural policies were an *unusually* important element in the programs with Indonesia, Korea, and Thailand. In particular, reforms in the financial and corporate sectors were needed to address the root causes of the crisis with a view to restoring confidence and preventing a recurrence.'[169] In this connection, a substantial restructuring of domestic financial systems (bank restructuring and recapitalization) was mandated in all IMF-supported programs. The US Treasury staunchly supported the IMF's involvement with structural problems. As Robert Rubin and Weisberg (2003, p. 219) put it in his memoirs, 'to restore the confidence of both domestic citizens and foreign creditors, the government needed to address both macroeconomic problems and structural flaws in the economy – not just its overvalued currency but its weak financial sector, which had contributed to a real estate and investment boom financed in foreign currency. ... Only when sound policies were pursued would confidence – and investment capital – return and economic recovery take place.'

IMF-supported programs were unusual in another respect: the size and modalities for disbursement. Indeed, the programs approved for Thailand, Indonesia, and Korea allowed those countries to withdraw funds for hundred times their quotas. The IMF programs with Thailand, for instance, announced on 24 August 1997, amounted to $17.2 billion, with the country withdrawing from the Fund more than 500 percent of its quota. In Indonesia, where the program was approved on 4 November following the deterioration of market conditions, the total size of the program was $40 billion, with the amount provided by the Fund equaling almost 500 percent of Indonesia's quota. The largest package ever approved, though, was the one for South Korea on 4 December totaling $57 billion. In this case, the country withdrew almost 2000 percent of its quota.

All financial packages were made up of two lines of financing. First, there was the multilateral assistance provided by the IMF, the World Bank, and the Asian Development Bank (ADB).[170] Second, financial assistance was provided through bilateral loans, the greatest bulk of which was provided by Japan. However, when it became clear that the announcement of the IMF programs did not help restore market confidence, the IMF, with the support of the G7, attempted to persuade private banks to continue rolling over their outstanding loans. This was the case for South Korea where, at the end of December, commercial and investment banks agreed to roll over their credits for the next month under the pressure of the US Treasury (Rubin and Weisberg, 2003, ch. 8).

IMF-supported programs became the targets of considerable criticism. As this chapter explains at greater length below, the IMF was accused of providing rescue packages which were too small (Ito, 2007) or, at the other extreme, of providing bail-outs which were too big (International Financial Institution Advisory Commission, 2000). The emphasis on structural adjustment and fiscal retrenchment was also severely criticized (Radelet and Sachs, 1998). The 'lack of credibility effect' of IMF programs in restoring market confidence (Ito, 2007, p. 25), combined with the difficulties in implementing IMF programs, also contributed toward discrediting the international response to the crisis. Political considerations, including presidential elections and government-business parental linkages, hindered the progress of implementation.[171] In this atmosphere, discussions were held on the possibility of setting up an Asian Monetary Fund (AMF), which would have helped countries in the region to cope with financial crisis by providing foreign exchange. To put it differently, the AMF would have replicated the IMF's financial activity on a regional scale. The proposal, however, was not followed through at the insistence of the US, China, and the IMF.[172] Before moving on to assess the implications of the criticisms leveled at the IMF on its capital policies, it is now timely to investigate how the IMF interpreted the crisis.

5.2   The IMF interprets the crisis

As the previous section showed, both domestic and international factors contributed to the crisis. Macroeconomic imbalances and weaknesses in domestic financial and corporate systems, on the one hand, and the volatility of international capital flows, on the other, combined in a mix that contributed to the speed and virulence of the crisis. While analysts recognize the interaction between these factors, their explanations vary according to whether emphasis is placed on one set of factors over the other.

The IMF put the emphasis on shortcomings in domestic policies. In a replication of what had been argued in the case of Mexico, the predominant view within the Fund was that policy inadequacies were the main culprit of the crisis. Capital movements certainly played a major part in the crisis, 'but it was not open capital accounts per se that led to problems,' as Jack Boorman, Director of the Policy Development and Review Department, forcefully remarked (IMF, 1998b). Although market participants took some part of the blame, Stanley Fischer (1998a) nonetheless noted, 'the problems of [the Asian] countries were mostly homegrown.'

In the December World Economic Outlook (IMF, 1997c, p. 2), for instance, the IMF staff pointed to two factors as the 'most important' to explain the build-up of the crisis: 'shortcomings and inconsistencies in domestic macroeconomic and exchange-rate policies.' The maintenance of a fixed exchange rate was particularly pernicious, in that it provided a level of guarantee that led to the mispricing of risks and excessive capital inflows. In the words of an internal staff document, 'in some countries, the prolonged maintenance of pegged exchange rates may have been seen as implicit exchange-rate guarantees and encouraged external borrowing. This, in turn, led to excessive exposure to foreign exchange risks in the financial and corporate sectors and increased vulnerability to a sudden change in market sentiment.'[173]

In addition to the choice of a fixed exchange rate, IMF staff forcefully contended that 'various structural weaknesses, particularly in the financial sector, ... made these economies and especially their financial systems increasingly fragile and vulnerable to adverse developments.' In other words, as Radelet and Sachs maintain (1998, p. 1), the IMF sponsored an interpretation of the crisis that 'assigned primary responsibility to the shortcomings of East Asian capitalism' – weaknesses in Asian domestic financial markets and the corporate sector. Specifically, the voice coming from the IMF repeatedly pointed to the inadequate supervision of corporate and financial systems as reflected in the substantial foreign borrowing by the private sector and a weak and over-exposed banking system (Fischer, 1998a; IMF, 1998c; 1997c).

From the view of the IMF, another prominent factor helped explain the origins and the severity of the Asian crisis: the sense of denial among national authorities in the region (Fischer, 1998a). Camdessus (1997c) put it thus, 'what we had here was an unprecedented "denial syndrome".' As the Managing Director continued to explain, 'after so many years of outstanding macroeconomic performance, it was difficult, if not impossible, for the authorities in Thailand – and other countries – to recognize that serious underlying deficiencies could jeopardize their track record.' Hence, there was significant delay in taking convincing policy action to restore market confidence, as attested by the 'reluctance to tighten monetary conditions and to close insolvent financial institutions' (Fischer, 1998a).

Delays in disclosure of crucial data, such as the data on foreign exchange reserves, and lack of transparency about government and central bank operations, about the true state of financial sectors, and about the links between banks, industry, and government, further complicated the crisis by undermining market confidence (IMF, 1998c).[174] Pushing these views to their logical conclusions, private markets could not be considered as the main culprit of the crisis. Camdessus (1997c) put it thus, 'in the absence of sufficient information, markets are entitled to fear the worst and to doubt the capacity of governments to take corrective action.'

In sum, the IMF pinned the blame for the severity of the crisis on domestic authorities and domestic policy choices. In 1995, Fischer (1995b) noted that Mexico was 'the case of a government that ignored advice and got into trouble.' Substitute Mexico for Asia, and that proposition still applied within the Fund in 1997–98. In particular, Thailand had long been warned about the danger of an impending crisis but had been postponing appropriate responses (Fischer, 1998c). The International Capital Market Report (IMF, 1998a, p. 46) makes clear, IMF management and staff repeatedly but vainly 'pressed the Thai authorities to take urgent action to correct problems in the balance of payments, recommending an adjustment of the exchange rate combined with a firming of monetary and fiscal policy to aid current account adjustment and resist a collapse of confidence.'[175]

The initial similarities between the Mexican and the Asian crises from the Fund's perspective are also evident from the first IMF response to the events in Asia. As the staff of the Policy Development and Review Department (PDR) put it in their analysis of IMF-supported programs in Asia, at the beginning, Thailand was seen through the lens of the typical currency crisis. In the words of the staff: 'Thailand ... was closer to the classic case: the exchange rate was widely viewed as somewhat over-valued, with the external current account deep in deficit, and the fiscal position had swung into deficit in the run-up to the crisis' (Boorman, et al., 2000, p. 5). A correction in its balance of payments was thereby deemed sufficient to restore market confidence. This position was ech-oed in the US Treasury. 'We discussed Thailand's difficulties at length,' Rubin and Weisberg (2003, p. 218) writes in his memoirs, 'and felt that the IMF could handle what we viewed at that point as a familiar kind of financial crisis that occurs when an exchange rate gets seriously out of line and a country is importing too much.'

This is not to say that the IMF did not see market excesses at play in the region. In the December 1997 World Economic Outlook (IMF, 1997c, p. 2), for instance, staff conceded that 'changes in market sentiment... cannot be fully explained, especially with regard to their timing, by economic fundamentals alone'– thereby suggesting that the shift in market sentiment was something more than a rational mar-ket response to fundamentals. Nevertheless, in the repartition of blame between domestic and international factors, the latter received com-paratively less attention in explaining the origins of the crisis. Rejecting the accusations most famously leveled by the Malaysian Prime Minister at international speculators, Camdessus (1997c) noted, 'it is true that sometimes the herd instinct of the markets generates all kinds of unfounded suspicions.' However, 'accusations of widespread manipula-tion and conspiracies' appeared to be 'hitherto unsubstantiated.' From the IMF's perspective, indeed,

> speculators appear to have played a relatively limited role in the cri-ses. Perhaps they determined the timing of the eruption of crisis in some countries, but investors who profited did so primarily by *cor-rectly* perceiving unsustainable and inconsistent economic policies, financial sector fragilities, and overvalued property and stock mar-kets. (IMF, 1997c, p. 41, emphasis mine)

Hence, Camdessus (1997c) concluded, 'from what we know so far, it would be a mistake to blame hedge funds or other market participants for the turmoil in Asia.'[176] 'Markets have overreacted,' in that 'the amount of exchange-rate adjustment of the Thai baht, the Indonesian rupiah, and the Korean won, among other currencies, far exceeds any reasonable estimate of what might have been required to correct their initial overvaluation.' But 'contagion does not strike out of the clear blue sky' (Camdessus, 1998).

In sum, the IMF's interpretation of the crisis was still firmly informed on the idea of *orderly liberalization*. Indeed, IMF management and senior staff officials made the point that the crisis did not prove that capital account liberalization was welfare-reducing. In the words of Camdessus (1997d),

> The lesson to be drawn from recent developments is not about the risks of globalization, but rather about the importance of approaching markets in a responsible manner – with sound macroeconomic fundamentals that give markets confidence and do not invite reckless market behavior; with respect for the signals that markets provide; and with transparent and market-friendly policies that allow markets to allocate resources efficiently.

Hence, from the IMF perspective, there was no doubt about the need to proceed along the path of liberalization. Rather, the problems in Asia reflected a problem of 'flawed capital liberalization' (Boorman, 1998). To put it simply, capital liberalization appeared to have been mishandled. 'East Asia succeeded in large part through being open and by opening up,' Stanley Fischer (1999a) remarked, 'but some of its problems were caused by opening the capital account in an inappropriate way.'

Still, from the IMF's perspective, the crisis did not call into question the view that capital controls were inefficient policy instruments to cope with large and volatile capital flows. For instance, the voice coming from the Fund consistently stressed the lack of significant evidence to corroborate the hypothesis that controls, such as those imposed in Malaysia or in place in India and China, were effective in stemming capital flight. As the staff of the PDR put it (Boorman et al., 2000, pp. 9–10), 'Malaysia's capital controls were introduced in September 1998, after market conditions stabilized and capital outflows abated.' Hence, 'they hardly provide a test of the usefulness of capital controls in handling a crisis.'

Controls were still viewed as harmful too. In the words of the IMF staff, 'the actual or threatened imposition of controls on capital outflows during the crisis may also have served to further undermine investor confidence' (IMF, 1997c, p. 17). 'Controls – and threat of controls – on market activity,' Camdessus (1997c) argued, 'tended to reinforce the view that governments were addressing the symptoms, rather than the causes, of their problems, and accelerated investors' run for cover and set back other efforts to restore confidence.'

Finally, from the Fund's perspective, the crisis underscored the importance of the IMF's involvement with the process of global financial integration. For instance, the fact that some member countries 'mis-handled' the process of liberalization or that insufficient information was made available to member countries spoke to the importance of the Fund's role. Specifically, these facts called for the strengthening of Fund surveillance so that the IMF can help member countries adopt appropriate domestic banking regulation and supervision while providing timely information to the markets (Fischer, 1999b). Furthermore, the financial support extended to the crisis-hit countries spoke to the need for a strengthened role of the Fund in crisis resolution. As Camdessus (1997f) explains, 'recent experience has demonstrated once again that early warnings cannot always prevent crisis from blowing up. This makes it indispensable for the international community to strengthen the financial capacity of its central monetary institution to assist countries in a crisis situation.'

In conclusion, similarly to what happened after the Mexican crisis, the idea of *orderly liberalization* emerged unscathed within the IMF in 1997. In contrast to what happened after the Mexican crisis, however, there was no longer a complacent audience for the IMF's ideas across the Fund's social constituencies for legitimation. This time around, member countries and market investors did not eagerly accept the IMF-sponsored interpretation. Rather, the IMF became a target of criticism and a hostage of its own rhetoric in a political environment in which contending interpretations gradually gained visibility and acceptance. Reviewing the mobilization of opposition to the IMF and to the idea of *orderly liberalization*, it is important to bear in mind that what was at stake was more than a battle for the 'right' interpretation of the origins of the Asian crisis. What was really at stake were the policies to be pursued to govern an international financial system characterized by widespread financial linkages. Different interpretations of the crisis implied different responses about how to prevent and manage future crises and about the role of the IMF in crisis prevention and management.

5.3 The mobilization of opposition against the idea of orderly liberalization

The crisis gave the IMF an incredible notoriety. In the words of Stanley Fischer (1998a), 'As the crisis has unfolded..., the IMF has become, at least for this brief moment in history, almost a household name.' However, notoriety did not come with good reputation. Member countries, the economic profession, and the private sector called into question the IMF's activities. In other words, the actors forming the Fund's social constituencies for legitimation grew increasingly skeptical of the benefits of liberalization and sympathetic to calls for capital controls. The role of the IMF as a manager of global financial flows was also hotly contested.

This contestation was the most trenchant as the crisis spread to those countries that the IMF had long praised as 'highly successful developing countries' (Fischer, 1999a, p. 13) and 'models of orderly development' (Camdessus, 1997c), for whose economic success the IMF had repeatedly taken credit. That is, the East Asian countries had been presented as examples of those emerging market countries 'that follow the policies advocated by the Fund [thereby] attracting substantial amounts of private foreign investment' (Camdessus, 1996c). When the capital outflows economically disrupted the region, these words could not be taken back. The IMF became responsible for the ill advice given in the past as well as for failing to 'give a seal-of-approval effect to financial markets to stop capital outflows' (Ito, 2007, p. 43). In this atmosphere, the stock of legitimacy of the Fund started being consumed.

Capital controls back on screen

According to a first line of criticism, the IMF's view on the ineffectiveness of capital controls in managing financial crises had proved wrong. Rather, capital controls appeared as being of help to cope with large capital flows. In the most well-known formulation, the argument in favor of capital controls was laid out by Paul Krugman (1998a). Pointing to the failure of the IMF-US supported strategy in Asia, which consisted of large conditional disbursements and high interest rates to keep capital in the region, Krugman invited the international community to start considering an alternative. 'Plan B involves giving up for a time the business of trying to regain the confidence of international investors and forcibly breaking the link between domestic interest rates and exchange rate.' In simple terms, Plan B involved the imposition of exchange controls, 'a solution so unfashionable, so stigmatized, that hardly anyone has dared suggest it.' In order to substantiate his point, Krugman noted that China, which had not been fully caught in the regional crisis, had currency controls through its inconvertible capital account.

Krugman was not alone in his advocacy for the use of controls. Individual investors and private-sector representatives advanced similar arguments. George Soros (1998, pp. 192–3), for instance, a financier who made his fortune thanks to open financial markets, suggested 'some form of capital controls may ... be preferable to instability even if it would not constitute good policy in an ideal world.' Even the Institute of International Finance (IIF), the world global association of financial institutions, became sensitive to the arguments in favor of controls. While controls on outflows were still catalogued as 'generally difficult to justify on efficiency or welfare grounds,' controls on inflows, such as the market-based controls used in Chile, appeared more acceptable than they had been before. In a report released in 1999, for instance, the IIF noted that 'rushing to liberalize is as ill advised as rushing to impose controls' (Institute of International Finance, 1999a, p. ii). Specifically, 'as economies begin to be viewed as an attractive destination for private capital flows, they may well be advised to consider controls on certain inflows to reduce their vulnerability to "excessive" amounts' (Institute of International Finance, 1999b, p. 13).

The advocacy of capital controls coming from the academic and financial establishment added to the more 'radical' advocacy articulated by non-governmental organizations (NGOs) and representatives of developing countries. Indeed, the Asian crisis fuelled the greatest opposition to market opening and, as a consequence, to the IMF as the organization embodying the principle of openness. The IMF was accused of insisting on more liberalization in countries where an open capital account was the main culprit of the crisis.[177] The fact that the IMF programs in Korea requested the authorities to continue opening the country's capital account exposed the Fund to the charge that it was simply following the biddings of the Wall Street-Treasury complex.[178]

These views were echoed in the actions of the Malaysian Prime Minister Mahatir Mohamad, who introduced capital controls in September 1998.[179] 'Malaysia had no choice but to change direction,' Mahatir (Mohamad 1998) commented on the choice to impose capital controls. 'What we have done is merely to insulate ourselves from the predatory speculators.' Not only were international investors the main target of Mahatir's accusations. The IMF was viewed as their accomplice. According to one source (Mckenna, 1998), 'the Malaysian Prime Minister accused the IMF of "economic colonialism," of supporting programs that undermined national economic sovereignty in favor of international investors.'

Although the Malaysian controls did not provide definitive proof that restrictions on capital flows were effective in reducing the impact of the crisis, they nonetheless proved an important point. They proved that an alternative to the predominant thinking existed. Krugman (1999) put it thus,

> Until the Malaysian experiment, the prevailing view among pundits was that even if financial crises were driven by self-justifying panic,

there was nothing governments could do to curb that panic except to reschedule bank debts...and otherwise try to restore confidence by making a conspicuous display of virtue. Austerity and reform were the watchwords. The alternative – preventing capital flight directly, and thereby gaining a breathing space – was supposed to be completely impossible, with any attempt a sure recipe for disaster. Now we know better.

In conclusion, the crisis provided a 'window of opportunity' for ideas previously relegated to the sidelines to gain prominence in the debate on international financial liberalization. In particular, capital controls gained new legitimacy as a means to cope with capital flows. While the IMF's interpretation of the crisis pinned the blame on domestic policies, an increasing number of actors apportioned the blame to the intrinsic volatility of international capital markets. In this atmosphere, the idea that capital liberalization is the 'appropriate' policy choice, as the IMF would put it, lost its persuasiveness. As Camdessus (1998) himself conceded, 'The Asian crisis has cooled the enthusiasm for liberalizing capital flows.'

Downsize the IMF

A second line of criticism was directed at the IMF. On the one hand, several analysts pointed to the IMF-supported process of financial-sector liberalization initiated before the crisis as one of the factors that contributed to worsen the risk performance of the East Asian countries (Radelet and Sachs, 1998; Stiglitz and Charlton, 2005). A decade after the crisis, some observers still criticize the IMF for having played a prominent role in 'pushing hard for swift capital account opening for several years before the crisis' (Yoon, 2007). On the other hand, the IMF was accused of having mismanaged the crisis. In this connection, three criticisms were addressed at the IMF: the IMF suggested the wrong medicine, the IMF interfered with national sovereignty, and the IMF nurtured moral hazard.

The first criticism can be summarized as follows: by imposing the traditional austerity program – monetary and fiscal retrenchment – to countries that were experiencing a liquidity rather than a solvency crisis, the IMF sharpened the slowdown, inflicting undue sufferance to the population. Instead of demanding that countries raise interest rates to defend their currencies, the IMF should have suggested instead to keep interest rates low, thereby helping a real economic recovery (Radelet and Sachs, 1998; Sachs, 1998).

The charge that the IMF was strangling domestic economic recovery was popular and was not confined to the usual IMF critics such as the Malaysian Prime Minister, who commented that the measures suggested by the IMF to cope with the crisis 'worsened the economic situation' (Mohamad, 1998). For instance, the then Thailand Deputy Prime Minister Supachai Panitchpakdi was reported as having said that the IMF was causing more harm than good by forcing the government to slash spending while the economy was already contracting (Mckenna, 1998). Even in the industrialized world, distinguished voices attacked the IMF's cure. Reflecting the division between the US Treasury and the State Department, former US National Security Advisor and Secretary of State Henry Kissinger went public, saying that 'the IMF cure would have been very good if it was applied three years ago.' In the current circumstances, however, 'we have to be careful that the economic realities don't lead to a wave of nationalism and eventually anti-Americanism in which the cure is worse than the disease.'[180] Furthermore, virtually all NGOs dealing with economic globalization condemned the IMF for its programs in the East Asian countries. Specifically, the IMF's prescription to raise interest rates and taxes and to cut public expenditures was forcefully condemned for deepening the crisis and fueling unemployment and poverty.[181]

The second criticism leveled at the IMF concerned its involvement with structural reforms in the crisis-hit countries. In particular, the structural prong in the IMF-supported programs was regarded as an undue intrusion into member countries' domestic economic policies. In a well-known criticism of the IMF, Martin Feldstein (1998) argued that, by emphasizing structural and institutional reforms in its programs throughout the Asian region, the IMF had gone beyond its traditional mandate of correcting balance of payments problems and had unduly entered into the sphere of member countries' economic sovereignty.

Finally, the last set of criticisms revolved around the problem of 'moral hazard'. Large IMF funding, the argument went, distorts the behavioral incentives for policy makers and international investors alike. Specifically, the IMF programs were considered a source of moral hazard in that they induced policy makers to delay policy adjustment. They also encouraged investors to take excessive risks in the future, building on their experience of rescue from large losses in the present (Calomiris, 1998). 'Allowing international banks to avoid the risks they undertake by imprudent lending,' Alan Meltzer (1998), Chairman of the International Financial Institutions Advisory Commission (IFIAC), put it thus, 'the IMF encourages the behavior that creates the problems.'[182]

Although the IMF strongly rejected the accusation of inducing moral hazard, the criticism was widespread. For instance, the Nobel Prize winner Milton Friedman sarcastically commented that the IMF-US strategy to provide large rescue packages 'is hurting the countries they are lending to, and benefiting the foreigners who lent to them.'[183] The US Congress was particularly vociferous in this respect. The Fund was accused of supporting moral hazard at the expense of US taxpayers by bailing out imprudent international banks and investors (US Congress, 1998b). These charges became increasingly difficult to dismiss particularly because of the ongoing debate over the increase in Fund resources.

Indeed, as we have seen in the previous chapter, after the Mexican crisis, IMF members had agreed on an increase of their quotas, as one of the policy measures to withstand potential financial crises. The quota increase, which was strongly supported by the Clinton administration, provided the US Congress with substantial political leverage over the Fund in that such an increase requires Congressional approval – an approval that was very difficult to get. Indeed, in a replication of what had happened during the Mexican crisis, opposition came from disparate quarters disregarding conventional Democrats-Republicans division. Specifically, the Fund came under fire from across the political spectrum for reasons ranging from the protection of workers' rights and environmental concerns to the lack of transparency and accountability in its decision-making (US Congress, 1998b).

The opposition voiced in the US Congress to the IMF spilled over to the proposal to amend the IMF's Articles of Agreement. Indeed, increasing skepticism emerged about expanding the mission of an organization that was regarded as already possessing too much power. On the one hand, US lawmakers interpreted the amendment as an attempt 'to impose the Multilateral Agreement on Investments,' which, as Congressman Donald Manzullo remarked, was an agreement that the US Congress had fiercely opposed.[184] On the other, the proposal was regarded with suspicion by several Democrats who questioned the need to enshrine the principle of capital mobility in the IMF's Articles. In an open letter to the US Secretary Robert Rubin, a number of Congressmen described themselves as 'troubled' and 'surprised to learn of the Administration's support of an amendment to the IMF's basic charter.' Their concern was justified on the basis of the recent experience in Asia. 'We believe that the rapid mobility of capital, especially short-term capital, greatly exacerbated the recent crisis in Asia,' they wrote to Rubin, adding that 'serious consideration should be given to the adoption of measures that retard this volatility' (Gephardt, et al., 1998).

The proposal to amend the Articles also started to be skeptically regarded by the private sector. According to IMF archival documents, during a seminar organized at the IMF headquarters in March 1998, 'some private sector representatives pressed for greater transparency in the Fund's deliberations on an amendment' and 'representatives appeared particularly concerned about Article VIII, Section 2(b)' concerning the enforcement of private contracts.[185] Indeed, according to Article VIII (2b) of its Articles, the IMF is allowed to approve exchange restrictions introduced by a member that would result in countries suspending current account payments, including payments for private contracts. Private-sector actors worried that the same provision would apply to capital account transactions. In other words, they were concerned that the enforcement of private contracts would be at the mercy of an international political body, had the amendment won support.[186] As a result, the final report prepared by the IIF Working Group on the Liberation of Capital Movements clearly concluded against 'any amendment that would formally extend the jurisdiction of the IMF over capital movements' (Institute of International Finance, 1999b, p. 22).

Private-sector opposition to the amendment may further be inferred from the preference for the word *progressive* to the word *orderly*. '"Orderly" – the modifier used most often by the IMF... – is certainly preferable to "disorderly" liberalization, but has overtones of gradualism and official intervention,' the IIF argued, sarcastically noting that 'Brazil... has remained in the IMF's "transition" status for 50 years... This approach to liberalizing payments for current account transactions may be orderly, but is not progressive' (Institute of International Finance, 1999a, p. 5).

In sum, the debate on the role of the IMF in an era of globalized finance that was initiated after the Mexican crisis spilled into the global arena after the Asian crisis. While the discussion on the future of the IMF had been hitherto confined to government representatives and economists, the crisis enlarged the number of the actors involved. In this arena, alternative ideas to the idea of *orderly liberalization* flourished.

5.4   Failure of the amendment to the Articles of Agreement

As a result of the criticism received during and after the crisis, the IMF is more vocal in pointing out the risks of rapid capital account liberalization. While such cautionary notes have always been present in IMF advice, today they are much more likely to be given greater prominence. (Dawson, 2002)

With these words, the former Director of the IMF External Relations Department captures the adjustment in the Fund's thinking on capital liberalization that took place under the pressures of the criticisms leveled at the IMF. Indeed, the opposition coming from member countries, private-sector and social actors, and academic economists created unprecedented momentum for a far-reaching repositioning of the Fund. Nowhere is this shift in thinking more evident than in the negotiations within the IMF Board that led to the failure of the amendment to the Articles of Agreement.

Indeed, since early 1998, public perception of the IMF's activities in capital-related issues acquired salience in the Board's discussion. In particular, Executive Directors made the issue of responding to the criticisms leveled at the IMF a primary policy concern.[187] As the German Executive Director Bernd Esdar forcefully remarked, the Fund should attempt to demonstrate to be 'in the process of reviewing its approach ... Otherwise, the Fund might be blamed for ignoring its critics.'[188] Similarly, the Canadian Director Thomas Bernes invited the IMF 'to show some humility,' suggesting a thorough rethink on capital account liberalization in an attempt to meet the criticisms coming from outside the Fund.[189] By and large, the claim that the IMF should 'acknowledge the role of...fora [other than the IMF] in the international debate, and to welcome their contributions,' as the US Executive Director put it, was widely shared among Executive Directors.[190]

One of the most visible attempts made by the Fund to respond to the external criticisms was the seminar held in March 1998 to discuss capital account liberalization and the role of the IMF in promoting it. As the *IMF Survey* (IMF, 1998b) records, 'the seminar was held at the behest of the IMF Executive Board to elicit views from a wide range of private and official opinions outside the IMF.' Boorman (1998) put it thus, 'the idea [was] of inviting a broader group of people in to hear views from the private sector, from some academics and so forth.' Hence, participants included government officials, banking and investment officials, academicians, and staff from international organizations. The discussions reveal a significant caution on the issue of capital liberalization and on the role of the Fund in promoting it. As Fischer (as quoted in IMF, 1998b) noted in his summation of the discussions, there were ' "severe doubts" either as to whether capital account liberalization per se was a good idea, or whether advocacy was not sufficient and legalized jurisdiction too painful, complicated, and unnecessary.'

In this atmosphere of widespread skepticism on the role of the IMF as a manager of globalized finance, shoring up the organization's legitimacy took pride of place in the Board's discussions. In particular, it now seemed appropriate to postpone the extension of the Fund's jurisdiction to regain member countries' confidence and support. As the Moroccan Director Mohammed Dairi remarked, for instance, postponing the amendment would have signaled that the IMF was taking 'a more prudent and cooperative approach.' Similarly, the Canadian Director suggested the need to 'proceed cautiously' to ensure the necessary majority to approve the amendment.[191]

In sum, after the Asian crisis, the growing skepticism on the role of the IMF as the anchor of global financial stability spilled over to the IMF Executive Board. Specifically, the Board was receptive to the external policy debate and explored new ideas and policy proposals as a means through which to respond to the crisis of legitimacy that the Fund was facing. In other words, the Board adjusted its position on capital account liberalization not as a function of US economic interests or as a function of a change in the Fund's bureaucracy. For instance, the US Executive Directors Karin Lissakers was still personally favorable to the amendment and her national authorities still in favor of supporting capital mobility on a global scale (Summers, 1998). Likewise, IMF management was still firmly behind the proposal to amend the Articles. In the April 1998 meeting, for instance, Camdessus still advocated that 'the Asian crisis had been a powerful argument for added jurisdiction,'[192] while Fischer (1998b, p. 2) reaffirmed his view that 'an amendment of the Fund's Articles of Agreement is the best way for the international community to help ensure that capital account liberalization is carried out in an orderly, non disruptive way.' Hence, what made Executive Directors willing to question previously taken decisions, including the amendment to the Articles, was a factor different from the US interests and the staff's technical expertise. The rethink worked its way inside the Board through the criticisms leveled at the IMF in its social constituencies for legitimation.

In picking out the criticisms coming from the Fund's social constituencies for legitimation, Executive Directors engaged in a process of clarification on several issues related to the amendment. In particular, issues that had been deliberately left ambiguous until the 1997 September declaration, when the Board was mandated to proceed with the amendment, occupied the Board's agenda in early 1998. The crisis showed that some of the ambiguities in the Fund's thinking on capital account liberalization needed urgent clarification had the international community to reduce the likelihood of capital account crises. The stance of Malaysian national authorities, for instance, who vehemently opposed the IMF's 'orthodoxy' by introducing capital controls to stem capital flight, vividly called for specifying the conditions under which the IMF and its members can legitimate their use. Still, the fact that financial and corporate-sector weaknesses and hastened liberalization contributed to the crisis along with macroeconomic imbalances spoke to the importance of clarifying the prerequisites for successful liberalization. Finally, the fact that the IMF disbursed large financial packages that proved unable to restore market confidence raised the issue of specifying the role of the IMF as a manager of globalized finance.

Clarifying outstanding ambiguities became a matter for debate within the IMF Board. As archival documents reveal, several Directors now gave the issue of specifying the conditions to (re)introduce capital controls the greatest prominence. For instance, the French Executive Director forcefully remarked that the 'regulation of short-term capital flows deserves to be addressed. It is a serious issue. It is not only a technical point; it is a serious *policy issue.*' Similarly, the Brazilian Director Alexandre Kafka emphasized the importance of clarifying 'the distinction between controls and regulation on the one hand and prudential measures on the other.'[193] The Australian Director, in turn, invited the Board 'to carefully and clearly delineate the specific circumstances under which [controls] might be considered.'[194]

The issue of preconditions and sequencing, then, jumped on top of the Executive Directors' remarks. Several Directors called for 'practical measures and advice' as well as clarifications on 'appropriate prerequisites.' As the representative of the African constituencies, Barro Chambrier explicitly put it, 'we need also to pay particular attention to the timing and the sequencing of the liberalization of capital movements.'[195] The Canadian Executive Director was the most explicit on this point,

> The Fund had to consider clearly the detailed prerequisites of liberalization – a strong regulatory framework, a sound banking system, an adequate supervisory structure – as well as the appropriate sequencing of liberalization measures.[196]

Finally, clarifying the exact implications of the expansion of the Fund's mission to the promotion of capital liberalization became a top concern.

In this connection, a number of Directors argued that agreement could not be reached 'without ample discussion based on a detailed staff paper' on the implications of granting jurisdiction to the Fund.[197] Specifically, the implications in terms of size of IMF resources became the object of close scrutiny. For instance, some Directors peremptorily noted that 'during the recent crisis... it had rapidly become apparent that the Fund did not have the resources to adequately help those members in need,'[198] thereby strengthening the arguments that a number of Executive Directors had raised in the past on the importance of knowing how much help a country should expect from the IMF in the event of capital flight.

In an attempt to address the concerns raised by Executive Directors, IMF staff submitted a number of papers to the Board during 1998 that tried to qualify the IMF's previous thinking on capital account liberalization.[199] However, whereas the ambiguities in the Fund's thinking had helped forged consensus in 1997, the push for dissipating them made consensus difficult to achieve. In particular, the attempt to reach an agreement on the conditions under which to impose capital controls, on the prerequisites for liberalization, and on the ability of IMF to stem capital outflows exacerbated the divide between industrial and developing countries. The position of industrial and emerging/developing countries on capital controls is illustrative here.

On the one hand, the UK, the US, and the German representatives were particularly active in preventing capital controls from being introduced into the language of the IMF staff-prepared report to the Interim Committee.[200] Bernd Esdar, German Executive Director, for instance, noted that 'the Fund needed to avoid giving the impression that the institution was prepared to rethink its entire approach just because a couple of members had introduced capital controls.' His position was echoed in the statements issued by the UK Director, while the United States representative on the Board staunchly opposed any suggestions that the Board might endorse staff papers where the conditions for the use of capital controls would go too far.[201]

On the other hand, developing countries asked for more flexibility in the use of controls and for specifying the conditions of their reintroduction. For instance, while acknowledging the risks entailed in 'unilaterally backsliding on capital market liberalization,' the Chilean Director Eyzaguirre forcefully argued that 'all the major financial crises of the past 20–25 years had resulted from premature liberalization.'[202] Hence, he invited the Board and IMF staff to recognize the effectiveness of 'relatively well-accepted measures such as prudential regulations aimed at discouraging excessive short-term capital flows.'[203] Interestingly, within the G7 countries, there were significant divisions too. Substantially modifying the Japanese stance on the Board, Yoshimura remarked that in light of the events in Asia, 'the Fund could not say that no reversals of capital account liberalization were appropriate.' He thereby concluded that the issue 'needed to be discussed further.'[204]

While IMF staff and management continued their persuasive battle to include capital liberalization within the purposes of the IMF,[205] the differences between and within groups of countries grew parallel to the efforts of clarifying the ambiguities related to the extension of the Fund's jurisdiction over capital flows. The Spanish Director summarized a widespread opinion within the Board, that the IMF 'should refrain from amending the Articles' until the 'detailed operational criteria' of such mission expansion are specified.[206] In the politicized environment of the post-Asian crisis, however, specifying those criteria proved all the more difficult. Therefore, in spite of the continued advocacy of the IMF management, the Interim Committee issued a declaration that slowed down the Fund's involvement with international financial liberalization. In the communiqué released in October 1998, the Interim Committee invited the Executive Board to 'review the experience with the use of controls on capital movements, and the circumstances under which such measures may be appropriate' (Interim Committee, 1998). Not only did the language of liberalization recede in favor of the language of controls; the issue of the amendment is also absent – even though it had been high on the Fund's agenda over the previous two years.

5.5 Conclusion

In contrast to what had happened after the Mexican crisis, after the Asian crisis the idea of *orderly liberalization* was profoundly challenged in its normative and procedural dimensions. Capital liberalization no longer appeared as automatically beneficial nor capital controls as intrinsically bad. The IMF, then, came to be perceived as part of the problem rather than an instrument of its solution (Stiglitz, 2002b). That is to say, the crisis challenged the presumption that governing the risks of the global financial system required a strengthened role for the IMF. As soon as the crisis turned the benefits of liberalization into substantial losses, the organization that had long emphasized the benefits of liberalization found itself entrapped in its own rhetoric. Specifically, the IMF faced a severe crisis of legitimacy as evidenced in the variety of criticisms leveled at the Fund in the wake of the 1997–98 crisis.

These criticisms are the most important in that they shaped the trajectory of the IMF's ideas and policies in the aftermath of the crisis. Rather than being driven by powerful members of influential bureaucrats, policy change was triggered by the input coming from the Fund's social constituencies for legitimation. Indeed, in an attempt to respond to the criticisms coming from member countries, economists, and the private sector, the Executive Board started reconsidering the IMF's position on capital account liberalization. Specifically, Executive Directors put at the top of the agenda those items from 1995 to 1997 that had been discussed without any definitive conclusions. Clarifying the outstanding ambiguities in the Fund's thinking – on the conditions to (re)impose capital controls, the preconditions for successful liberalization, the size of Fund resources and the exact contours of its potential jurisdiction – became a primary policy concern within the Board. The process of clarification, however, brought to the surface the dividing line between industrial and developing countries. Differences between the two constituencies grew markedly, making the attainment of consensus all the more difficult.

The failure of the amendment, which embodied the principles of the policy idea of *orderly liberalization*, can thereby be read as the manifestation of the contestation to the existing policy consensus. In particular, once the presumption on the role of the IMF as an anchor for global financial stability was called into question, the policies that aimed at making the IMF the fulcrum of international financial governance seemed no longer appropriate. Along with contestation, however, new ideas gained prominence in the political debate. Specifically, new ideas were proposed about how to govern the risks of global financial integration. As the next chapter will show, those ideas proved influential in the post-Asian context, marking a shift from the view that effective oversight of the international financial system requires a concentration of powers in the IMF to the view that managing global capital flows requires a decentralized system of governance.

6
The Subprime Crisis: Towards a New Consensus

Since the Asian financial crisis, major changes have taken place in the international financial system and in policy ideas about how to ensure international financial stability. Against the backdrop of a global economy characterized by growing financial linkages and innovation, a new consensus emerged around what can be defined as the policy idea of *market-led liberalization*. Evolving out from the contestation sparked in the aftermath of the Asian crisis, three procedural principles about how to contain systemic financial risks provided the foundations to the policy idea of *market-led liberalization*: market discipline, self- and light-touch regulation, and the dispersion of supervisory and regulatory authority among various international bodies. The wide international agreement around the new policy idea is well reflected in some of the most well-known policies adopted since the end of the 1990s. Indeed, the international financial standard initiative in the late 1990s and the Basel II accord in 2004 were both largely based on the principles of market discipline and private-sector self-regulation. In contrast, the role of governments along with that of traditional intergovernmental organizations was downsized, with the IMF increasingly marginalized as the anchor of global financial cooperation. Instead, new international bodies, such as the G20 and the Financial Stability Board (FSB), were created with the responsibility of supervising the international financial system.

In 2007–8, however, the subprime crisis put the post-Asia international financial governance framework on trial. Not only did the financial turmoil highlight the vulnerability of domestic systems to financial integration; the crisis has also shown the inadequacy of some of the rules that govern international capital markets. In light of the serious shortcomings brought to the surface by the crisis, there has been pressure from world leaders to intensify work on a complete overhaul of the institutional and regulatory architecture of the global financial system – a sort of Bretton Woods II.

In other words, the subprime crisis showed weaknesses in the international system of crisis prevention and management as it evolved after the Asian crisis. In particular, the three pillars underpinning the governance of the international financial system are in question as the crisis unfolds. Hence, like the Mexican and the Asian crisis, the subprime crisis has called into question the contours of the international financial architecture. In this respect, the ongoing crisis is profoundly different from the other crises that punctuated the international financial system since 1997, such as the financial crises in Argentina or in Turkey. The subprime crisis was more profound. It was not just a financial and economic crisis but a political crisis because it called into question the principles of international financial cooperation among states. The subprime crisis thereby raises similar questions to the ones that have been tackled in preceding chapters: Why were the policies that govern the system questioned? What direction did the reforms to the international financial architecture take in the aftermath of the crisis? How can we account for the scope and direction of reform? Did political feedback play a role?

Although it is too soon to speculate about the direction of the reforms adopted in response to the crisis, we cannot but notice an emerging intellectual position calling for tightened international regulation and for a strengthened IMF. That is to say, after years of marginalization, the signs coming from the Fund's social constituencies for legitimation indicate a renewed interest in the activity of the Fund as a mechanism to ensure global financial stability.

This chapter thereby tackles the issue of the reform of the international financial regime in the aftermath of the subprime crisis by assessing whether the mood in the international community is turning against the principles that underpinned the system of the market-led financial governance towards a renewed system of centralized governance. In other words, tracing the debate about regulatory measures adopted with the aim of assuring global financial stability, I will attempt to assess whether the global economic crisis has shifted the climate of ideas against the principles of market discipline, self- and light-regulation, and the dispersion of supervisory authority at the international level.

The chapter is organized as follows. In the next section, I review those market and policy developments that took place in the years leading to the crisis. Specifically, I will focus on the policy idea of *market-led liberalization* and its principles of market discipline, self- and light-regulation, and dispersion of supervisory and regulatory authority. These principles underpinned the international financial system until the crisis burst. The second section will introduce the subprime crisis against the backdrop of the new approach to international financial governance. The third section details the IMF's interpretation of the crisis. That is to say, as I have done in preceding chapters, I will identify the lenses through which policy makers interpreted the crisis and acted on to prevent future ones. Contrary to what happened after the Asian crisis, however, after the subprime crisis, the voice coming from the Fund found a receptive audience among world leaders, academic economists, and even private-sector actors. Finally, I will analyze the policy measures adopted to respond to the crisis, showing the relationship between those policies and the interpretation of the crisis that came to prevail in the international community.

6.1   After the Asian crisis: The policy idea of market-led liberalization

Since the Asian financial crisis, several changes have taken place in the international financial system. On the one hand, financial integration proceeded apace leading to increasing linkages between financial institutions, both within and across countries. The integration of emerging market countries with global financial markets rose steadily with net private capital flows to emerging markets growing from 1 to 5 percent of emerging markets' GDP in the period from 2000 to 2007 (IMF, 2009a, p. 7). To provide a further measure of the growing financial linkages, foreign claims by banks from five major advanced countries (France, Germany, Japan, UK, US) increased steadily from $6.3 trillion in 2000 to $22 trillion by June 2008. In mid-2008, claims by these banks on emerging markets exceeded $4 trillion (Bank of International Settlements, Banking Statistics).

On the other hand, financial innovation and, in particular, the process of securitization marked the development of international financial markets over the past decade of global finance. Indeed, the issuance of asset-backed securities (ABS) expanded strongly since the end of the 1990s, supported by low interest rates on the supply-side and investors' search for yields on the demand side.[207] Against this scenario, global securitization issuance hit €1564 billion in 2007, an amount twice as large as global government bond issuance (European Securitisation

Forum, 2008). Only in Europe, securitization issuance grew tenfold between 2000 and 2008. Securitized assets also became an important asset class for international investors, accounting for 21.2 percent of the Lehman Aggregate Index as of the end of 2008.[208]

Alongside these developments in international markets, major changes were taking place in the policy ideas underlying international financial governance. Whereas until the Asian crisis the political debate mainly revolved around the question of whether and how financial liberalization is welfare-enhancing, since the end of the 1990s an increasing number of policy makers, practitioners, and economists came to regard financial markets not only as welfare-enhancing forces but also as stability-maximizing ones. Provided that they are free to operate, the predominant view was that financial markets would have contributed to domestic and international financial stability. In sum, using the distinction between the normative and the procedural dimension applied to investigate the idea of *orderly liberalization*, the normative dimension of the policy idea of *market-led liberalization* was that financial liberalization had both beneficial effects for domestic economic growth and a stabilizing impact on the international financial system.

At the procedural level, instead, the idea of *market-led liberalization* revolved around three principles that came to characterize the governance of the international financial system in the late 1990s: market discipline, self- and light-touch regulation, and the diffusion of supervisory and regulatory powers among international bodies mandated with the task of promoting global financial stability.

First, market forces were widely conceived as efficient mechanisms to ensure global financial stability and thereby to mitigate the risks associated with the integration of the world's capital markets. Under the favorable economic environment of the time, not only did markets appear able to allocate resources efficiently and to boost economic growth; they also appeared able to withstand the risks of financial integration and prevent instability. In particular, the dispersion of risk associated with financial innovation, mainly through securitization and derivatives, seemed to greatly enhance the ability of global financial intermediaries to manage market and credit risks (the so-called originate-to-distribute model). Government officials and regulators thereby recognized the significant benefits that securitization would have brought to both the domestic economy and international financial system. For instance, US Secretary Henry Paulson (2007) described securitization as 'a process that has been extremely valuable in extending the availability of credit to millions of homeowners.' Along similar lines, José Manuel Gonzales-Paramo (2008), member of the executive Board of the European Central Bank (ECB), hailed securitization as 'an effective mechanism' to mitigate the risks of liquidity transformation that banks ordinarily face and to provide banks with 'an additional source of funding to expand lending.' In sum, risk dispersion and diversification in credit markets had become the conventional wisdom giving market forces pride of place in the list of mechanisms to ensure both economic growth and global financial stability.

Building on the widespread faith in market discipline as a stabilizing force, new policies were adopted to strengthen international financial cooperation. Specifically, the international community embarked on what has been defined as the international 'regulatory project' (Walter, 2008). That is to say, since the late 1990s, several international bodies were mandated with the task of developing standards and codes of conduct in the areas of fiscal transparency, monetary and financial policy, among others.[209] These standards would have helped national authorities, especially in emerging market countries, in the management of their domestic financial system thereby contributing to the minimization of systemic risk that may have arisen from inappropriate domestic policies. In sum, the logic behind the international standard project was that bringing domestic financial-sector regulation in line with international standards would have helped foster international financial stability.

One of the crucial aspects of the process of international standardization is the involvement of the private sector. Indeed, the success of international standardization is perceived as being critically dependent on the activities of private-market participants (Financial Stability Forum, 2000; Mosley, 2003). Specifically, the argument was that market participants' use of international standards in their analyses and investment decisions might have provided a compelling incentive for states to comply with those standards. For instance, if the terms on which countries can borrow depend on their compliance with international standards, countries would have faced a strong incentive to adjust their financial system in line with the international guidelines reducing the likelihood of a financial crisis.

The second principle that constituted the policy idea of *market-led liberalization* is closely related to the principle of market discipline. Indeed, having accepted the argument that market actors force discipline and due diligence while searching for profits, the logical corollary was that regulation should be kept to a minimum. The principles of light-touch and self-regulation thereby gained currency and were institutionalized in the rules governing international financial markets. The light regulation of the growing derivatives industry well illustrates this point. Indeed, over the past decade, most over-the-counter (OTC) securities, including credit default swaps, were traded in almost totally unregulated markets. As Mark Brickell, a former lobbyist for the derivatives world was reported saying, Wall Street acted on the assumption that the industry had 'slammed the door shut' on government controls (Tett, 2009).

The adoption of the Basel II agreement, then, offers an apt illustration of the international acceptance of the principle of private-sector self-regulation to govern the international financial system. The Basel accord, initially negotiated in 1988 and profoundly revised in 2004, pursues two objectives. On the one hand, the accord aims at enhancing the safety and soundness of internationally active banks. On the other hand, it is meant to promote competitive equality among banks from different countries. In doing that, the Basel agreement set the standards governing the capital adequacy of internationally active banks. That is to say, the agreement specifies the formulas and mechanisms that banks should follow in setting aside capital as a ratio of their assets. Whereas there was a common capital requirement under the Basel I framework, Basel II introduced a risk-sensitive approach to calculate capital requirements – the so-called advanced internal risk-based (IRB) approach. In other words, capital requirements became a function of the different risk profile of banks' portfolios. In the attempt to align regulatory capital requirements to the risks that banks really face, however, the 2004 accord granted international banks significant room for maneuver. Indeed, the new accord allows banks to use their own internal measures and models to determine the riskiness of their portfolios (the IRB approach).[210] The higher the risk the higher the capital requirements will be, where the level of risk is decided by the banks themselves.[211]

Finally, building on the poor performance of the IMF in restoring international financial stability in the face of the 1997–98 crisis, the governance of the international financial system became increasingly informed on the principle of decentralized cooperation in crisis prevention and crisis management. That is to say, the supervisory and regulatory authority in the international financial system became either dispersed among public- and private-sector bodies (Porter, 2005) or increasingly left to the private sector (Cutler, et al., 1999; Hall and Biersteker, 2002; Higgott, et al., 2000).

As pointed out in the preceding chapter, the Asian crisis unleashed a profound contestation of the IMF that eroded trust in the Fund's ability to guarantee global financial stability. Governments thereby opted for policies premised on the assumption that actors other than the IMF could play a stabilizing role in the governance of the international financial system. In this connection, the private sector was recognized as playing a preeminent role. The proposal of creating a Sovereign Debt Restructuring Mechanism (SDRM), along with the already mentioned international standard initiative, well reflects the importance of private actors' involvement with the management of an international financial system. Indeed, although the proposal has not yet been translated into an actual policy, the SDRM was based on the recognition that governments are increasingly dependent on international markets to raise the capital they need for domestic investments and consumption. The SDRM thereby suggested the creation of an international bankruptcy framework and the inclusion of collective action clauses in private-sovereign contracts to prevent a few minority of creditors from holding out on the agreement reached between sovereign and a qualified majority of creditors.[212] In sum, the underlying assumption was that sovereign debt restructuring required the coordination of private creditors with or without the IMF's help in coordinating the claims of private creditors in case of sovereign default.

In this atmosphere, the IMF progressively was eclipsed as the preeminent institution in the system of international financial cooperation (see, for instance, Truman, 2006). To make matters worse for the Fund its internal governance had become a serious burden for the organization's role in the global economy. Since its decision-making had not seriously changed from the time of the Fund's creation, the argument is that the IMF is no longer the appropriate international forum that can effectively deal with the challenges of a changed international economy.[213] Furthermore, under the favorable economic environment of the early 2000s, the IMF suddenly appeared as a useless tool in the management of the global financial system. Major member countries, such as Russia, repaid their debts with the Fund while several emerging economies accumulated large international reserves to cushion against potential capital account crises and to avoid resorting to the Fund for financial assistance. In sum, at the beginning of the 2000s, the IMF ran out of clients; since the Fund relies primarily on income from its lending operations to finance its work, the sharp drop-off in lending activity was set to threaten the Fund's very existence.[214]

As the IMF was progressively discredited and its role streamlined, the international community opted for the creation of new international bodies to be involved in the governance of the international financial system: the G20 and the Financial Stability Board (FSB). The G20 was created in November 1997 at the initiative of US President Bill Clinton. Originally called the G22,[215] the group was transformed into the G33 in early 1999 before being named G20 later in the year.[216] As the G20 website put it, the group 'was created as a response both to the financial crises of the late 1990s and to a growing recognition that key emerging-market countries were not adequately included in the core of global economic discussion and governance.'[217] Indeed, the group brings together the finance ministers and central bank governors of both industrial and emerging market countries with the aim of identifying and discussing systematic financial vulnerabilities. Along with member representatives, the President of the World Bank, the Managing Director of the IMF, and the chairs of the International Monetary and Financial Committee and the Development Committee in the G20 meetings also participate in the workings of the G20.

Along with the G20, another international body was created in the aftermath of the Asian crisis as a forum in which to discuss issues related to global financial stability: the Financial Stability Forum (FSF), renamed as the Financial Stability Board in 2009. As it had been the case for the G20, the FSF was created at the initiative of the most advanced countries that mandated the President of the Deutsche Bundesbank, Hans Tietmeyer, to recommend reforms to the design of the international financial architecture. The recommendations of the Tietmeyer report were presented to the G7 countries in 1998 and suggested the creation of a new international body to make up for the shortcomings of the international financial architecture with the IMF as its sole fulcrum.[218] In this connection, the FSF was mandated 'to assess vulnerabilities affecting the international financial system; to identify and oversee action needed to address these; and to improve co-ordination and information exchange among the various authorities responsible for financial stability.'[219] The Forum was also tasked with the responsibility of fostering the adoption of internationally recognized standards. In particular, the FSF identified 12 key standards 'deserving of priority implementation depending on country circumstances.'[220]

Similarly to the G20 system of representation, the FSF was created on the assumption that addressing the challenges to global financial stability required an active involvement of systematically important countries. The FSF membership thereby included representatives of

26 national financial authorities of both advanced and emerging market countries. Furthermore, membership includes the international financial institutions, international regulatory and supervisory groupings, committees of central bank experts, and the European Central Bank.[221]

In conclusion, ten years after the Asian financial crisis the policy ideas about how to govern the international financial system had evolved towards new guiding principles and were institutionalized into new rules and policies. Specifically, market discipline, self- and light-touch regulation became crucial elements in the governance of the international financial system as reflected in the international standard project and in the international banking and derivative regulation. Furthermore, governments around the world seemed to agree that fostering global financial stability was no longer an exclusive competence of the IMF. Rather, various international bodies, alongside the private sector, would have contributed to the goal of mitigating and managing financial instability. As has been noted, in the years preceding the subprime crisis, these ideas were so engrained that 'most investors, bankers and even regulators did not change their behavior to any significant degree' even when the first signs of financial instability started emerging in early 2006 (Tett, 2008). It is also important to note that the idea of *market-led liberalization* was not articulated and strongly advocated by the IMF as it had been the case for the idea of *orderly liberalization*. Rather, the idea of *market-led liberalization* was articulated outside the IMF in the international financial industry and regulatory circles. The fact that the IMF did not significantly contribute to this debate further attests to the discredit in which the IMF fell after the Asian crisis.

Against this changed system of international financial governance, the world witnessed one of the most sustained period of economic growth, low inflation, and financial stability. This positive outlook characterized advanced as well as emerging market economies, which were perceived to be the most vulnerable to systemic instability. Indeed, as already pointed out, the reforms to the IFA adopted in the late 1990s were staked on the premise that the main risk to the global economy was likely to materialize in the domestic financial system of emerging market countries. Hence, emerging market countries were encouraged to bring their domestic financial systems in line with those of the advanced countries following internationally recognized standards of financial conduct. In drafting international banking regulation, for instance, 'the BCBS [the Basel Committee of Banking Supervision] and other international standard setters drew heavily upon institutional designs and practices in the major developed countries, especially those with the most sophisticated financial markets.' In other words, it was 'implicitly assumed that [Western] regulatory systems had been operating efficiently' (Walter, 2008, pp. 22, 24). Nevertheless, the subprime crisis proved these assumptions wrong. The Western world expected the crisis to erupt in a developing crisis. In fact, it did erupt in the most sophisticated financial market in the world, where market discipline and self-regulation were the most widespread. As a result, the key principles that underpinned the 21st international financial system started cracking vigorously.

6.2   The subprime crisis

After the emerging market crises of the 1990s, it has been publicly understood that integrated financial markets can allow the transmission of shocks.[222] The subprime crisis, however, demonstrated the risks associated with the integration of the world's financial markets in an unprecedented way. Indeed, although the crisis started with defaults in a marginal segment of the US financial services industry, it quickly spread to virtually all assets and all countries. From being a US-only event, the crisis became global.[223] To understand the magnitude of the contagion, it is thereby necessary to analyze the different factors that contributed to the crisis.

Contrary to the Mexican and the Asian crisis, the subprime crisis was not a currency crisis in an emerging market country triggered by a reversal in market sentiment. Rather, the crisis was first and foremost a credit crisis in the industrialized world caused by the deterioration of loan underwriting standards and by poor regulation of financial institutions.[224] Indeed, in the run-up to the crisis, financial institutions primarily based in the US loosened their credit standards as well as risk pricing on loans. In other words, they started rolling over an increasing number of loans to borrowers with low income and poor credit scores. For instance, it has been calculated that US subprime mortgages rose from about 9 percent of all mortgages originations from 1996 through 2004 to 21 percent from 2004 through 2006.[225] Mortgage lenders even proposed 'teaser' interest rates to their clients in the form of adjustable rate mortgages (ARM). That is to say, interest payments were fixed for a predetermined period, followed by market interest rates for the remainder of the mortgage's term. In doing so, loans were attractive to borrowers in the short-term, but risky and onerous in the long term. Why did financial institutions contribute to the deterioration of the creditworthiness of loans?

Setting aside regulatory incentives,[226] there are at least three factors that may help explain financial institutions' reckless behavior. First, there was the assumption that house prices would continue to increase. Hence, risk was perceived as being contained. In other words, the fact that US house prices had increased every year since 1991 to 2006, even during the recession of 2001, led financial institutions to believe that borrowers' potential repayment problems would have been eliminated by higher market prices for the collateral. If the borrower were unable to meet his/her redemption and interest payments, the home's increase in value would have allowed the bank to sell the house at a higher price and use the proceeds to reclaim its funds.[227] In sum, booming housing prices led to excessive optimism by lenders and investors.

The second factor that contributed to the loosening of the underwriting standards is extensive recourse to securitization. Indeed, in the run-up to the crisis, lenders massively transformed their loans in asset-backed securities (i.e. mortgage-backed securities, MBS) that derive their value from mortgage payments and housing prices. Low-quality loans also made their way into the pools of securitized assets. To provide a measure of the growing size of the mortgage market, consider that US financial institutions securitized approximately 46 percent of the total credit they originated from 2005 to 2007.[228] In Europe, issuance of mortgage-backed securities rose from €183 billion in 2005 to €590 billion in 2008.[229] Nevertheless, by selling off the risk of balance-sheet assets on to other investors, banks probably faced fewer incentives to check on the quality of the underlying asset,[230] thereby contributing to the accumulation of risk in the financial system.

Mortgage-backed securities, which were also sliced and diced to be inserted in collateralized debt obligations (CDOs), were then rated by credit rating agencies to be sold on to domestic and international investors. In light of the optimism that reigned in the market, the IMF calculates that as of April 2008 the three credit rating agencies had overestimated the performance of securitized subprime loans, attributing them elevated investment ratings (IMF, 2008a, pp. 61–3). Record volumes of securitization characterized by high ratings opened up the market of mortgage-backed-securities to all kinds of investors. Along with banks, hedge funds, pension funds, and mutual funds became the holders of mortgage loans. These investors, in turn, purchased insurance on mortgage instruments via credit derivatives issued by insurance companies. In sum, a dense network of financial interconnections was perilously built up.

Finally, another factor contributed to the deterioration of banks' lending decisions: the favorable macroeconomic outlook characterized by ample liquidity and low real interest rates. The upshot of this environment, fueled by the global imbalances, was to encourage demand for housing and to increase risk-appetite. In other words, the benign economic conditions 'provided fertile ground for financial excesses, including high leverage,' leading 'some firms to overestimate the market's capacity to absorb risk' as the global association of financial institutions itself concedes (Institute of International Finance, 2008a, pp. 111, 31). Indeed, in an environment characterized by low interest rates, investors' search for high-yield returns led them to invest in highly-remunerated mortgage-linked securities often with insufficient capital. For instance, a significant portion of mortgage-backed securities was held in off-balance-sheet vehicles, the special investment vehicles (SIVs) or conduits. These conduits, which were highly dependent on the liquidity of the short-term money market for their funding, did not need as much capital as banks need to meet regulatory requirements.[231] Putting subprime-related securities in the 'shadow banking system' thereby allowed banks to free capital and increase their leverage. Hence, the ultimate consequence of the favorable macroeconomic outlook was that a period of strong growth resulted in excessive risk-taking.[232]

Around the end of 2006, however, interest rates began to rise and US house price indexes stopped rising and then started declining more steadily. Under these changed circumstances, many borrowers could no longer refinance their mortgages, and loan delinquency and fore-closures started rising. With interest and debt repayment unpaid, the price of many mortgage-backed securities was severely curtailed and with it the financial health of investors that held them. Furthermore, the decline in mortgage payments caused serious turbulence for the money markets. Indeed, fearing massive withdrawal of investors from the asset-backed securities, money market funds shifted their portfolios away from medium- and long-terms assets (such as bank deposits and commercial paper) to assets with very short-term maturity. This defensive move, however, increased demand for short-term liquidity and contributed to freeze the commercial paper market, which was the source of funding for the special investment vehicles. Banks, pension funds, hedge funds, and other financial institutions suddenly found themselves exposed to the turmoil. On 9 August 2007, the European Central Bank injected $150 billion-worth of funds into the money markets to prevent borrowing costs from spiraling sharply. The US Federal Reserve followed suit. Despite these early actions, however, the crisis burst.

The drying up of the funding market for the SIVs forced banks either to lend to or to bring those vehicles onto their balance sheets primarily because of reputational concerns. Supporting their off-balance-sheet vehicles, however, banks became unsure about their liquidity and capital needs. As a result, banks started hoarding cash, reducing the periods at which they would lend to other banks. Although these moves reflected the loss of confidence in their counterparts, banks' hoard for cash exacerbated market illiquidity by bringing the interbank market in the major currencies to a halt. In sum, US chaos in housing and mortgage markets rippled into the wholesale market, where banks raise short-term finance, with devastating consequences for banks' financial stability.

On 14 September 2007, Northern Rock, a British mortgage lender that relied on the interbank market for its funding, was forced to seek emergency support from the Bank of England, precipitating its collapse and nationalization.[233] The stock market started suffering heavily with equity prices of financial institutions leading the decline. In less than a year, market capitalization of global banks fell by more than half from $3.6 trillion at the end of 2007 to $1.6 trillion at the end of 2008 (IMF, 2009a, p. 32).

The stock-market crash further exacerbated banks' liquidity and capital needs. Indeed, with investors becoming increasingly risk-averse, financial institutions that needed to raise more capital to strengthen their balance sheets had to confront higher costs of both equity and debt. In March 2008, an illustrious victim gave a graphic dimension to the crisis. Indeed, after weeks of financial difficulties that had wiped out its cash reserves, one of Wall Street's symbols, the fifth-largest US investment bank Bearn Stearns, was forced to sell itself to JPMorgan Chase for $2.1 billion with the support of the Fed and the US Treasury.

Beyond the banking system, insurance companies and pension funds were also severely hit by the crisis because of their exposure to assets whose value was deteriorating sharply. The situation was further aggravated by the use of fair value accounting that forced banks to readjust their books after every price change. As debt prices plunged, the market-to-market rule thereby contributed to severe write-down and to fire sales of debt portfolios.

To make matters worse, the opacity and complexity of mortgage-related products made it difficult to gauge losses in the financial sector. Estimated losses on US subprime loans and securities were initially estimated at about $250 billion as of October 2007. This estimate, however, was revised upward several times as credit conditions worsened. By

April 2008, global losses in the financial sector were estimated to have reached almost $1 trillion (IMF, 2008a). In January 2009, the IMF raised its estimate of the potential deterioration in the assets held by financial institutions from $1.4 billion, as calculated in October, to $2.2 trillion. In April, the same estimate rose to $2.7 trillion for US banks and $1.1 trillion for European ones (IMF, 2009a).

Against this background of high uncertainty, the availability and cost of funding for banks continued to deteriorate. Conditions even worsened after the bankruptcy of one of the icons of Wall Street investment banks: Lehman Brothers. Starting in early September, Lehman was witnessing a virtual collapse of its share price while the cost of its credit insurance was rising sharply. On 14 September, Lehman was forced to file for bankruptcy protection after it emerged that Bank of America abandoned takeover talks, deciding to buy another Wall Street investment bank instead: Merrill Lynch. Not only had three investment banks disappeared from the Wall Street landscape; the two remaining investment banks, Goldman Sachs and Morgan Stanley, were transformed into depository institutions.

Lehman's collapse had profound effects outside the United States. Around the world, bank prices collapsed and credit default swap spreads, which measure default probability, surged. At the same time, overnight interbank rates significantly rose, liquidity became scarce, and demand for dollar funding became acute. Financial institutions across Europe experienced severe difficulty. Among them, Fortis, Hypo Real Estate, and Dexia were rescued by the combined efforts of several governments. Still, what happened to Lehman, which was an important financial counterparty in many derivative transactions, exacerbated the situation in the credit derivative markets, pushing insurance conglomerates such as AIG close to collapse.

With financial institutions around the world recording vast losses, the real economy started to be severely affected too. Indeed, the deterioration in the banks' capital base reduced their ability to provide loans and thus finance activities like investments and consumer spending. In other words, the intensification of the banking crisis led to a decline in credit to the private sector, intensifying the vicious circle between the financial sector and the real economy.[234] With the supply of credit contracting sharply, firms thereby slashed their investments and unemployment rose. In this gloomy scenario, consumer demand also weakened as a result of both tighter credit conditions and growing uncertainty (IMF, 2009a). The slump in consumption especially affected sectors such as housing or auto manufacturing that had traditionally benefited from massive credit financing. In sum, economic activity decelerated and many advanced countries were reported to be in recession. At the same time, the pace of economic growth lost momentum in emerging market countries, adding downward pressure to the global economy.

Indeed, the crisis eventually broadened to emerging market countries at the expense of the decoupling scenario. While until late in 2008, emerging markets were regarded as insulated from the crisis, at the end of the year they were drawn into the storm. The crisis was transmitted to the emerging economies by the two channels of trade and finance. On the one hand, with global demand slowing, the corporate sector in several emerging market countries faced large drops in export volumes. In Latin America and Asia, for instance, sharp drops in export revenues increased firms' funding needs, straining domestic financial systems. On the other hand, the crisis and, in particular, the credit crunch were transmitted to the emerging market countries via the contraction of cross-border lending. For instance, the IIF estimates that net private capital flows to emerging economies had dwindled at end-2008 and are now projected to be $165 billion in 2009, 82 percent below the 2007 level (Institute of International Finance, 2009). That is to say, the crisis propagated to emerging markets in the form of a reduction of international capital flows since international banks slashed their funding in an effort to satisfy their liquidity needs. The drying up of international capital particularly hit those countries with high current account deficits, such as many countries of central and Eastern Europe.

Essentially, similarly to what happened in Asia, an initial shock, such as default on the subprime mortgages, became a sort of wake-up call for investors. When problems emerged in the specific category of US subprime assets, this triggered a process that ultimately led to a repricing of risk of several asset classes. Deleveraging took place across the board from the mortgage-related structured credit markets to the money markets and to emerging market assets. The increasing risk aversion among investors was ultimately reflected in the contraction of capital flows. As it was the case in Mexico and Asia, the volatility of international capital flows was 'a powerful factor in crisis contagion' (Pisani-Ferry and Santos, 2009, p. 10).

The (short-term) response to the crisis

The global financial crisis propelled a variety of national responses primarily aimed at restoring financial market stability and at avoiding spill-over effects to the real economy. In this connection, monetary policy provided the first line of defense. Indeed, several central banks lowered interest rates to relieve pressures on borrowers and facilitate the access of households and business to credit. For instance, by the spring of 2009, the Federal Reserve had lowered its main rate at a rate close to zero whereas the ECB brought interest down to 1 percent.

Central banks, then, expanded the traditional monetary tools to include unconventional measures meant to provide liquidity to the stressed financial system. In particular, several central banks in the advanced economies loosened the terms and availability of their liquidity facilities, widened the range of counterparty financial institutions, and swapped liquid government securities for illiquid assets held by banks. Still, central banks expanded the range of collateral eligible for liquidity support operations to include securitized assets. With the aim of providing short-term funding, the European Central Bank, for instance, accepted securitization notes as eligible collateral for repo transactions.[235]

A few central banks, such as the Federal Reserve and the Bank of Japan, also opted for expanding their balance sheets to finance the purchases of mortgage-backed securities and commercial paper by borrowers and investors. Central banks also opted for quantitative easing, buying corporate and government debt. In March 2009, even the Bank of England, in coordination with the UK Treasury, agreed to create new reserves for the purchase of corporate and governments bonds.

National governments also played an active role in response to the crisis in the attempt to tackle both liquidity and solvency problems that emerged in the domestic financial system. To address the liquidity concerns, some governments pursued the path of the purchase of illiquid loans and securitized assets. In order to restore confidence, national regulators and supervisors also opted for restricting short-selling on financial-sector shares several times during the fall of 2008. One of the most prominent examples of governments' measures to address liquidity problems is the initial US rescue plan: the $700 billion Trouble Assets Relief Program (TARP). Indeed, when TARP was initially proposed in September 2008 by US Treasury Secretary Henry Paulson, the assumption was that the crisis was essentially one of liquidity. Hence, in order to restore confidence, government intervention was necessary to create a market for the most deteriorated assets (i.e. the mortgage-backed securities), thereby purchasing them. In early 2009, then, the incoming Obama administration expanded on TARP's original mission, launching a similar initiative: the public-private investment fund for cleaning up banks' balance sheets from toxic assets.

When liquidity problems gave way to solvency concerns, governments expanded their intervention introducing guarantees for bank debt and injecting capital into domestic banks. The development of the Trouble Assets Relief Program well illustrates the expansion in the scope of governments' intervention. Indeed, in November 2008, the US Treasury asked Congress to use the remaining TARP funds to invest in domestic banks. In other words, the idea was to recapitalize troubled financial institutions. At the same time, the US administration announced the creation of a new facility to sustain the credit markets and facilitate the flow of credit: the Reserve's Term Asset-Backed Securities Loan Facility (TALF). Under the TALF, the Federal Reserve Bank of New York (FRBNY), with the Treasury support, would have provided up to $200 billion of loans to finance the purchase of securities collateralized by credit-card, car, student and small-business loans.

Alongside these full-fledged measures to restart lending and the flow of credit, several governments put in place comprehensive and coordinated plans to support demand. These initiatives included programs to support the housing market, create new jobs, and cut taxes.

Finally, the actions taken to repair domestic financial systems and support demand were complemented by measures aimed at mobilizing resources for emerging markets. Specifically, liquidity to emerging market countries was provided by swap lines arranged with the central banks while the IMF heavily intervened to provide financial assistance to the crisis-hit countries, in particular in central and Eastern Europe. The G20 also decided to provide $250 billion in short-term trade financing to emerging economies to supplement the sharp drop in private-market financing. In spite of the unprecedented responses, however, the present downturn is widely regarded as the deepest global recession since the World War II.

Along with the immediate concerns to tackle the crisis, policy makers started questioning the design of the international financial architecture and, in particular, the policies that had been adopted in the late 1990s, building on the experience of the Asian crisis. In this connection, a series of questions were raised about the extent to which financial integration increased the risks of crises, and about the scope of reforms needed to overhaul the mechanisms of crisis prevention and management at the international level. In order to understand the long-term reforms to the governance of the international financial system, it is first necessary to detail the emerging policy consensus on the causes of the crisis so as to chart its implications for the financial architecture exercise. As I have done in previous chapters, the analysis is going to start from the IMF's interpretation on the origins of the crisis in order to assess the extent to which IMF ideas were embraced across its social constituencies for legitimation. As we are going to see in the next sections, contrary to what happened in the aftermath of the Asian crisis, in the aftermath of the subprime crisis, the IMF's interpretation resonated with the larger political environment.

6.3   The IMF interpretation of the crisis

Several factors contributed to the origins and virulence of the subprime crisis including macroeconomic imbalances, poor risk management in systematically important institutions, and inadequate international financial regulation. In order to address the crisis, and design the policies to promote financial-sector stability, national governments called on several international bodies to analyze the interaction among the multiple factors that caused the crisis and to propose recommendations for the reform of the international financial architecture. In this connection, international bodies such as the International Monetary Fund (IMF), the Financial Stability Board (FSB), and the G20 have all been involved in understanding the causes and elaborating a series of measures to address the shortcomings brought to the surface by the subprime crisis.

As far as concerns the IMF, the Fund published a series of reports and papers in early 2009 with the aim of contributing to the public debate and, specifically, to the G20 spring meeting. Some of this work, which includes specific recommendations on the long-term reforms to the international financial architecture,[236] was presented to the International Monetary and Financial Committee (IMFC) as part of the paper 'The recent financial turmoil – Initial assessment, policy lessons, and implications for fund surveillance' (IMF, 2009e). Furthermore, the IMF made its views known through the analyses conducted in the Global Financial Stability Reports and in ad-hoc publications. The public pronouncements of senior IMF officials, then, offer another source to gauge the IMF's interpretation of the subprime crisis.

As has already been noted for the other crises analyzed in this book, interpreting the causes of a financial crisis is a crucial exercise that helps explain the policies adopted in response. Furthermore, while crises are often the results of the interaction among multiple factors, interpreting them involves a process of intellectual simplification through which certain factors are recognized to have more explanatory weight than others. For instance, after the Mexican turmoil, the IMF emphasized weaknesses in domestic macroeconomic policies, and after the Asian crisis the emphasis was put on weaknesses in domestic financial and corporate systems. The IMF interpretation of the subprime crisis was also focused on a number of factors. Specifically, according to the IMF, market discipline proved pointless in preventing financial excesses, light-and self-regulation were harmful for systemic stability, and international financial supervision was too fragmented to detect the early signs of the crisis. In what follows, I elaborate on each issue in turn.

To start with, from the Fund's perspective, market discipline did not work. In an economic context characterized by low interest rates and financial innovation, 'market discipline failed as optimism prevailed, due diligence was outsourced to credit rating agencies, and a financial sector compensation system based on short-term profits reinforced the momentum for risk-taking' (IMF, 2009b, p. 2). In other words, the Fund saw the signs of market failure on two fronts. On the one hand, there was the failure of 'the loan brokers and originators, who had little incentive to screen risk that they sold on.' On the other hand, the failure of market discipline is evident in the behavior of 'end-investors, who relied on optimistic statistical analyses by credit rating agencies – less so own due diligence – to assess asset quality' (IMF, 2009b, pp. 2–3). Although the Fund still acknowledged that the private sector had a central responsibility in the good functioning of financial markets 'by improving risk management, including through attention to governance and remuneration policies,' the Fund nonetheless concluded that 'system-wide stability is a public good that will be undervalued by private institutions' (IMF, 2009a, p. xviii). In other words, markets cannot be stabilizing forces on their own and the 'failure' of investors' ability to perform due diligence was thereby seen as 'a major contributor to the present crisis' (IMF, 2009a, p. xx).

Building on these observations, the Fund pinned the blame of the crisis on the type of financial regulation that had developed from the adherence to the principles of market discipline and light-touch intervention. Indeed, from the Fund's perspective, the crisis 'undermined the effectiveness of a regulatory model that rested, at least in large part, on transparency, disclosure, and market discipline to curb excessive risk-taking' (IMF, 2009d, p. 3). As IMF staff members put it in one of the papers prepared to draw lessons from the crisis, financial regulation 'was not equipped to see the risk concentrations and flawed incentives behind the financial innovation boom' (IMF, 2009b, p. 1). For instance, the limited scope of regulation of the shadow banking system was widely interpreted as having helped the spread of the crisis.

The fact that banks used large, unregulated off-balance-sheet vehicles to accumulate complex financial products led to a perilous concentration of credit and liquidity risk. In the words of the Fund, 'regulation may have been the better tool in theory, but in practice huge risks were amassed below the regulator's radar, in the shadow banking system' (IMF, 2009b, p. 7).

Having interpreted the crisis largely as a result of poor regulation, the IMF has been a strong advocate of strengthening international and domestic regulation. In the 2008 Global Financial Stability Report (IMF, 2008b, p. 54), for instance, IMF staff called for 'more robust foundations for the global financial system', suggesting that 'regulation and supervision should be designed according to the type of financial activities being performed by regulated institutions, and less by the type of intermediary.' That is to say, regulating the activities of actors such as hedge funds and investment banks was required. Still, in a staff position note (Carvajal, et al., 2009, p. 5), a group of IMF staff members encouraged the expansion of the perimeter of financial regulation and disclosure obligations for systematically important financial institutions. 'The key objective should be to ensure that all financial activities that may pose systemic risks are appropriately overseen.' Along similar lines, José Viñals, Financial Counsellor and IMF Director, Monetary and Capital Markets Department, encouraged the international community 'to add a Chapter to the rulebook [of financial regulation and supervision], with the aim of increasing the likelihood that the systemic risks posed by unregulated or less-regulated financial sector segments are identified and addressed alongside risks in the regulated sector' (Viñals, 2009). In sum, contrary to the arguments positing that market discipline and self-regulation would provide an effective way to ensure systemic stability, the IMF clearly put its weight behind the expansion of prudential regulation.[237]

Still, the voice coming from the Fund in the aftermath of the subprime crisis questioned existing rules on capital requirements, that is to say, the rules embodied in the Basel II framework. As one IMF staff paper summarized what needed to be done to reform existing rules, 'capital, provisioning and liquidity norms should be more demanding in good times to build buffers that in bad times can help to offset procyclical pressures'(IMF, 2009d, p. 5).

Finally, the Fund's view was that the crisis reflected important coordination gaps in the international financial architecture. In the words of the Fund, 'a lack of global policy coordination stoked the crisis, reflecting in part the limitations of available structures' (IMF, 2009c,

p. 7). Specifically, the Fund identified gaps in the international cooperative efforts related to both crisis prevention and crisis management. On the prevention front, the Fund blamed the crisis on the segmented international supervisory arrangements grown out of the Asian crisis. The repartition of international surveillance among the IMF, the G20, and the Financial Stability Forum proved unable to detect the vulnerabilities that were accumulating in the run-up to the crisis. As one of the IMF papers prepared to analyze the crisis put it, 'none of [existing] arrangements provided sufficiently robust warnings in the run up to the crisis' (IMF, 2009c, p. 2).

On the crisis management front, the crisis revealed several weaknesses in cross-border cooperation. As the Fund put it, 'coordination of macroeconomic policies across governments did not produce the international leadership needed for a concerted response to the global risks identified.' In other words, there was a 'lack of mechanisms to coordinate initial policy responses' (IMF, 2009c, pp. 1 and 7). Absent 'an effective forum where relevant policy makers could actively engage,' countries did not always respond in a coordinated manner to unfolding events in the financial sector.

Nowhere is the lack of international cooperation more evident than in the orderly resolution of cross-border bank insolvencies. Indeed, from the Fund's perspective, national governments resorted to 'defensive moves,' such as ring-fencing of foreign banks assets, which did not contribute to withstand the impact of the crisis but further undermined confidence. For instance, as the crisis intensified in the fall of 2008, UK supervisors ring-fenced Icelandic bank assets, in the absence of assurances that UK bank liabilities would be fulfilled. Similarly, German authorities froze Lehman's assets after the latter started its bankruptcy proceedings. Still, 'countries rushed to protect their banks' assets and liabilities with government guarantees, they put pressure on less protected systems in neighboring countries, exposing them to risks of deposit runs unless they too adopted guarantees' (IMF, 2009c, pp. 7, 10).

From the Fund's perspective, the crisis thereby revealed the urgency of improving the mechanisms of financial cooperation. Strauss-Khan (2009a), for instance, called for an 'agreed framework of cooperation for dealing with cross-border firms that would address conflicts of interest – this would include harmonizing national legislation where necessary.' According to the Managing Director, this financial coordination framework should have dealt with a number of issues including the harmonization of domestic financial regulation and depositors' protection schemes, the development of resolution tools for cross-border institutions, and the elaboration of information-sharing mechanisms among national regulators and supervisors. Although the Managing Director did not claim Fund leadership in managing the proposed common framework in favor of the Financial Stability Board and the Basel Committee, he nonetheless pointed to the crucial role that the IMF can play in monitoring and implementing the resolution framework.

In sum, in interpreting the crisis, the IMF clearly identified those factors that above others had contributed to the scale and scope of the crisis. Failures in market discipline, financial regulation, and international coordination were the factors upon which the IMF put its emphasis. In contrast, global imbalances seemed to have played an ancillary rather than a causal role in the financial meltdown. Although it has been noted that IMF emphasis on poor regulation rather than on global imbalances partly reflect the Fund's guilty contribution to the build-up of imbalances (*The Economist*, 2009e), what is relevant for the purposes of this study is that there are several possible interpretations of the same event 'crisis'. Hence, it is necessary to assess how far a specific interpretation becomes predominant. In order to understand the extent to which the IMF position was shared in its operating environment, thereby legitimating it, the next section analyses how member countries, academic economists, and private-sector representatives reacted to the crisis.

6.4   The international financial architecture exercise: Ideational contestation and policy debate

Contrary to what happened in 1997, when the IMF's interpretation of the Asian crisis did not find a receptive audience among the actors that form the Fund's social constituencies for legitimation, after the subprime crisis, policy makers, academic economists, and even private-sector actors shared the diagnosis of the crisis as put forward by the Fund. In other words, the interpretation stressing the failures of market discipline, self-and light-regulation, and poor international financial cooperation resonated with the broad political environment in which the IMF operates. In what follows, I thereby trace the signs of the contestation of existing policy ideas about how to ensure systemic financial stability under conditions of globalization. Specifically, I review the main reports issued in response to the crisis as well as the decisions taken during the international summits convened to redesign the international financial architecture. In doing so, this section attempts to gauge how far the contestation anticipates the shift to a new intellectual consensus on the policies with which to govern the risks of the global financial system.

As the financial turmoil was still unfolding, several world leaders called on international bodies or formed ad-hoc working groups to draw lessons from the crisis and to advance proposals to reform the international financial architecture. In this climate of reform, several authoritative reports were produced. For instance, suggestions about the scope and direction of reform to the international financial system came from the reports prepared by the G30 Working Group on Financial Reform led by Paul Volcker, the former Federal Reserve chairman (G30, 2009). Still, the group chaired by the former governor of the Banque de France, Jacques de Larosière (de Laroisiere, 2009), and the recommendations prepared by the Financial Stability Board, are among the most well-known works issued in the spring of 2009 with the aim of contributing to the global efforts to restore financial stability and reform the international regulatory system.

Despite the variety of the reform proposals that flourished in the aftermath of the crisis, virtually all reports and comments show a remarkable consensus on the failure of the existing policies governing the functioning of the global financial system. In particular, the crisis seemed to have shaken the belief in several, if not all, the principles underlying the policy idea of *market-led liberalization.*

The first principle that came to be questioned was the assumption that market discipline is a viable mechanism to ensure international financial stability. Rather, the view according to which market failure greatly contributed to the current financial crisis became widespread. 'The financial crisis has challenged the intellectual assumptions on which previous regulatory approaches were largely built, and in particular the theory of rational and self-correcting markets,' the Chairman of the British Financial Services Authority (FSA), Lord Turner, declared. 'Much financial innovation has proved of little value, and market discipline of individual bank strategies has often proved ineffective' (FSA, 2009a).

Along similar lines, and in line with the position expressed by the IMF, the G20 leaders concluded that 'during a period of strong global growth, growing capital flows, and prolonged stability earlier this decade, market participants sought higher yields without an adequate appreciation of the risks and failed to exercise proper due diligence.' Even market actors recognized several of the mistakes committed by the financial industry in the years that preceded the crisis. In the words of a joint report prepared by a group of associations of the securities industry, as early as the first half of 2007, 'the industry was aware of a gradual deterioration in origination and overall credit standards. But market players did not feel sufficient responsibility for ensuring discipline across all parts of the securitization value chain.' The report thereby concluded that market actors lacked 'a sense of shared responsibility for the integrity of the system as a whole.'[238]

A specific example of market failure in imparting discipline and thereby contributing to international financial instability is provided by the behavior of the credit rating agencies (CRAs). While it was believed that the CRAs would have helped markets in assessing financial products and pricing risk, credit ratings played a big part in exacerbating the crisis. Indeed, CRAs failed to sufficiently appreciate the risks inherent in complicated financial instruments, notably, assets linked to subprime mortgages.[239] By giving AAA ratings to complex and opaque structured financial products, CRAs lowered the perception of credit risk among investors. The fact that regulators required certain institutional investors to invest only in AAA-rated products, then, magnified CRAs' weaknesses when the issuer defaulted on its interest and principal payment.

Not only the credit rating agencies but also market investors did not assess risk properly. They over-relied on credit rating models, further weakening public faith in the markets. As the Chairman of the FSB Mario Draghi (2008) put it, there was a 'collective blindness' among market actors. In this connection, the Commission of the European Union condemned both the agencies and the market participants. As the Commission put it, the 'failure by CRAs to produce sound and accurate ratings was combined with an imprudent and non-judicious approach of the investors, who relied blindly on credit ratings.' Hence, 'credit was granted even if it was not justified by economic fundamentals' (EU Commission, 2008).

Alongside market discipline, the crisis questioned the second pillar of the post-Asian consensus. That is to say, the idea that markets and market actors could safely be left to self-correct no longer found a receptive audience. As we have seen, the IMF clearly spelled out the limitations of existing international regulation. Nevertheless, the voice coming from the Fund was not an isolated one but several policy makers and economists joined in the chorus, calling for re-regulation of the markets. The debate on financial regulation that is taking place within the European Union is particularly relevant here. Indeed, the EU is calling for a regulatory framework that covers 'all financial markets, products and participants' (Bryant, 2009) first and foremost within the Union but also at the international level. For instance, the EU institutions have developed a number of proposals to centralize supervision of financial firms at the EU level (de Laroisiere, 2009) and to tighten controls on hedge funds, tax havens, and credit rating agencies at the international level (Hall and Mackintosh, 2009).[240] In short, the EU is supporting a series of reforms to the international financial architecture according to which the oversight approach of the 1990s is clearly replaced by an approach based on regulation. Whereas it was believed that market actors could look after themselves and contribute to international financial stability, the predominant view in Europe today is that markets require strong regulatory mechanisms to function effectively. The French President Nicolas Sarkozy even concluded that 'a page has been turned' on an era of post-war 'Anglo-Saxon' capitalism (as reported in Parker, et al., 2009).

Interestingly, then, this view also appears on the rise outside of the EU. Several analysts, for instance, have pointed out that the Anglo-Saxon model of capitalism has been seriously questioned (Buiter, 2008). According to Nouriel Rubini, then, the pillars of the financial supervisory system of the past decade have all failed, including the principles of self-regulation and market discipline (Roubini, 2009). Stressing the irrationality of markets, two respected economists, George Akerlof and Robert Shiller (2009), have recently argued to rebuild the orthodox economic doctrine, keeping in due consideration what Keynes used to define 'animal spirits.' That is to say, markets are perceived as destabilizing forces that must be contained and not as agents of financial stability, as the intellectual paradigm of the late 1990s have forcefully argued. Even in countries long associated with a regulatory approach favoring the financial industry, the condemnation of the regulatory model developed since the aftermath of the Asian crisis was not less severe. The Director of the US National Economic Council Larry Summers, for instance, has been reported as saying that the view that the markets are inherently self-stabilizing had been 'dealt a fatal blow.'[241]

The Financial Stability Board, in turn, started working to ensure that financial systems would be subject to more effective regulation to increase capital ratios and decrease leverage. This would imply, *inter alia*, reducing the procyclicality of the regulatory framework and its reliance on 'self-regulation' by market participants, as the Chairman of the FSB Mario Draghi (2008) pointed out.

The representatives of the financial industry were themselves aware of the limitations of self-regulation and of the political climate against it. For instance, in presenting one of the reports prepared by the Institute for International Finance (IIF) in response to the financial turmoil, Chairman Josef Ackermann felt the need to stress that the report should not be intended as 'an exercise in self-regulation.' Rather, he recognized that 'it is essential for the industry to reform and that there is an emerging consensus on the benefits of reinforcing these efforts through effective regulatory incentives and structures' (Institute of International Finance, 2008b). Similarly, Tom Ryan, the Director of SIFMA, the association of the securities industry, went public, admitting that 'the industry accepts its share of responsibility for its role in the economic crisis' (Ryan, 2009).

The upshot of the criticisms raised at the principle of self-regulation was a profound rethink on the perimeter of financial regulation. In other words, the evidence provided by the crisis called into question the principle of light-touch regulation that had marked the decade preceding the subprime crisis. Even in the UK, where the doctrine of light-touch regulation was probably the most embedded, authoritative voices were raised to cast doubt on its efficiency. The report prepared by Lord Turner, head of the British Financial Service Authority (FSA), for instance, called for expanding regulation of the European banking market (Financial Services Authority, 2009b).

Finally, the crisis brought into relief the weaknesses of existing global cooperative arrangements in crisis prevention and crisis management. In other words, the system of decentralized financial cooperation, which had dominated the governance of the system since the late 1990s, came to be perceived as inadequate to the task of ensuring global financial stability. On the one hand, the crisis showed that the international network made up by FSB, the G20, and the IMF missed the systemic implications of the growing interconnectedness among financial institutions. This is not to say that these bodies were caught offguard by the crisis. The problem was rather that the warning signals coming from these bodies were either weak or unheard. As the De Laroisiere report put it, 'the key failure in the past was not so much a lack of surveillance, although the messages emerging from the surveillance could have been sharpened, but a lack of policy action' (de Laroisiere, 2009, p. 63). That is to say, warnings did not activate policy makers, financial regulators and supervisors, and market participants' response. On the other hand, the magnitude of the crisis revealed the limited armory at the IMF's disposal after years of international marginalization. As the crisis threatened several emerging market economies, a question was raised whether the IMF would have had enough resources to extend its financial assistance and thereby helping the global recovery.

In sum, the experience of the subprime crisis seemed to have disrupted the policy consensus that had emerged in the late 1990s around the idea of *market-led liberalization*. As a result, the role of markets in ensuring global financial stability, the principle of light- and self-regulation, and the dispersion of supervisory authority in the international financial system were deeply challenged. Stressing the emerging shift in the climate of economic ideas, the G20 (2009a) even referred to 'the desirability of a new global consensus on the key values and principles that will promote sustainable economic activity.'

Building on the contestation of previous policy ideas and of their institutionalization into the policies governing the international financial system, specific policy proposals have been advanced to reform the international institutional and regulatory set-up. These policy recommendations depart significantly from the policy consensus built in the aftermath of the Asian crisis in that they primarily suggest reducing the scope of private-sector self-regulation, enlarging the scope of financial regulation, and re-centralizing the governance of international financial cooperation by strengthening the Fund's role. That is to say, contrary to what happened in the aftermath of the Asian crisis, after the subprime crisis the IMF was again at the center of the reform process to the international financial architecture. Not only did the Fund's intellectual position on the origins of the crisis and on its remedies find a receptive audience across the actors that form its social constituencies for legitimation, but member countries called on the IMF to manage the crisis and pledged to strengthen its role in the governance of the international financial system. In other words, after years at the margins, the subprime crisis unleashed a positive feedback for the Fund whose emergence is traced in the next sections. Specifically, in what follows, I analyze two main areas of proposed reforms, bringing to the surface the connections between each of them and the contestation of the previous policy ideas about how to govern international finance.

From market discipline to market regulation

Reflecting the weakening faith in self-stabilizing property of markets, the first set of policy recommendations around which a broad convergence of views is emerging relates to the scope of financial regulation. Specifically, policy makers seem interested in reducing the scope of market self-regulation. The most illustrative examples of this trend are the suggestions to revise the Basel accord and to increase scrutiny over credit rating agencies.

As far as concerns the Basel rules, several policy makers and analysts have pointed to the fact that even well-capitalized banks according to the Basel standards were nonetheless forced to raise capital to survive the financial turmoil.[242] Since large banks enjoy the possibility of manipulating the level of capital requirements using internal risk management models to assess portfolio risk, the logical conclusion drawn from the crisis has been that the use of internal models needs to be substantially reduced. In this connection, it has been suggested, for instance, that an approach close to that of standardization typical of Basel I be adopted, according to which all banks are subject to common minimum capital requirements independent from the risks of their portfolios. 'Its very simplicity makes [the standardized approach] deserving of consideration as one element of an international capital regime' (Tarullo, 2008, p. 228). Along similar lines, the Financial Stability Board recommended national and international regulators to use simple ratios of equity to assets in their judgment on the soundness of domestic banks. As one of the reports prepared to identify the principles to strengthen financial systems reads, 'the BCBS [Basel Committee of Banking Supervision] should supplement the risk-based capital requirement with a simple, non-risk based measure to help contain the build-up of leverage in the banking system' (Financial Stability Board, 2009b). Simple measures of capital to assets were also used by the Federal Reserve and the US Treasury in the 'stress test' exercise carried out in the spring of 2009 to identify the capital needs of major US banks. In sum, banking regulation is one of the areas widely regarded as most in need of a substantial re-regulation. As *The Economist* (2009d) put it, 'it hasn't got to the stage of taxi drivers demanding a crackdown on tier-one capital, but in general terms the world agrees that banks need to be regulated until they weep.'

Another area of reforms that aims at limiting private-sector involvement with the task of ensuring international financial stability regards the activities of the credit rating agencies. Indeed, beyond the failure of credit rating agencies in warning investors about the risks associated with complex financial products, the crisis also unveiled the discretionary power given to the agencies. In particular, several policy makers and analysts suggested that it was the lack of formal control by public authorities that led the CRAs to questionable practices, scarce transparency, and conflicts of interest (G20, 2009c). Stressing the fact that the activities on the CRAs are only based on the voluntary *Code of Conduct Fundamentals for Credit Rating Agencies* developed by the International Organization of Securities Commissions (IOSCO) in 2004, the EU

Commission, for instance, concluded that the code 'has failed as a self-regulatory framework.' In particular, the 'CRAs are free not to respect certain obligations stemming from the Code...There is no robust mechanism of control of the CRAs' activity' (EU Commission, 2008).

Against this backdrop, in April 2009, the European Union proposed new rules to regulate rating agencies, improve transparency, and avoid conflicts of interest. The text of the proposed legislation introduces a legally binding registration system for credit ratings agencies operating in the EU and the obligation to accept unannounced inspections (EU Commission, 2009). In the United States the proposals for regulating the CRAs have not been absent. Mary Schapiro, chairman of America's Securities and Exchange Commission, called for an 'intense review' of the function of credit rating agencies in the markets (*The Economist*, 2009c). Although we still have not reached an international agreement about how to regulate the activities of CRAs, the steps taken in the EU and in the US nonetheless indicate the potential direction of international reforms.

Alongside the proposals to adjust existing regulation, several policy makers and observers have suggested expanding the perimeter of international financial regulation. The French President Nicolas Sarkozy, for instance, claimed that tightening up on financial regulation must be regarded as an 'immense progress' in international financial cooperation (Hall, et al., 2009). Similarly, German officials expressed their preferences for tough international regulatory measures (Benoit, 2008). In particular, it has been proposed to extend regulation to hedge funds, tax havens, and to the derivative industry.

As already pointed out, after having long-embraced the principle of light-touch regulation, the calls for tightening regulation were voiced even in the United States and in the United Kingdom, whose financial model of capitalism has traditionally been characterized by an arms-length relationship between markets and the state. For instance, the US Treasury Secretary has called for 'new rules of the game' to regulate the domestic financial system and not just minor repairs at the margins (Braithwaite and Guerrera, 2009) and has initiated a profound overhaul of the US domestic financial system. Building on these changes in the intellectual climate, an observer has even concluded that 'there is consensus that the laissez-faire era of financial sector regulation is over' (Kaufmann, 2009).

These claims are probably premature but they nonetheless signal important discontinuities with the policy ideas that had been at the heart of the governance of the international financial system until recently. These discontinuities also emerge from the proposed reforms on bankers' pay and incentives,[243] that is to say, areas that have not traditionally fallen within the responsibility of governments in a market economy. A review of the conclusions of the G20 leaders also unveils the extent of the emerging consensus that significantly departs from the erstwhile approach to international finance.

Indeed, the G20 meetings, which took place to discuss measures to tackle the crisis, focused on the reforms to financial regulation at both the national and international level. Among other measures, the G20 has called for a review of the scope of financial regulation. The November communiqué, for instance, dedicated 'a special emphasis on institutions, instruments and markets that are currently unregulated, along with ensuring that all systemically important institutions are appropriately regulated' (G20, 2008). Having identified the 'fundamental causes of the crisis' in 'major failures in the financial sector and in financial regulation and supervision,' the G20 leaders agreed to 'extend regulation and oversight to all systemically important financial institutions, instruments and markets.' In this connection, the April summit declaration pledged to crack down on tax havens, extend regulation of the financial system to large hedge funds, and curb 'risky' bank pay and bonuses (G20, 2009a). Furthermore, regulation was said to be extended to oversee credit ratings agencies. As the April communiqué put it, the G20 would extend 'regulatory oversight and registration to credit rating agencies to ensure they meet the international code of good practice, particularly to prevent unacceptable conflicts of interest.'

In sum, whereas at the end of the 1990s policy makers and practitioners discussed how to let markets operate freely, now the question is how international finance has to be controlled.

International cooperation: The Fund's comeback

Not only do pillars of market discipline and self-regulation look in tatters in the aftermath of the subprime crisis; the system of international decentralized cooperation is also under close scrutiny. As I pointed out, after the Asian crisis, the international community supported the decentralization of supervisory powers in the governance of the international financial system. Building on the perceived failure of the centralized governance that had been established after the Mexican crisis, member countries decided to downsize the Fund's central role as the guardian of global financial stability in favor of a constellation of organizations, including the G20 and the FSB.

In the aftermath of the subprime crisis, however, policy makers started reassessing the decentralized system of governance because of its apparent inability to prevent the crisis. Specifically, existing governance arrangements suddenly looked ill-equipped to live up to the task of global surveillance that had been the primary motivation behind the creation of forums such as the G20 and the FSB. In light of the ineffectiveness of the existing financial governance framework, several world leaders called for new arrangements in the international institutional set-up – a sort of Bretton Woods II or a new world order (Porter, et al., 2009). In doing so, they reaffirmed their faith in international financial cooperation as a way to address the problems posed by a deeply integrated global financial system. 'A global crisis requires a global solution,' coupled with 'unshakeable commitment to work together' (G20, 2009a). Nevertheless, world leaders also recognize the need to change existing mechanisms of cooperation. In particular, global leaders have called for a strengthening of the system-wide perspective of international financial cooperation. In other words, global institutions have been called on to refocus the scope of their supervisory task in order to take into due consideration the assessment of systemic risk. In this connection, the G20 agreed to institutionalize the activities of the FSF, transforming the Forum into a Board with a Chairman, a Steering Committee and a Plenary, supported by Standing Committees and ad-hoc working groups. The mandate of the FSB has also been strengthened by clarifying its responsibilities in assessing and detecting financial vulnerabilities and in promoting information exchange among national authorities responsible for financial stability. At the same time, the FSB membership has been extended to include all G20 countries, FSF members, Spain, and the European Commission. Finally, member countries expressed their preference for institutionalizing the cooperation between the Board and the IMF, calling on the former to work in close consultation with the IMF to provide early warning of macroeconomic and financial risks and to suggest the actions needed to address them (Financial Stability Forum, 2009).

Alongside the calls for inter-organizational cooperation, it is possible to detect the signs of a renewed attention to the workings of the IMF. That is to say, while the role of the IMF as a manager of the international financial system had been discounted since the Asian crisis, after the subprime crisis the Fund is catalyzing governments' and other actors' attention. In particular, there are several signs coming from the Fund's social constituencies for legitimation that unveil the existence of a positive feedback for the Fund.

In the communiqué prepared by the G20 leaders in April, for instance, significant space is devoted to the role that the IMF can play in the governance of the international financial system. Interrupting the irrelevance of the recent past, G20 leaders called on the IMF 'to assess regularly the actions taken and the global actions required' to maintain international financial stability. Leaders also pledged to 'support, now and in the future, candid, even-handed, and independent IMF surveillance' of domestic economic and financial systems and financial sectors. Specifically, they publicly accepted the involvement of the IMF in assessing the impact of domestic policies on others, and its evaluation of 'risks facing the global economy.'

Following the objective of strengthening the IMF, the G20 agreed to increase the resources available to the IMF in order to channel capital to emerging market countries. In particular, leaders pledged to increase the Fund's resources by $500 billion to $750 billion, supporting the issuance of $250 billion-worth of its own currency, the Special Drawing Right (SDR), to ease liquidity in emerging and developing economies.[244]

Setting aside the question of whether the new resources will actually be allocated, what the G20 proposals nonetheless show is the emergence of a rethink about the role of the IMF in the international financial system. In other words, world leaders did not simply decide to increase IMF resources. They also decided that the Fund has to play a more prominent role in the management of the global financial system. And 'that is a huge shift from the recent past, when the fund seemed to be fading towards irrelevance'(*The Economist*, 2009a). As the US Treasury Secretary remarked, 'the IMF has a special responsibility to help us all fulfill our collective obligations by offering independent assessments of our policy efforts, and their impact on a more balanced and sustainable recovery' (Geithner, 2009). The G8 Finance Ministers further reaffirmed this position in June 2009, when leaders stressed their commitment to 'reforming the IMF to enable it to carry out its critical role in the modern global economy' (G8, 2009).

Along with G20 leaders' support, there are other signs of renewed interest in the activity of the Fund. For instance, the US Congress, which after the Asian crisis had raised its voice to streamline the activity of the Fund, has now softened its previous stance. Indeed, in June 2009, Congress approved legislation containing important provisions for the IMF's role in the global financial system.[245] For instance, US lawmakers authorized an expansion of the US credit arrangement with the Fund up to about $100 billion. In short, the US has committed to increase its funding to the IMF to allow the organization to manage financial crises effectively. In this connection, they also agreed to a new income model for the Fund that will provide the organization more independence from its principles that it has been granted thus far. Indeed, a key element of the model is to create an endowment through the limited sale of some IMF gold.[246]

Nonetheless, a renewed sign of trust in the IMF activity can be detected from member countries' stance towards IMF financial assistance. Indeed, a number of member countries, including Mexico, Colombia, and Poland, decided to accept a precautionary credit line from the IMF to withstand the effects of the subprime crisis. While this fact may appear meaningless in light of the mandate of the Fund that tasks the organization with the responsibility of providing financial assistance to its members, we should interpret this phenomenon in relation to the distrust towards the IMF that has characterized the attitude of several emerging countries in the decade before the subprime crisis. As already pointed out, after the Asian crisis, several emerging market countries drew the conclusion that they had to self-insure against future crises rather than relying on IMF assistance. They thereby accumulated large foreign exchange reserves in the hope of avoiding going to the Fund 'cap in hand.' Member countries also declined to accept IMF help even when the Fund created new facilities to make up for the mistakes of the past. For instance, drawing from the experience of the Asian crisis, the Fund attempted to reform its lending and conditionality framework by creating the Contingent Credit Line (CCL) in 1999. The facility was meant to 'be a new instrument of crisis prevention' by providing 'a precautionary line of defense readily available against future balance of payments problems that might arise from international financial contagion.' The facility would have been available for countries with 'strong economic policies' (IMF, 1999). In other words, the CCL aimed at ensuring that IMF assistance address effectively the underlying causes of countries' balance of payments financing needs, particularly the withdrawal of external capital flows in emerging market countries. Despite the good intentions, no country applied. The IMF crisis of legitimacy was in full swing and no member seemed to trust the Fund.

In 2009, however, the Fund developed a new facility – the Flexible Credit Line (FCL) – designed in a manner similar to the CCL: to provide near automatic access to IMF lending in a crisis that the IMF deems to be in good economic health but that are facing temporary financing difficulties. This time around, however, a number of countries decided to trust the Fund and take advantage of its financial support, signaling a renewed faith in the Fund's activities. According to Alejandro Werner,

Mexico's deputy finance minister, for instance, Mexico 'was attracted not just by the flexibility and size of the new facility, but also by the fact that the IMF consulted emerging economies while designing the program to ensure that it met their needs.'[247] The positive market reaction following the decision of Mexico, Colombia, and Poland to accept the IMF program under the FCL is another sign of the increasing support for the IMF. Even academic economists, who in the aftermath of the Mexican crisis, called for streamlining the role of the Fund, now suggest that the organization be tasked with new responsibilities in the management of the international financial system (Eichengreen, 2009).

These are probably small signs of a return of confidence in the Fund and we still do not know how wide member countries' support will be. Nevertheless, it is clear that the Fund is again on the rise. The activity of the IMF in providing financial support to the crisis-hit countries in Eastern Europe, for instance, has been widely appreciated. 'The IMF intervened in a timely manner and with massive resources,' Marco Annunziata, chief economist at Unicredit banking group, for instance, declared.[248] 'In sum, 'under the pressure of the current crisis, the international community is carving out a new role for the IMF' (Lombardi, 2009).

In conclusion, the subprime crisis unleashed a profound rethink of the principles that had governed the international financial system since the Asian financial crisis. In light of the failure of market discipline and of the decentralized system of governance, policy makers called into question erstwhile ideas and seemed to have moved towards a new approach for the governance of the international financial system. The new approach is based on an acknowledgement that the market cannot be counted on to limit financial excesses and that the IMF still has a fundamental role to play in the system in both crisis prevention and crisis management.

6.5   Conclusion

> Among the many contrasts between World War I and World War II nothing is more remarkable than the profound change in economic thinking. (Alvin Hansen)[249]

The change in thinking from *orderly* to *market-led liberalization* is probably not as remarkable as the one that the Keynesian economist refers to in the above remark. Nevertheless, it was a profound change with important policy implications for the IMF and the international financial architecture. Indeed, acting on the principles underlying the idea of *market-led liberalization*, the international community adopted a series of policies, including the international standards initiative and the creation of new international bodies, which disempowered the IMF as a guarantor of global financial stability in favor of market-based mechanisms.

This chapter has traced the trajectory of the idea of *market-led liberalization*: its emergence, institutionalization, and contestation. Similarly to what happened after the Asian crisis to the idea of *orderly liberalization*, after the subprime crisis, the idea of *market-led liberalization* lost the social support it had enjoyed thus far in the internal community and its principles were contested. In this context, a global regulatory debate is underway to address the perceived failures that have caused the subprime crisis. While the debate on the reform to the international financial architecture is too recent to draw firm conclusions, something of a consensus seems to be emerging about the origins of the crisis and the cure needed to avoid repetition in the future. Specifically, the bulk of the reform proposals advanced to reform the international financial architecture in response to the subprime shock seems to have called into question several, if not all, the principles that have marked the governance of the international financial system since the late 1990s.

On the one hand, the validity of market discipline and private-sector self-regulation as mechanisms to ensure global financial stability have been questioned. Indeed, an increasing number of political actors have realized that markets do not always set the incentives right or provide the information they needed to make efficient decisions. Markets are not even able to rescue themselves. As one commentator put it, public 'willingness to trust the free play of market forces in finance has been damaged' (Wolf, 2009). On the other hand, there is a renewed attention towards the Fund as the manager of global financial stability. As the Managing Director Strauss-Khan (2009b) put it, 'the world community has placed its trust in the IMF.' Specifically, world leaders, academic economists, private-sector actors, and even the US Congress have all taken position in favor of a strengthened IMF. In this connection, reversing the irrelevance of its recent past, the Fund has been granted an increase in its resources and has been publicly recognized as playing a primary role in crisis prevention and crisis management.

In sum, this chapter has brought to the surface the important changes that are emerging in the policy consensus related to the governance of international finance as far as concerns both crisis prevention and management. In particular, this chapter has argued that, as compared to the late-1990s reform project, today we are assisting towards a shift from a governance project based on the dispersion of supervisory authority to one based on regulation and political centralization.

7
Conclusions: Past and Future of International Financial Governance

This book has addressed three sets of questions. First, it asked why and how economic ideas influenced the policies adopted to ensure global financial stability. Specifically, this work identified competing versions of the policy idea of international financial liberalization – *orderly* and *market-led liberalization* – and investigated how these ideas shaped the policies that the IMF adopted to govern the risks deriving from the free movement of international capital flows. Second, the book asked why IMF Executive Directors take particular decisions over rival alternatives. Hence, the book addressed the issue of the policy-making within the Fund by tracing the process through which the ideas proposed by IMF staff are endorsed by the IMF Board. Finally, the book asked how the IMF has adapted to the challenge of financial globalization. The increasing importance to the global economy of capital flows, in terms of both size and composition, has indeed affected the IMF's activities and has called into question the Fund's capacity to discharge its global responsibility. Investigating what courses of action member countries took to make the IMF respondent to the challenge of growing financial integration since the early 1990s, the book touched upon the question of what is the role of the IMF within the framework of the international financial architecture.

The three questions have been held together by this book's argument: that the policies that the IMF pursued to govern the risks of financial globalization have been driven by the evolution of the ideas on financial liberalization that came to command consensus in the 1990s and in the early 2000s – the idea of *orderly* and *market-led liberalization*, respectively. In what follows, I will summarize the story developed in the preceding chapters to extrapolate the empirical findings.

7.1   Theoretical argument and alternative explanations

The story narrated thus far is a story about how economic ideas influence policy choices. In other words, the institutional variation exemplified in the different set of policies that the IMF was requested to follow since the early 1990s has been explained in light of competing versions of the policy idea on international financial liberalization. Supporting this ideational explanation, the book suggests that it is a significant exaggeration to argue that the policies that the IMF follows systematically reflect the economic interests of powerful member countries. Furthermore, the book reveals that it is a mistake to assume that all actors involved in IMF policy-making react to material changes, such as the growing volume of international capital flows or a financial crisis, in the same way. Rather, actors need to interpret reality before acting on it. Economic ideas serve exactly this interpretive purpose.

This book is thereby clearly informed on a constructivist approach that gives pride of place to the role of ideas as an explanatory variable of policy choices. Ideas provide the lens through which actors interpret the structural changes in the international financial system and through which actors define their economic interests. The book, however, departs from constructivist approaches applied to the IMF in particular and to the IOs in general that explain the policies pursued by an IO in terms of the ideas held by its staff. This bureaucratic approach, indeed, is static and tends to evacuate politics from the analysis. In other words, the bureaucratic approach tends to disregard the fact that the ideas developed by IMF staff, like any other idea, are not fully formed but continuously transformed through the interaction with the 'ecology' in which they are floated.

Drawing on these insights, the book advanced an evolutionary approach whereby previous ideas, and the policies built on them, constitute the foundations for policy change. Indeed, what this book has argued and illustrated is that a specific set of economic ideas are influential to the extent that they raised new expectations that provided the foundations for old ideas to be dismissed and for its sponsor to be trapped into its own rhetoric when expectations were disappointed. In particular, the idea of *orderly liberalization* raised expectations across the Fund's constituencies about the growth effects of the free movement of international capital flows and about the role of the IMF in containing the risks deriving from financial integration. These expectations, however, were severely disappointed in the aftermath of the Asian crisis, prompting a backlash against the IMF and the process of liberalization.

Indeed, having long preached the benefits of liberalization and the cru-cial role of the IMF in governing its risks, IMF staff had built a rhetorical trap around themselves. When the benefits turned into losses, the IMF could not fend off the criticisms, leading to the rejection of the poli-cies adopted in reflection of the idea of *orderly liberalization*. In other words, the idea of *orderly liberalization* provided the foundations for the contestation of the sponsor: the IMF. Similarly, the idea of *market-led lib-eralization* raised a number of expectations, including the expectation that market discipline and self-regulation would have avoided episodes of financial distress. The disappointment of these expectations in the aftermath of the subprime crisis led to the contestation of previously adopted policies allowing competing ideas to be brought front and cen-ter in the policy debate. In short, the institutionalization of the idea of *market-led liberalization* set the stage for its backlash.

Hence, what this book shows is how important it is that policy ideas, whether they are sponsored by IMF staff or other actors, gain policy makers' acceptance about what works and what does not in economic policy. In other words, this book has drawn attention to *legitimacy feed-backs* as a mechanism through which ideas are influential over time. For instance, what ultimately mattered for the IMF to follow specific poli-cies was not that those policies were based on the economic interests of powerful members or on the accumulated knowledge of the IMF expert community. Rather, what mattered was that the policy idea underlying those policies resonated with the larger political environment made up of member countries, academic economists, and the private sector that constitute the Fund's social constituencies for legitimation at the elites level. The feedback coming from these actors, expressed in the form of consent and opposition, was pivotal in shaping the trajectory of the role of the IMF as a manager of the risks of global financial integration.

It is also important to know that, although the book has drawn atten-tion to the relationship between ideas and the environment or the ecol-ogy in which ideas are floated, this is not meant to suggest that the external environment instructed policy makers about what policies to adopt in order to ensure global financial stability. In particular, the idea-environment relationship is not meant to suggest that the process of policy change is simply the result of experiential learning according to which change takes place in light of better information, new evi-dence, or policy failures (Cyert and March, 1963, p. 283; Levy, 1994). Experiential learning is thereby conceived of an epiphenomenal pro-cess in which all actors draw the same inferences from experience and act accordingly on them.

The explanation of change supported in this book builds on an alternative explanation to the experiential learning one. Specifically, under an evolutionary approach, actors do not necessarily draw the same inferences from historical evidence but their conclusions are colored by the continuous transformation of the global economy and by their understanding about how the economy works. History, indeed, is not seen here as a given fact but as an event that needs to be interpreted (Best, 2005, p. 5; Widmaier, 2007). As Friedrich Kratochwil (2006, p. 21) put it, 'history is not simply there' but 'it is always viewed from a particular vantage point.' In other words, experience is rarely available in explicit and uncontested form. Seen from this perspective, the experiential learning suffers from some major pitfalls. In particular, it seems unable to tell us how experience is assessed (what does constitute relevant evidence?) and how policy failure is identified (what does constitute failure?). For instance, it would have been plausible to interpret the Mexican crisis as an example of policy failure – i.e. the failure of the ideas favoring market opening. Nevertheless, in the aftermath of the Mexican crisis, policy makers sitting at the IMF tables decided not to stop the process of global financial integration but to intensify it by giving the Fund the powers to promote liberalization. Similarly, despite the successful experience of the Chilean capital controls, until the late 1990s ideas in favor of controls did not retain intellectual respectability.

Since reality needs interpretation, for learning to occur at the collective and not at the individual level, we need a mechanism through which different actors draw the same lesson from the real world. Ideas offer this kind of mechanism by providing the cognitive map through which actors interpret experience, select among empirical evidence, and dismiss discrepant ideas – as the impact of the ideas of *orderly* and *market-led liberalization* attest.

In the empirical analysis, I not only tested my hypotheses on the interaction between ideas and the environment in which they are floated but I also sought to gauge the relative explanatory power of competing explanations of how ideas are institutionalized into IMF policies. Not surprisingly, the findings reveal that the economic preferences of the US and other industrialized countries are an important factor determining whether an idea will influence policy outcomes. However, the historical record suggests that US support has substantially less of an impact than it is conventionally assumed. For instance, the idea of *orderly liberalization* gained currency and, later, was unseated within the Fund even in the absence of an active US advocacy. The findings also offer only limited support for explanations that emphasize organizational culture as the key mechanism through which ideas shape the IMF's policies. For instance, the amendment failed in advance of substantial turnover of IMF staff. IMF management and senior staff officials continued advocating for it until late in the 1990s.

More broadly, the relatively weak support for these alternative explanations is the result of their attempts to identify a single actor (the US) or a community of actors (IMF staff) as the only mechanism through which ideas get established into IMF's policies. As this book argued and illustrated, there are instances in which ideas gain leverage over Fund policies without any of these mechanisms being present. This is not to suggest that they are not at work but that other mechanisms, such as the inputs coming from the Fund's political realm, may well shape organizational outcomes too. In other words, existing scholarship has thus far neglected the role played by an organization's social constituencies for legitimation. Hence, in future analysis on IOs and their policies, we should ask not only who drives changes in ideas over time but also who accepts them (Seabrooke, 2007c, p. 382), thereby assessing the relative weight of the inputs coming from the Fund's political environment.

Following this approach, however, there is still substantial work to be done. In particular, calling for a more holistic study of IOs that keeps in due consideration the global public sphere in which IOs operate, raises a number of theoretical and empirical questions that will need further examination. For instance, there is a need to set the boundaries of the Fund's social constituencies for legitimation, to identify the actors that belong to these constituencies and to identify the channels through which different actors can make their views known and support the IMF's activities. Furthermore, it is important to specify the conditions under which the IMF is respondent to the external environment, whether, for instance, an economic crisis is a necessary condition.

7.2 Ideational innovation, ambiguity, and the international financial architecture

After having summarized the story narrated thus far and having detailed the theoretical framework behind the narrative, in this section I extrapolate the findings of the book. The findings are organized into three sections according to the research agenda they relate to. Specifically, this section looks at how the findings of the book relate to the research agenda on institutional change, on the inner workings of international organizations, and on the reform to the international financial architecture.

Ideas and policy outcomes

The literature on the influence of economic ideas on institutional change has provided interesting insights about the conditions under which and the mechanisms through which economic ideas influence institutional outcomes (IOs) across countries as well as across policy domains.[250] Tracing the emergence of specific ideas and their influence in terms of policies has also become part of the research agenda of the scholarship that investigates the inner workings of international organizations. Indeed, scholars have used IOs as a laboratory to identify the mechanisms through which ideas emerge and are instantiated into the activities of IOs (Barnett and Finnemore, 2004; Broome and Seabrooke, 2007; Park, 2005; Vetterlein, 2007, 2008a; Weaver, 2007). Despite their shared assumption on the importance of ideas, scholars have nonetheless advanced distinct explanations of the mechanisms through which ideas become influential. On the one hand, drawing on the literature on epistemic communities, some scholars have drawn attention to the quality of the ideas elaborated by staff members of an IO – the so-called expert authority (Barnett and Finnemore, 2004). The fact that ideas are 'technical' helps account for their influence on policy makers. On the other hand, another group of scholars has drawn attention to the identity of the sponsor of economic ideas. Seen from this perspective, among other factors, ideas are deemed to be influential within an IO to the extent that they are backed up by prominent staff members (Abdelal, 2007, ch. 6) or by powerful member countries (Wade and Veneroso, 1998).

One of the findings of this book, however, is that the influence of economic ideas is not closely dependent on the inherent quality of the idea in question – whether the idea is highly specific – or on the identity of the sponsor – whether the sponsor is a powerful member country or IMF management. The idea of *orderly liberalization* became politically dominant within the IMF even in the presence of substantial ambiguities on the effects of capital account liberalization for economic growth and on the role of the IMF as a manager of the risks of globalized finance. Likewise, the idea of *orderly liberalization* lost its influence despite the continuous support of powerful member countries and prominent IMF staff members. Instead, the findings of this book suggest that the influence of economic ideas is mostly determined by the reception of the idea in the environment in which the idea is floated. Specifically, the book shows how political actors' support of the ideas of *orderly* and *market-led liberalization* was crucial for ideas to become legitimate and effective.

The finding on the interaction between policy ideas and the environment in which they are floated has important implications for our understanding of the influence of ideas. Indeed, if we accept the argument that the influence of ideas is a function of their acceptance by the agents at the receiving end of persuasion, the logical conclusion is that the influence of ideas is highly contingent. Since agents can both accept and reject ideas, studying the influence of ideas requires historical as well as spatial contextualization. It requires acknowledging that ideas are not fully formed but shaped through contestation that varies across time and across actors. For instance, the acceptance of the idea of *orderly liberalization* varied across the 1990s and was differently regarded by member countries, academic economists, and private-sector actors. These cross-time differences were also shaped by the institutional changes brought about in the first half of the 1990s. As evolutionary theory would point out, institutional changes shape the strategic environment in which actors devise policy solutions (Rothstein and Steinmo, 2002). That is, as already pointed out, the policies adopted in the aftermath of the Mexican crisis raised expectations on the effects of financial liberalization for economic growth and on the efficacy of the IMF in guaranteeing the stability of the international financial system. Unmet expectations, however, engender disappointment and lead to dissolution of relationships. Hence, when the Asian financial crisis triggered a period of sluggish economic growth and proved the limits of the role of the IMF in an era of globalized finance, the expectations raised by the idea of *orderly liberalization* as instantiated in the post-Mexico policies engendered profound disappointment across the actors that form the Fund's social constituencies for legitimation, leading to the contestation of the Fund's activities. Likewise, the practice of private-sector involvement in the governance of the international financial system, which took form after the Asian crisis, set the foundations for the disappointment that followed the subprime crisis. Indeed, the crisis showed market excesses rather than markets' stabilizing property.

Recognizing the contingent nature of economic ideas also calls for the acknowledgement of the pattern of ideational innovation along with that of institutional innovation. That is to say, ideas not only have varying degrees of influence over institutional choices over time; ideas themselves also vary over time. This book, for instance, showed the ideational change from *orderly* to *market-led liberalization*. In this respect, the book showed that *market-led liberalization* did not displace *orderly liberalization*, as several studies on the influence of economic ideas seem to suggest. For instance, it is common to think of the evolution of economic theories in terms of displacement. In this light, Keynes's General Theory is assumed as having unseated classical liberalism and monetarism as having displaced Keynesianism in the 1970s. Nevertheless, the findings here suggest that *orderly liberalization* engendered the idea of *market-led liberalization*, meaning that the former was transformed into the latter by a process of adjustment. Hence, the book suggests that although it is often assumed that economic theories are set up to be toppled, economic ideas are often transformed rather than completely unseated and substituted with other theories. As Yves Surel (2000, p. 507) points out, 'the spread of new ideas, principles of action and forms of action does not come about in a "revolutionary" way from scientific development, but rather from a more or less radical re-evaluation of ways of legitimizing groups and social exchanges.'

Finally, the findings of this book relate to the debate on the merits of financial liberalization. Indeed, by tracing the evolution of the consensus on the topic, the book found that what has changed over time has not been faith in the beneficial effects of financial liberalization. Although the use of capital controls and sequencing issues has received renewed theoretical and empirical attention (Eichengreen, et al., 1999; Leiteritz and Moschella, forthcoming; Prasad and Rajan, 2008; Prasad, et al., 2003), financial liberalization is still regarded as an inevitable and desirable economic policy choice for countries to pursue. Nevertheless, what has really changed in the debate on international financial liberalization over time has been the consensus on the mechanisms through which to ensure financial stability. In other words, using the repartition used for analyzing the idea of *orderly liberalization*, the normative component of the policy idea has remained almost unchanged whereas its procedural dimension has been profoundly revised. In sum, there has been a substantial revision of the policies to govern the risks of financial integration, not on the opportunity to proceed with such an integration.

The inner workings of the IMF

The findings of the book also speak to the inner workings of the IMF. In particular, the book has explored the process through which the Executive Directors sitting on the IMF Board adopt the ideas produced by IMF staff. In this connection, two findings are worth attention here.

First, with regard to IMF staff's ideas to 'walk their way' into the IMF Board, ambiguity plays a crucial role. In contrast to the bureaucratic explanation that accounts for the influence of IMF staff's ideas by pointing to the degree of specialization and expertise embedded in those ideas (Barnett and Finnemore, 2004), the findings of the book suggest that ideas are influential because they fail to provide technical answers to controversial issues – where controversy here refers to those issues loaded with distributional outcomes. For instance, battling for the amendment to the Articles, IMF staff left many questions unresolved including the use of capital controls, the sequence of liberalization, and the financial implications for IMF resources. Rather than weakening IMF staff's negotiating position, the ambiguities in the IMF economic thinking were pivotal in forging consensus within the IMF membership. Specifically, these ambiguities played a constructive role in accommodating the different interests represented on the IMF Executive Board. Indeed, by bracketing the most contentious issues, the ambiguities in the ideas produced by IMF staff projected different things to different groups of countries, thereby facilitating coalitional alignments between industrial and developing countries.

Seen from this perspective, the ambiguities in the IMF's thinking are not theoretical anomalies but part and parcel of the process of consensus-building inside the IMF. Hence, the book found that ambiguity is one of the instruments that IMF staff use to influence the negotiations within the Executive Board. Contrary to a well-established conclusion that IMF staff members influence policy by virtue of their technical and highly specialized expertise, the book suggests that IMF staff members may well be influential even when their theoretical and empirical arguments are not neatly articulated. IMF staff strategically use ambiguous knowledge to facilitate coalitional alignment within the IMF Board, thereby influencing the policy decisions that Executive Directors take.

In this connection, my findings add to the work developed by Catherine Weaver (2008a, pp. 5, 6) on the World Bank. Indeed, ambiguity is a 'strategic tool' used by IMF staff members to the same extent that the World Bank's 'hypocrisy' is. That is to say, ambiguity, like Weaver's hypocrisy, arises when the organization has to reconcile 'multiple political masters with heterogeneous preferences.'

Second, Executive Directors adopt IMF staff's ideas if they perceive those ideas as being in line with the 'climate of economic opinion' that prevails in the Fund's social constituencies for legitimation. As the negotiations for the amendment to the Articles have shown, for instance, Executive Directors are sensitive to the inputs coming from the Fund's operating environment which is primarily made up of member countries, academic economists, and private sector actors. These external inputs work their way within the Board via the concerns for IMF legitimacy. In other words, Executive Directors are not only state representatives.

They are also IMF representatives, in the sense that they are responsible for conducting the day-to-day business of the IMF – a task that requires Executive Directors have permanent residence at the IMF headquarters in Washington DC. Discharging their task, Executive Directors are therefore also concerned about preserving the legitimacy of the organization vis-à-vis its member countries. As a result, Executive Directors are sensitive to the inputs coming from the outside, especially if those inputs take the form of criticisms that seem to impair the legitimacy of the organization. For instance, the criticisms leveled at the IMF in the aftermath of the Asian crisis rapidly spilled over to the negotiations on the amendment to the IMF's Articles. Executive Directors became increasingly sensitive to the criticisms coming from across the Fund's political realm. Public perception of the IMF's activities in capital-related issues acquired salience in the Board's discussion, leading to the failure of the negotiations.

Drawing attention to the influence of external inputs on IMF policies, the findings of this book cast doubt on the conventional image of the IMF that Ngaire Woods (2006) captures with the term 'globalizer,' that is, an organization that shapes the policies of its member countries by constituting social reality, fixing meanings in the social world, and articulating and diffusing new norms around its membership (Barnett and Finnemore, 2004). The empirical findings here suggest that the IMF is also itself subject to globalizing pressures. Its staff and Executive Directors are receptive to the policy debate going on outside the Fund, and open to policy change to retain the organization's legitimacy. Hence, although IMF staff members enjoy considerable autonomy in shaping the agenda of the Board by framing the issues for discussion, the autonomy of IMF staff is limited by the quest for legitimacy of the organization. That is, the IMF needs to find the acquiescence of the agents forming its social constituency for legitimation, including states and non-state actors, to have its policies translated into operational practice. It thereby follows that the Fund's social constituency for legitimation is an important stimulus for the elaboration of the Fund's policies and not simply a passive recipient of them as the 'globalizer' hypothesis would lead us to expect.[251]

The international financial architecture

Finally, the findings of the book also speak to the debate on the reforms to the international financial architecture. Indeed, studying the process of policy change within the Fund also bears on the study of the changes in the international financial system. As Louis Pauly (1997, p. 8) put it, 'the IMF reflects a long and continuing struggle to design the political architecture for global capital markets.' In other words, it is possible to use the IMF as a laboratory to get at some bigger questions on the changes that have taken place in the regulatory management of the global financial system.

To start with, the book suggests some of the conditions under which reforms are more likely to take place, including the availability of economic ideas and the validation of those ideas by states and non-state actors. For instance, the fact that domestic actors, such as the US Congress, and transnational actors, such as private-sector representatives, played a role in the failure of the proposal to amend the Articles of Agreement in 1998, and in the renewed interest in the IMF's activities in 2008–9, suggests that reforming the international financial architecture is not solely a matter for intergovernmental negotiations. Rather, bringing about reforms to the architecture seems to require national policy makers to reach out to a wide variety of actors. The acquiescence of private-sector actors, for instance, seems to be a crucial variable for reforms to be adopted and implemented.

Still, one of the major findings of the book is the disclosure of the pattern that led to the governance of the international financial system from the adoption of centralized mechanisms to govern the risks of global financial integration to decentralized mechanisms. Indeed, as the empirical analysis showed, what we witnessed from the early 1990s onwards had been a progressive contraction of the role of the IMF as the primary mechanism to ensure global financial stability. In particular, in the first half of the 1990s the policies in the area of crisis prevention and crisis management revolved around the role of the IMF. The decisions to strengthen IMF surveillance, increase IMF resources, and amend the Articles of Agreement to give the IMF jurisdiction over cross-border capital flows well indicate the central role reserved to the IMF in the area of the management of international capital flows. Starting at the end of the 1990s, however, a new set of policies has been pursued, including the initiative of international financial standardization as a mechanism of international surveillance and the involvement of private-sector actors as a mechanism of crisis management. Furthermore, the proposal to amend the Articles has been abandoned. In contrast to the policies pursued in the first half of the 1990s, the policies pursued after 1998 indicate a progressive disempowerment of the IMF as a mechanism to govern the risks to international financial stability.

This shift from a centralized to a decentralized system of governance, where the responsibility for minimizing the risks deriving from financial integration is no longer the exclusive domain of the IMF, points to a significant change in the governance of the international financial architecture. Specifically, this shift suggests that the pattern of international financial cooperation moved from a form of interstate cooperation towards a form of public-private governance, where the elaboration of policy solutions to the problems that states face required the involvement of international public actors such as intergovernmental organizations, international private actors, and domestic public actors including national regulators and supervisors.

The subprime crisis, however, has raised doubts about the maintenance of the decentralized system of governance. Indeed, the reform proposals that have gathered momentum in the aftermath of the crisis have called into question the international financial architecture as conceived in the aftermath of the Asian crisis. For instance, reformers have called for increasing capital requirements, the checking of bankers' compensation frameworks, and increasing scrutiny of ratings agencies, among others. In other words, reformers have called for a reduction in the room for maneuver in the private sector in contrast to the earlier faith in market forces as an antidote to financial instability. Furthermore, in contrast to the recent past, reformers have called on the IMF to strengthen the mechanisms of crisis prevention and management. In sum, there are signs of a renewed preference for some form of centralized governance of the global financial system.

Tracing the current debate on the reform to the international regulatory framework, the book has thereby brought to the surface the important changes that are emerging in the policy consensus related to the governance of international finance. While the post-Asia intellectual and policy consensus emphasized the importance of markets in enforcing compliance with a universal set of financial *standards*, after the subprime crisis it seems that the faith in the role of markets has been seriously undermined in favor of an approach that strengthens international and domestic *rules*. Although there are some reservations about the transfer of regulatory responsibilities to the international level (Rodrik, 2009), it seems as if the crisis has challenged the intellectual assumptions on which the governance of the international financial system was built, and in particular the belief of self-stabilizing markets. In sum, the *moralizing turn* of the late 1990s (Best 2003), which recognized the ultimate value of the markets in ensuring international financial stability, has not gone unscathed in the aftermath of the recent crisis.

This is not to say that we have already reached a time in which policy makers reconceive the parameters of political possibility. In other words, despite the important signals of an intellectual rethink that is emerging from the current debate, it is too soon to identify a paradigmatic shift. Indeed, as Thomas Kuhn (1962) has noted in his explanation of the evolution of science, the trajectory of a given intellectual consensus cannot be solely derived from the contradictions of the old consensus with the observable reality. In other words, contrasting evidence is not a sufficient condition to trigger ideational change. Hence, we cannot predict the path of ideas and institutional change that will follow the subprime crisis by simply pointing to the inadequacy of the old consensus in addressing the sources of the current turmoil. What this book thereby suggests is that we are assisting towards a moment of ideational contestation unleashed by a crisis (Blyth, 2002). This contestation is of help in identifying important discontinuities with the recent past, but the 'tipping point' in which a critical mass of states and non-state actors adopt a new norm has not been reached yet (Finnemore and Sikkink, 1998).

7.3 The role of the IMF in the global financial system

The International Monetary Fund was created in 1944 to preside over the international monetary and financial system. Today, however, in a number of important respects, the IMF is significantly different from the organization that the Bretton Woods' fathers envisaged. Created to preside over a fixed exchange-rate system, and to provide financing to countries facing temporary current account deficits, the Fund has gradually taken on new responsibilities, developed new means to achieve its goals, and enlarged its membership. At various times, the role of the IMF in the international monetary system has been debated and the rationale for its own existence called into question. Nevertheless, as one of the former IMF Managing Directors points out, 'one of the lessons of IMF history is that the organization has survived by a process of adaptation to new demands and new challenges' (De Rato, 2006). Adapting to the growing integration of world capital markets certainly figures in the list of challenges the IMF has been lately confronted with.

Indeed, the increasing integration of world capital markets raises significant challenges to the Fund's activities. On the one hand, growing capital flows call into question the traditional scope of IMF surveillance, which focuses on macroeconomic policies, requiring the organization to expand the scope of its analysis to financial issues and their linkages with the real economy. On the other hand, the massive volume of capital flows that everyday moves from one country to another questions the ability of the IMF to provide financial assistance at times of trouble to member countries. In particular, the phenomenon of financial globalization raises doubts about whether the IMF is able to provide rescue packages large enough and readily available for short-term support to stop a creditor run.

Not only has financial globalization questioned IMF surveillance and financial assistance; the very rationale of its role in the international monetary system has also been disputed. Until recently, the argument was that in an economic environment characterized by increasing capital flows the time for the Fund has passed (Schwartz, 1998). Indeed, in an environment where liquidity abounded, so that emerging economies enjoyed easy access to private capital and built up huge reserves, the IMF seemed to be losing its relevance both as a financier of current account deficits and as a lender of last resort. The problems of the IMF were then aggravated by the public perception of the IMF as an organization controlled by industrial countries and resistant to change. The discredit of the Fund's role in the governance of the international financial system was also attested by the creation of two international bodies, i.e. the G20 and the FSB, which, similarly to the IMF, have the responsibility of ensuring global financial stability and thereby preventing the emergence of financial crisis.

The subprime crisis, however, played into the IMF's hands. On the one hand, several emerging market countries found themselves again in the position to ask for IMF financial assistance. This is particularly the case for the countries of Eastern Europe, which were severely hit by the capital flight that followed the subprime crisis. From the start of the crisis, the IMF has rolled over around $157 billion in lending commitments.[252] It has also created new financing facilities such as the Flexible Credit Line (FCL) and has been endowed with new financial resources. On the other hand, the international community felt the need to understand the causes of the crisis in order to draw the lessons for reform. The IMF, with its in-house research capacity, has thereby become a crucial reference point for identifying the causes of the crisis and distilling the lessons that can be drawn from it. Indeed, the IMF has published numerous papers providing policy advice and forecasts for the global economy.

In this context, since the early start of the crisis, several policy makers have called on the IMF to play a more active role in the process of international financial supervision and regulation than it had done in the recent past.[253] In particular, as the empirical analysis has shown, the IMF has been called on to develop early warning exercises in collaboration with the FSB and to make recommendations for reforming the international regulatory set-up. In short, in contrast to the marginalization of the previous years, the governance of the international financial system seems leaning again towards a central role for the IMF.

Nevertheless, the governance of today's international financial system is significantly different from the one created in 1944, when the IMF was virtually the only international body mandated with the responsibility of fostering financial cooperation among states and presiding over the international financial system. Rather, current arrangements for the supervision of the international financial system are based on the collaboration among various international bodies that share responsibility for promoting the stability of the financial system. These bodies include both the international financial institutions (i.e. the IMF and the World Bank), international groupings of regulators and supervisors (BCBS, IOSCO, IAIS), and private-sector bodies, whose members include representatives of accountants, service, industry, and commerce (i.e. IASB).[254] The G20 and the Financial Stability Board (FSB), which bring together financial regulators and supervisors of industrial and emerging market countries, are tasked with the responsibilities of identifying systematic financial vulnerabilities and overseeing the action needed to address them. In sum, the governance of international finance is distributed among multiple transnational public and private international institutions (Porter, 2005).

In light of the fragmented system of international financial governance, where several bodies share responsibility for the surveillance of the international financial system, a question can be raised about the effectiveness of inter-organizational cooperation or even about the usefulness of so many international bodies for the governance of the system. Although it is widely recognized that international financial cooperation is no longer the exclusive competence of states or formal intergovernmental organizations such as the IMF, a question can still be raised whether we are assisting towards cooperation or rather duplication in the governance functions at the international level. These are all open questions that need to be addressed in the international financial architecture exercise because of their implications for the role of the IMF and for the governance of the international financial system at large.

Annex: List of Interviewees

International Monetary Fund

Jacques J. Polak, Director of the Research Department [1958–80], Economic Counsellor [1966–80], Executive Director [1981–86]
Leo Van Houtven, Secretary [1977–96], Economic Counsellor [from 1987]

Executive Board

Thomas A. Bernes, Executive Director, Canada (and Antigua and Barbuda, the Bahamas, Barbados, Belize, Dominica, Grenada, Ireland, Jamaica, St. Kitts and Nevis, St. Lucia, St. Vincent, and the Grenadines) [1996–2001]
Bernd Esdar, Executive Director, Germany [1996–2001]
Enzo Grilli, Executive Director, Italy (and Albania, Greece, Malta, Portugal, and San Marino) [1994–18]
Willy Kiekens, Executive Director, Belgium (and Austria, Belarus, Czech Republic, Hungary, Kazakhstan, Luxembourg, Slovak Republic, Slovenia, and Turkey) [1994 to present]
Karin Lissakers, Executive Director, United States [1993–2001]
Abbas Mirakhor, Executive Director, Iran (and Afghanistan, Algeria, Ghana, Morocco, Pakistan, and Tunisia) [1990 to present]
Aleksei Mozhin, Alternate Executive Director, Russia [1992–16], Executive Director, Russia [1996 to present]
Abdel Shakour Shaalan, Executive Director, Egypt (and Barahin, Iraq, Jordan, Kuwait, Lebanon, Lybia, Maldives, Oman, Qatar, Syrian Arab Republic, United Arab Emirates, Republic of Yemen) [1992 to present]
B. P. Misra, Executive Director, India (and Bangladesh, Bhutan, Sri Lanka) [2003 to 2006]
Amal Uthum Heart, Alternate Executive Director, Bangladesh, Bhutan, India and Sri Lanka [to present]
J. Onno de Beaufort Wijholds, Executive Director, Netherlands (and Armenia, Bosnia and Herzegovina, Bulgaria, Croatia, Cyprus, Georgia, Israel, Macedonia, Moldova, Romania, and Ukraine) [1994–2003]

Policy Development and Review Department

Jack Boorman, Director [1990–2001]
James Boughton, Assistant Director and Official Historian of the IMF

Research Department

Andrei Levchenko, Economist (EP), 2004–5

Paolo Mauro, Research Department [1999–2005], Chief of Strategic Issues Division [since 2005]
Michael Mussa, Director [1991–2001], Economic Counsellor [1991–2001]

Independent Evaluation Office (IEO)

Thomas A. Bernes, Director [2005 to present]
Shnji Takagi, Team leader for the IEO's Evaluation Report on the IMF's Approach to Capital Account Liberalization [2005]

G24

Ariel Buira, Staff G24 Secretariat
Laura Dos Reis, Staff G24 Secretariat

Institute of International Economics

John Williamson, Senior Fellow
Michael Mussa, Senior Fellow

Institute of International Finance

Yusuke Horiguchi, First Deputy Managing Director and Senior Economist Institute of International Finance [to present]
Lex Rieffel, Chairman of the IIF Working Group on the Liberalization of Capital Movements [1998–99]

United States Department of Treasury

Caroline Atkinson, Senior Deputy Assistant Secretary for International Monetary and Financial Policy [1997–2001]
Edwin M. Truman, Assistant Secretary for International Affairs [1998–2001]

Notes

1 Introduction: The IMF and Global Financial Governance

1. In this book, I use the terms international financial liberalization and capital account liberalization interchangeably to indicate the removal of restrictions in the flows of foreign direct investments (FDI), portfolio flows, and short-term bank loans.

2. About the transfer of regulatory authority to the private sector see, for instance, Cutler, Haufler, and Porter, 1999 and Higgott, Underhill, and Bieler, 2000. About the involvement of the private sector in crisis management, see also Baker, 2005, p. 71.

3. Originally confined to surveillance over members' exchange-rate policies, the scope and modalities of surveillance have changed over time. Today, Article IV consultations generally cover not only exchange-rate policies, but also a broad range of macroeconomic and structural policies.

4. Statistics on IMF staff's recruitment are available at the IMF's webpage http://www.imf.org/external/np/adm/rec/workenv/aboutst.htm#Recruitment Statistics.

5. For some of the works on the history of the Bretton Woods agreement, see Best, 2005; Helleiner, 1994; Horsefield, 1969; and James, 1996.

6. See, for instance, the historical account in Helleiner, 1994, pp. 101–7.

7. For instance, in 1971–72, a group of finance ministers and central bank governors, 'the Committee of 20,' discussed the future of the Fund, including the possibility to extend its powers on capital transactions. See, for instance, the account in De Vries, 1986. Thereafter, in 1977, the Executive Board issued a decision that extended the scope of the Fund's surveillance from its narrow focus on exchange rate to a wide range of policies that might influence the pattern of capital flows.

8. Although the liberalization of the capital account was a policy far more controversial than the other policies included in the Washington consensus, the inventor of the term, John Williamson, nonetheless noted that the 1990s economic opinion represented in Washington could hardly entertain the thought that liberalization was not good for economic growth. Williamson, 2003, p. 49.

9. IMF Archives, SM/95/164, pp. 8–9 and 10.

10. About the importance of studying policy persistence and change simultaneously see, for instance, Capano, 2009.

11. For noticeable studies that have explicitly addressed the question of ideational innovation, see Bierkester, 2002 and Steinmo, 2003.

12. Many constructivist works on norm diffusion have investigated how norms/ideas are replaced by new norms/ideas. Examples include Acharya, 2004; Keck and Sikkink, 1998; Klotz, 1995.

13. About the 'constructive role' of ambiguity in shaping political outcomes in the realm of global finance, see Best, 2005.
14. On the strategic use of ambiguity by IMF staff in the policy area of current account convertibility see also Broome, forthcoming.

2 Evolutionary Policies: Economic Ideas and Legitimacy Feedback

15. The IEO is the body that conducts independent evaluations of Fund policies and activities.
16. For the 'political sponsorship' argument see Goldstein, 1993.
17. See, for instance, the difference in the list of economic reforms suggested in Williamson, 1990a; Kuczynski and Williamson, 2003.
18. On the issues of representation, political involvement, and participation in the IMF's decision-making see, for instance, Woods and Lombardi, 2006; Bini Smaghi, 2004.
19. The premium placed on small groups of activists is in line with most of the literature on the diffusion of new ideas. See, among others, Hall, 1989; Keck and Sikkink, 1998. For an example of diffusion at the regional level, see, for instance, McNamara, 1998.
20. According to the IMF Archive's disclosure policy, 'the public has access to a substantial range of information including: Executive Board documents, which are available to the public under 5, 10 or 20-year rules except for classified items; Other institutional archives, which are available after 20 years' as quoted on the IMF website http://www.imf.org/external/np/arc/eng/archive.htm, date accessed 31 January 2009.
21. Until 2001, the GFSR was known as the International Capital Markets Report (ICMR).
22. The search involved articles from the *Financial Times, The Economist*, and *the Wall Street Journal*. In addition, other sources include the articles published in the *New York Times* and the *Washington Post*.

3 The 1990s Consensus on International Financial Integration

23. Financial globalization, or globalized finance, is here used to indicate the sum of global linkages created by cross-border financial flows. It is interesting to note that it is possible to distinguish between financial globalization and financial integration – whereas the latter refers to 'an individual country's linkages to international capital markets' (Prasad, et al., 2003).
24. On the history of the international financial system in the decade 1970–80, see Helleiner, 1994, part II and Frieden, 2006, ch. 14–6.
25. For a thorough analysis of the 1980s debt crisis, its managements and consequences, see Boughton, 2001. See also Cline, 1995.
26. For an estimate of capital flight from developing countries during the 1980s, see data in World Bank, *World Debt Tables*, various issues; International Monetary Fund, *Balance of Payments Yearbook*, various issues. Some of the

studies on the patterns of flows to developing countries include Rojas-Suàrez, 1991, and Calvo, Leiderman, and Reinhart, 1995.

27. The United States decidedly moved to international financial liberalization in 1974, the United Kingdom in 1979, and Japan in 1980. Australia and New Zealand removed their capital controls in 1983 and in 1984 respectively, and extensive liberalizations took place in the context of the European Monetary Union. Complete decontrols were adopted in the Netherlands (1986), Denmark (1988), France (1989), Belgium, Ireland, Italy, and Luxembourg (1990). Several members of the EFTA – Sweden (1989), Austria, Finland, and Norway (1990) – followed suit. Finally, liberalization took place in Portugal and Spain in 1993; in Greece in 1994, and Iceland in 1995.

28. The US Federal Reserve left federal funds at a rate of 3 percent from September 1992. It started raising the rate by 25 basis points in February 1994. By September, the federal funds rate rose by 175 basis points, following projections of domestic economic recovery. See, IMF, 1994b, pp. 32–36, and IMF, 1995a, p. 54. As it is explained at greater length below, the Clinton administration, which took office in 1992, strongly promoted a policy of low interest rates in the effort to pursue deficit reduction – with the active support of the Fed Chairman, Alan Greenspan. The underlying logic was that low interest rates were essential to boost private investments, thereby productivity and economic growth, and to reduce the budget deficit by curtailing debt-servicing costs.

29. Several studies emphasized the importance of domestic factors to explain the surges of capital inflows into many developing countries. See, for instance, IMF, 1994b, p. 55, and Schadler, et al., 1993.

30. Portfolio capital flows include international placements of bonds, issues of equities in international markets, and purchases by foreigners of stocks and financial market instruments in developing countries' domestic markets.

31. For an analysis of the surge of capital inflows to Latin America, see Calvo, Leiderman, and Reinhart, 1995, p. 339.

32. Specifically capital flows changed from a cumulative net *outflow* of about $15 billion during 1983–89 to a cumulative net *inflow* of $102 billion during 1990–94.

33. Asia here includes the following countries: India, Indonesia, Korea, Malaysia, the Philippines, and Thailand. IMF, 1995b, p. 44.

34. Latin American countries here include Argentina, Brazil, Chile, Colombia, Mexico, and Peru. Ibid., p. 44.

35. *The Economist*, 1994, p. 11.

36. These funds are defined as those that hold at least 60 percent of its assets in developing-country securities (ICMR, 1995, Annex I, p. 38, fn. 6).

37. As reported in Wayne, 1994.

38. For an interesting portrait of George Soros and his role in the attack of the British pound see Frieden, 2006, pp. 405–9.

39. For some of the best overviews of the shift from Keynesianism to monetarism, see Helleiner, 1994; Eichengreen, 1996; Kirshner, 1999; Best, 2005; Blyth, 2002; and Campbell and Pederson, 2001.

40. On the shift in economic doctrine in the US see Blyth, 2002 and Campbell, 2001. On the shift in the UK see Hay, 2001.

41. The inventor of the term, John Williamson, however, has repeatedly rejected the label neoliberalism for the list of 'consensual' policies he identified in the late 1980s. See, for instance, Williamson, 1994a, p. 18. Similarly, Williamson has made clear that he did not intend capital account liberalization to be part of the Washington consensus Williamson, 2004, p. 6.
42. The most influential studies on the topic include Williamson, 1983, and Cline 1983, 1984.
43. Williamson's essay, 'The Progress of Policy Reform in Latin America', has been re-published in several volumes. In what follows, I refer to Williamson, 1990b.
44. Boughton, 2001, pp. 522–3, and Fidler, 1988.
45. Virtually all IMF staff members and Executive Directors that I interviewed referred to Camdessus's willingness to put the IMF front and center in dealing with the economic challenges of the 1990s. A list of interviewees is provided in the Annex.
46. IMF Archives, EBM/98/38, p. 6.
47. The Policy Development and Review Department is the one that has to approve all IMF financial programs negotiated with member countries. Specifically, the Department checks the program for equality and consistency with previous programs before the submission to the Executive Board by a decision of the Managing Director.
48. IMF Archives, SM/98/233.
49. Economic growth refers here to a rise in real GDP.
50. IMF Archives, SM/95/164, pp. 8–9 and 10.
51. IMF Archives, SM/97/32, p. 4.
52. During the period 1990–94, there was an acceleration in the rate of acceptance of member countries' Article VIII obligation. That is, many countries, which had not yet done so, made their currency fully convertible. The growth of international trade, then, added opportunity to disguise controls through the practice of import- and export-invoicing.
53. IMF Archives, SM/95/164, Sup. 1, pp. 7–9; p. 17.
54. IMF Archives, SM/94/202, p. 20.
55. IMF Archives, SM/97/32, p. 6.
56. IMF Archives, SM/94/202, p. 25.
57. IMF Archives, MD/Sp/98/5.
58. IMF Archives, SM/94/202, p. 53.
59. For instance, the staff memoranda prepared in 1997 suggested alternative courses of action rather than a definitive list of criteria. See, among others, IMF Archives, SM/97/86 and IMF Archives, SM/97/173.
60. IMF Archives, SM/97/32, p. 25.
61. IMF Archives, SM/95/164, p. 4.
62. The first operational guidance notes to the staff in the area of capital convertibility were issued in December 1995.
63. IMF Archives, SM/97/173, p. 23.
64. As reported in Lippman, 1994.
65. As reported in Kristof and Sanger, 1999.
66. As reported in Ibid.
67. Specifically, the NEC had four main functions: to coordinate policy-making for domestic and international economic issues, to coordinate economic

policy advice for the President, to ensure that policy decisions and programs are consistent with the President's economic goals, and to monitor implementation of the President's economic policy agenda.

68. As reported in CNN, 'All Politics, Players,' available at http://www.cnn.com/ALLPOLITICS/1997/gen/resources/players/rubin/, date accessed 16 February 2007.
69. As reported in Kristof and Wyatt, 1999.
70. As reported in Walter, 2002, p. 4.
71. As reported in Kristof and Sanger, 1999.
72. As reported in Ibid.
73. Asian countries accounted for almost 20 percent of total US FDI flows in the 1991–95 period. Walter, 2000, p. 59.
74. According to the USTR (1996) report, 'Foreign banks are permitted to establish branches, only after one year has passed following the establishment of a representative office and subject to onerous individual branch capitalization requirements. Foreign banks face issuance limits for certificates of deposit based on branch vs. global capital, limiting their ability to obtain local currency funding. Foreign banks also face discriminatory treatment in the interbank market. Foreign banks are disadvantaged by a relatively non transparent regulatory system, and must seek approval for introducing new products and services.' With regard to securities firms, as of 1996, subsidiaries of foreign securities firms were not allowed, and foreign equity in joint ventures was limited to less than 50 percent.
75. Kristof and Sanger, 1999.
76. The account of the MAI negotiations drawn from the empirical analysis is carried out by Walter, 2000, pp. 55–7.
77. A compromise on a final text, however, was never reached and negotiations were discontinued in April 1998.
78. OECD countries at that time included Australia, Austria, Belgium, Canada, the Czech Republic, Denmark, Finland, France, Germany, Greece, Hungary, Iceland, Ireland, Italy, Japan, Korea, Luxembourg, Mexico, the Netherlands, New Zealand, Norway, Poland, Portugal, Spain, Sweden, Switzerland, Turkey, the United Kingdom, and the United States – as well as the European Community.
79. The openness of the MAI negotiations to non-members took the form of workshops and meetings in various locations where selected economies were invited to participate. For more details on the MAI negotiations see Smythe, 2000.
80. As reported in Wayne, 1994.
81. As reported in Kristof and Wyatt, 1999. About global investors' 'euphoria' during the period 1990–94 see also Krugman, 1995.
82. As reported in Wayne, 1994. For an overview of the EU financial sector industry's eagerness to invest in these emerging market countries see Atkins, 1995 and Southey, 1995.
83. As reported in Wayne, 1994.
84. As reported in Kristof and Sanger, 1999.
85. The conclusion drawn by the IEO's report is that 'the IMF undoubtedly encouraged countries that wanted to move ahead with capital account liberalization, and even acted as a cheerleader when it wished to do so, especially

before the East Asian crisis, but there is no evidence that it exerted significant leverage to push countries to move faster than they were willing to go.' IEO, 2005, p. 59.

86. As quoted in Naim, 1995, p. 45.
87. As reported in Kristof and Sanger, 1999.
88. The G24 is the body that coordinates the position of developing countries on monetary and financial issues.
89. As reported in Blustein, 1994.
90. The proceedings of the conference are collected in Boughton and Lateef, 1995.
91. IMF Archives, BUFF/94/106.

4 The Mexican Crisis: Testing the Consensus

92. As reported in Smith and Chandler, 1995.
93. The Code, which was adopted in 1961 and since then progressively expanded in scope, set an obligation for member countries to 'progressively abolish between one another' restrictions on the movements of capital 'to the extent necessary for effective economic cooperation' (Art. 1a). Article 2 specifies the transactions to be liberalized. For an analysis of the OECD Codes, see Abdelal, 2007, ch. 5.
94. According to the data provided in the 1995 International Capital Markets Report, in the period 1990–93, current account deficits averaged 1.9 percent in Argentina, –0.1 percent in Brazil, and 1.1 percent in the United States.
95. An exception was provided by the MIT economist Rudiger Dornbusch, who issued early warnings on the danger of the Mexican economy. See Dornbusch and Werner, 1994.
96. For an assessment of the impact of global interest rates on the pattern of capital flows to developing countries, see IMF, 1994b, pp. 53–54.
97. Before the devaluation, the peso-dollar exchange rate was allowed to fluctuate within a band consisting of a fixed lower limit (on the peso appreciation) and an upper limit that increased by MexN$0.0004 a day.
98. The transformation of government debt into foreign currency-denominated debt aimed at signaling to financial markets the government commitment to maintain the value of the exchange rate, since only a government that it is not going to devalue would transform its debt into foreign currency. According to Delong and Eichengreen (2004, p. 208 fn. 42) the Mexican government devised the *tesobonos* on the advice of the Weston Group, a New York-based group of financiers that specialized in peso investments.
99. At any rate, despite the early enthusiasm for *tesobonos*, 'barely nine months later, the very same international financial community would be pointing to the *Tesobonos* as a major vulnerability in the Mexican situation' (Sachs, Tornell and Velasco, 1996).
100. If not otherwise specified, economic data used in this section are drawn from the International Capital Market Report (August 1995), chapter II (pp. 2–11) and background papers II and III (pp. 53–78).

101. Upon joining the IMF, each member is assigned a quota based broadly on its relative size in the world economy, which determines its contribution to the IMF's financial resources and its borrowing capacity (its access limits). However, access may be higher in exceptional circumstances.
102. As reported in Smith and Chandler, 1995.
103. As reported in Sanger, 1995.
104. For an account of Congressional opposition see Delong and Eichengreen, 2004, pp. 213–4. In the end, the administration decided to use the Exchange Stabilization Fund (ESF) to extend $20 billion to Mexico. Indeed, the ESF was a pool of money – about $35 billion – that the Treasury had the mandate to use to help stabilize the dollar without Congress approval.
105. From the Managing Director's perspective, European opposition to the IMF loan was attributable to 'the prevailing diagnosis in Europe that the crisis was a regional problem, not a global one, which should be resolved within NAFTA.' Camdessus, 1995e. Similarly, Fischer (1995c) commented that 'the considerable opposition from some of the European countries' was due to the fact that they 'had the view that if Mexico was in trouble, it was up to the United States to fix it.'
106. IMF Archives, EBM/95/30, Marc-Antoine Autheman, Executive Director France, p. 33.
107. Ibid., pp. 22–6, 69–70, and 46–9.
108. Ibid., p. 47.
109. IMF officials, especially Camdessus and his Deputy Stanley Fischer, were perfectly aware of what expectations the US administration had on the size of financing to be made available to Mexico. In their regular meeting, Treasury and Federal Reserve officials made their views known to the IMF management (Rubin and Weisberg, 2003, p. 20).
110. Smith and Chandler, 1995.
111. In the words of the staff, maintaining the exchange rate 'would enable Argentina to continue attracting capital inflows from abroad.' IMF Archives, SM/97/32, Sup. 1, p. 34.
112. In contrast, Brazil tightened a number of controls to withstand the tequila effects.
113. As the IMF internal documents reveal, the staff was very supportive of the Argentinean authorities' response to the crisis and pointed to the choice of a fixed exchange rate as one of the crucial factors in the country's continued stability. In the words of the staff, 'in presenting the authorities' request or a stand-by arrangement in March 1996, the staff was again generally complimentary of the authorities' policy actions and supported the policy of maintaining the Convertibility Plan in Argentina. The staff felt that the authorities' commitment to the plan served the country well and enjoyed widespread support as a symbol of price stability and a safeguard against fiscal profligacy, and in light of Argentina's past inflationary experience the staff saw no credible alternative to the currency board arrangement.' IMF Archives, SM/97/32, Sup. 1, p. 34.
114. Ibid., p. 34.
115. IMF Archives, EBM/95/73, p. 69.
116. Ibid., Summing Up of the Acting Chairman, Stanley Fischer, p. 69.
117. IMF Archives, SM/95/164, p. 10.

118. IMF Archives, EBM/95/30, Karin Lissakers, Executive Director US, p. 42.
119. Ibid., Michel Camdessus, Managing Director, p. 49.
120. Ibid., p. 49.
121. IMF Archives, EBM/95/73, Summing Up of the Acting Chairman, Stanley Fischer, p. 68. Similar considerations applied to capital inflows.
122. Ibid., K. P. Geethakrishnan, Executive Director India (and Bangladesh, Bhutan, and Sri Lanka), pp. 57–8.
123. One of the most vocal supporters for more gradualism in opening the capital account was the Chinese Executive Director who warned against 'too much haste'. Ibid., Zhixiang Zhang, Executive Director China, p. 47.
124. Ibid., Summing Up of the Acting Chairman, Stanley Fischer, p. 69.
125. For an interpretation of the positive markets' reaction to the Mexican shock that looks at the regulatory framework for global finance to explain such a crisis-resilient attitude see Kapstein, 1996.
126. As reported in Fidler, 1994.
127. For instance, Paul Krugman recalls the climate of hostility and bemusement that Dornbush and him met when they had warned on the unsustainability of the Mexican exchange rates and on excessive market euphoria. Krugman, 1995, p. 36 fn. 1.
128. On the Mexican crisis as an example of 'a new kind of crisis in the global market era', see Calvo and Mendoza, 1996.
129. For an evolution of the scope of Fund surveillance see Guitián, 1992, and James, 1995.
130. See, for instance, Woods, 2006, pp. 56–63. Stanley Fischer, in contrast, argued that the crisis was not unexpected (Fischer, 1995b).
131. In the Halifax document, the G7 representatives argued that an effective surveillance 'requires an improved early warning system' which the IMF may contribute to by 'establish[ing] benchmarks for the timely publication of key economic and financial data; … a procedure for the regular public identification of countries which comply within these benchmarks; insist[ing] on full and timely reporting by member countries of standard sets of data.' G7, 1995.
132. Decision N° 10950 – (95/37), 10 April 1995.
133. Decision N° 10950 – (95/37), 10 April 1995.
134. IMF Archives, BUFF/96/50 Annex, Scope and Operational Characteristics of the Special Data Dissemination Standard, p. 3.
135. A copy of the cover memorandum was reproduced in IMF Archives, SM/97/32 Sup. 1, p. 50.
136. Ibid., pp. 50–1.
137. As of 1995, however, the issue of moral hazard was still not as compelling as it was about to become in the aftermath of the Asian crisis. For instance, in the aftermath of the peso crisis, Fischer (1995b) commented that 'Moral hazard is indeed a relevant issue, but one that is easily overplayed.'
138. The 11th Quota Review was concluded in 1998.
139. After many years of negotiations, the SDR allocation took place on 28 August 2009.
140. See Fischer, 1997b, and IMF Archives, SM/97/32.
141. IMF Archives, EBM/97/38, p. 39.

142. See, for instance, the reservations raised by Executive Directors in the following meetings. Ibid., IMF Archives, EBM/97/66, and IMF Archives, EBM/97/87.
143. See, for instance, IMF Archives, SM/97/86 and IMF Archives, SM/97/146.
144. IMF Archives, EBM/97/38, Chairman of the Meeting, p. 31. See also the statement prior to the meeting and the concluding remarks of the Chairman in IMF Archives, EBM/97/66.
145. Author's interviews with IMF officials in Washington DC, US, March–June 2006.
146. IMF Archives, EBM/97/93, Nicolas Eyzaguirre, Alternate Director Chile (and Argentina, Bolivia, Paraguay, Peru, Uruguay), p. 7.
147. IMF Archives, EBM/95/73, Alberto Calderon, Alternate Executive Director (Brazil, Colombia, Dominican Republic, Ecuador, Guyana, Haiti, Panama, Suriname, Trinidad and Tobago), p. 48.
148. Ibid., Zhixiang Zhang, Executive Director China, p. 46.
149. Ibid., Abdulrahman Al-Tuwaijri, Executive Director Saudi Arabia, p. 56.
150. For instance, the Indian Executive Director Geethakrishnan rejected the proposal to amend. 'Any attempt at enhancing the status of capital account convertibility in the Fund's mandate through an amendment of the Articles of Agreement would only lead to increased pressure for premature introduction of capital account convertibility and this will be disastrous.' Not only did he question the proposal to amend the Articles; he was also the only Director that questioned the normative argument about capital liberalization. 'Capital account convertibility [should] not be spoken of as a matter of dogma,' he remarked. Ibid., Geethakrishnan, Executive Director India (and Bangladesh, Bhutan and Sri Lanka), p. 58.
151. IMF Archives, EBM/97/38, Gus O'Donnel, Executive Director UK, p. 5.
152. Ibid., Benny Andersen, Alternate Director Denmark (and Estonia, Finland, Iceland, Latvia, Lithuania, Norway, and Sweden), p. 21.
153. Ibid., Sulaiman M. Al-Turki, Executive Director Saudi Arabia, pp. 24–5; Dinah Z. Guti, Executive Director Zimbabwe (and Angola, Botswana, Burundi, Eritrea, Gambia, Kenya, Lesotho, Liberia, Malawi, Mozambique, Namibia, Nigeria, Sierra Leone, South Africa, Swaziland, Tanzania, Uganda, Zambia), p. 27; and A. Shakour Shalaan Executive Director Egypt (and Bahrain, Iraq, Jordan, Kuwait, Lebanon, Libya, Maldives, Oman, Quatar, Syrian Arab Republic, United Arab Emirates, Yemen), p. 28.
154. Author's interviews with J. Onno de Beaufort Wijnholds, Executive Director Netherlands (and Armenia, Bosnia and Herzegovina, Bulgaria, Croatia, Cyprus, Georgia, Israel, Macedonia, Moldova, Romania, and Ukraine) [1994–2003], International Monetary Fund, Washington DC, 26 May 2006 and Author's interviews with Aleksei Mozhin, Executive Director, Russia [1996–present], International Monetary Fund, Washington DC, 30 March 2006.

5 The Asian Crisis: Questioning the Consensus

155. On the Asian miracle, see, for instance, Bloom and Williamson, 1998, and Hanna, Boyson, and Gunaratne, 1996.

156. See, for instance, Krugman, 1994. According to Krugman, the 'miracle' was overrated, leading him to hypothesize that the growth rates of the newly industrialized countries of East Asia would eventually slow down.
157. In Thailand, in each of the years from 1994 to 1996, short-term inflows became dominant amounting to 7–10 percent of GDP. IMF, 1997c, pp. 4, 6.
158. For instance, in 1997, international bank lending to Thailand amounted to $70 billion, with Japanese banks providing over $37 billion, European banks about $19 billion, and US banks $5 billion.
159. IMF Archives, EBS/98/44, p. 7.
160. The literature on the Asian crisis is extensive and references are simply indicative here. For detailed analyses of the Asian crisis from an economics perspective, see Krugman, 1998b; Radelet and Sachs, 1998; Goldstein, 1998; and Ito, 2007. For accounts of the crisis from a political economy perspective, see Haggard, 2000; Noble and Ravenhill, 2000; and Thirkell-White, 2005.
161. *The Economist*, 1998, emphasis mine.
162. If not otherwise specified, economic data used in this section are drawn from IMF International Capital Market Reports and World Economic Outlook (various years).
163. According to the IMF data, about '30 percent, of the finance companies' assets were in property development, a substantial proportion of all their loans were effectively in default beginning February.' IMF, 1998a, pp. 45–6.
164. For a discussion of how no observer predicted the devaluation see Irvine, 1997. Among those who warned that East Asia was vulnerable to the sort of capital reversals experienced in Mexico see Park, 1996.
165. Moody's downgraded the sovereign's credit rating below investment grade on 22 December 1997.
166. For instance, The Sammi group went bankrupt in March, followed by the near collapses of Jinro and Dainong. The Kia group went under bankruptcy protection in mid-July 1997.
167. As reported in Giles, 2007.
168. Created in 1993, the BIBF provided a mechanism by which domestic borrowers were able to access foreign capital. Foreign banks were encouraged to participate in the BIBF by a combination of tax incentives, and informal indications that future access to the domestic market would also be determined by the scale of individual banks' participation in the BIBF.
169. For a detailed analysis of IMF-supported programs in Asia see Boorman et al., 2000, and Lane et al., 1999.
170. As far as concerns Korea, financial assistance was disbursed through the just-created IMF Supplement Reserve Facility (SRF) that aimed at dealing with balance of payments disequilibria attributable to sudden loss of market confidence.
171. For an overview of the political factors hindering program implementation in Indonesia and in Korea see IEO, 2004.
172. On the US opposition to the Asian Monetary Fund see Golup, 2004, pp. 771–2.
173. IMF Archives, SM/98/172, p. 61.

174. See also IMF Archives, EBS/98/44.

175. Although IMF staff were aware of the problems in Thailand, staff members concede that the Fund 'did not forecast the recent crises, and in retrospect was too optimistic in its baseline projections' (IMF, 1997c, p. 40). Along the same lines, Fischer (1998c) concludes that the IMF 'failed to foresee the virulence of the contagion effects produced by the widening crisis.'

176. About the relative role of different investor groups (hedge funds, commercial and investment banks, international mutual funds, multinational corporations, and domestic banks and corporates) during the crisis see IMF, 1998a, pp. 41, 44, 48, 50 and 51.

177. See, for instance, the account in Thirkell-White, 2005.

178. Specifically, Asian programs provided for extensive opening to foreign participation in banking (Indonesia, Korea, Thailand), other financial services (Korea), telecommunications (Korea, Thailand), and distribution services (Indonesia). It is worth reminding, however, that in the years that preceded the crisis, Korean authorities have opened the short-term end of the capital account – i.e. the most volatile term. The long-term end, which includes foreign direct investments and is widely believed to be the source of stable and beneficial resources, remained subject to significant restrictions.

179. Malaysia was not the only country that introduced controls. In mid-1998, for instance, the Philippines introduced controls on selected capital transactions involving repatriation of capital. Even Hong Kong introduced a new regulatory system aimed at discouraging speculative capital flows.

180. As reported in Mckenna, 1998.

181. See, for instance, the reports posted on the website of Third World Network, Focus on Global South, or the Centre for Global Development. In this atmosphere, the environmental NGO community hit the street in Washington in January 1998, rallying against the Fund. In particular, the aim of the rally was to demand that the US Congress not approve the increase in Fund resources.

182. The International Financial Institutions Advisory Commission was established by the US Congress in November 1998 to recommend future US policy to a number of international organizations, including the IMF and the World Bank.

183. As reported in Kristof and Wudunn, 1999.

184. US Congress, 1998a, pp. 36–37.

185. IMF Archives, SM/98/75, p. 6.

186. Similar concerns were raised by the private sector during the discussion of the sovereign debt restructuring mechanism (SDRM) – i.e. a mechanism with which private creditors would be actively involved in sovereign debt restructuring.

187. For the debate within the Executive Board see also Abdelal, 2007, ch. 6, and Leiteritz, 2005.

188. IMF Archives, EBM/98/103, Bernd Esdar, Executive Director Germany, p. 12.

189. Ibid., Thomas Bernes, Executive Director Canada (and Antigua and Barbuda, Bahamas, Barbados, Belize, Dominica, Grenada, Ireland, Jamaica, St. Kitts and Nevis, St. Lucia, St. Vincent and the Grenadines), p. 13.

190. Ibid., Karin Lissakers, Executive Director US, p. 6. See also the remarks by Gregory Taylor, Executive Director of Australia (and Kiribati, Korea, Marshall Islands, Mongolia, New Zealand, Papua New Guinea, Philippines), p. 5.

191. IMF Archives, EBM/98/38, Mohammed Dairi, Alternate Director (Afghanistan, Algeria, Ghana, Iraq, Morocco, Pakistan, and Tunisia), p. 9 and Thomas Bernes, Executive Director Canada (and Antigua and Barbuda, Bahamas, Barbados, Belize, Dominica, Grenada, Ireland, Jamaica, St. Kitts and Nevis, St. Lucia, St. Vincent and the Grenadines), p. 9.

192. Ibid., p. 9.

193. Ibid., Marc-Anthoine Milleron, French Executive Director, p. 20 (emphasis mine) and Alexandre Kafka, Executive Director Brazil (and Colombia, Dominican Republic, Ecuador, Guyana, Haiti, Panama, Suriname, Trinidad and Tobago), p. 25.

194. IMF Archives, EBM/98/103, Gregory Taylor, Executive Director of Australia (and Kiribati, Korea, Marshall Islands, Mongolia, New Zealand, Papua New Guinea, Philippines), p. 12.

195. Ibid., Gregory Taylor, Executive Director of Australia (and Kiribati, Korea, Marshall Islands, Mongolia, New Zealand, Papua New Guinea, Philippines), p. 27, and Aldrandre Barro Chambrier, Alternate Director (Benin, Burkina Faso, Cameroon, Cape Verde, Central Africa Republic, Chad, Comoros, Congo, Cote d'Ivoire, Djibouti, Equatorial Guinea, Gabon, Guinea, Guinea-Bissau, Madagascar, Mali, Mauritania, Mauritius, Niger, Rwanda, Sao Tome and Principe, Senegal, Togo), p. 27.

196. Ibid., Thomas Bernes, Executive Director Canada (and Antigua and Barbuda, Bahamas, Barbados, Belize, Dominica, Grenada, Ireland, Jamaica, St. Kitts and Nevis, St. Lucia, St. Vincent and the Grenadines), p. 8.

197. Ibid., Gregory Taylor, Executive Director Australia, p. 28, and Alexandre Kafka, Executive Director Brazil (Colombia, Dominican Republic, Ecuador, Guyana, Haiti, Panama, Suriname, Trinidad and Tobago), p. 25.

198. Ibid., M. R. Sivaraman, Executive Director India (Bangladesh, Bhutan, and Sri Lanka), p. 9. See also IMF Archives, EBM/98/38, Dinah Z. Guti, Executive Director Zimbabwe (and Angola, Botswana, Burundi, Eritrea, Gambia, Kenya, Lesotho, Liberia, Malawi, Mozambique, Namibia, Nigeria, Sierra Leone, South Africa, Swaziland, Tanzania, Uganda, Zambia), p. 29.

199. IMF Archives, SM/98/172.

200. The Interim Committee is the advisory body to the Board of Governors – i.e. the highest decision-making body of the IMF, which normally meets once a year and where each member country is represented. In September 1999, the Interim Committee has been replaced by the International Monetary and Financial Committee (IMFC).

201. IMF Archives, EBM/98/103, Bernd Esdar, Executive Director Germany, p. 11, Jon Shields, Executive Director UK, p. 10, and Karin Lissakers, Executive Director US, p. 14.

202. IMF Archives, EBM/98/38, Nicolas Eyzaguirre, Alternate Director (Argentina, Bolivia, Chile, Paraguay, Peru, Uruguay), p. 12.

203. IMF Archives, EBM/98/103, Nicolas Eyzaguirre, p. 10.

204. Ibid., Yukio Yoshimura, Executive Director Japan, p. 14.

205. See, for instance, the statements from the IMF Managing Director in IMF Archives, EBM/98/38, p. 9.
206. Ibid., Jan Jose Toribio, Executive Director Spain (and Costa Rica, El Salvador, Guatemala, Honduras, Mexico, Nicaragua, Venezuela), p. 13.

6   The Subprime Crisis: Towards a New Consensus

207. ABS are debt securities collateralized by pools of assets, such as residential or commercial mortgages, car loans or credit card payments.
208. Securities Industry and Financial Markets Association (SIFMA), the American Securitization Forum (ASF), the European Securitization Forum (ESF), and the Australian Securitization Forum (AuSF), 2008, p. 2.
209. During the past decade, standards have been developed in a variety of areas. For instance, the IMF developed standards for fiscal transparency, and for monetary and financial policy transparency. Other standards and codes have been prepared in the areas of banking supervision (Basel Committee), corporate governance (the OECD), accounting (International Accounting Standards' Committee), insurance (IAIS), and securities markets (International Organization of Securities Commissions, IOSCO).
210. Specifically, it is up to domestic regulators to allow banks to use their internal risk models.
211. As has been noted, 'the accord brought about a major change in the basic method of making regulation...by completely overhauling the minimum capital requirements that have become central to prudential supervision' (Tarullo, 2008).
212. The arguments in favor of the creation of the SDRM can be found in Boorman, 2002; Krueger, 2001, 2002.
213. About some of the most recent proposals to overhaul the Fund's internal governance see, for instance, the Trevor report. Committee on IMF Governance Reform, 2009.
214. As a traditional bank, the Fund generates its income by virtue of the lending margin. That is to say, member countries that draw on the Fund's financial resources pay a higher interest rate than the Fund pays to its member country creditors. To tackle the problem posed by the reduction in its lending activity, the Fund even established a Committee of Eminent Persons with the mandate of suggesting new measures for the Fund to generate income. The Committee, created in 2007, was chaired by former general manager of the Bank of International Settlements, Andrew Crockett. The Committee's recommendations involved a package of measures aimed at generating new sources of income for the Fund. Among these measures, the Committee suggested a limited sale of Fund gold reserves.
215. The Group of 22 comprised finance ministers and central bank governors from the G7 industrial countries and 15 other countries (Argentina, Australia, Brazil, China, Hong Kong SAR, India, Indonesia, Korea, Malaysia, Mexico, Poland, Russia, Singapore, South Africa, and Thailand).
216. The membership of the G20 is made up of the finance ministers and central bank governors of 19 countries: Argentina, Australia, Brazil, Canada, China, France, Germany, India, Indonesia, Italy, Japan, Mexico, Russia,

Saudi Arabia, South Africa, South Korea, Turkey, the United Kingdom, and the United States of America; and the European Union.

217. G20 website, 'About G20', http://www.g20.org/about_what_is_g20.aspx, date accessed 26 March 2009.

218. In October 1998, the Finance Ministers and Central Bank Governors of the G7 countries mandated Hans Tietmeyer, President of the Deutsche Bundesbank, to recommend measures for enhancing cooperation to promote international financial stability.

219. FSF website, 'Mandate,' http://www.fsforum.org/about/mandate.htm, date accessed 26 March 2009.

220. FSF website, '12 Key Standards for Sound Financial Systems,' http://www.fsforum.org/cos/key_standards.htm, date accessed 26 March 2009.

221. The international supervisory groupings represented in the FSF are the Basel Committee on Banking Supervision (BCBS), the International Accounting Standards Board (IASB), the International Association of Insurance Supervisors (IAIS), the International Organization of Securities Commissions (IOSCO).

222. On the tendency of financial turbulence to spill across borders see, for instance, Wyplosz, 1999, and Eichengreen, 2006.

223. Despite the increasing interconnections among financial institutions around the world, the crisis was not simply caused by financial integration but by a combination of flawed incentives in the financial industry, inadequate regulations, and macroeconomic policies. The interaction among these multiple factors is analyzed below. For an accurate analysis of the emergence of the crisis see, for instance, Bank for International Settlements, 2008.

224. In this connection, the subprime crisis is similar to the Asian crisis in that it was largely caused by bad lending practices and inadequate supervision and regulation.

225. Securities Industry and Financial Markets Association (SIFMA), the American Securitization Forum (ASF), the European Securitization Forum (ESF), and the Australian Securitization Forum (AuSF), 2008, p. 4.

226. On the regulatory incentives that contributed to the crisis, see, for instance, Blundell-Wignall, Atkinson, and Lee, 2008.

227. On this point, see, for instance, Dodd and Mills, 2008.

228. Securities Industry and Financial Markets Association (SIFMA), the American Securitization Forum (ASF), the European Securitization Forum (ESF), and the Australian Securitization Forum (AuSF), 2008, p. 2.

229. European Securitization Forum (ESF), Securitization Data Report, Q4 2008.

230. Duffie and Zhou, 2001, and Gorton and Pennacchi, 1995.

231. Special investment vehicles were funded with short-term asset-backed commercial paper (ABCP) whose proceeds were used to buy longer-term assets.

232. Minsky, 1992.

233. Northern Rock is the first institution to be rescued by the Bank of England since its revision of powers in 1998.

234. For instance, the February ECB lending survey found tightening credit standard to households and firms in the last quarter of 2008. European Central Bank, 2009.

235. Following the regulatory incentive, it has been calculated that over 95 percent of all securitization issuance in Europe for 2008 was retained for transactions with the ECB. European Securitization Forum, 2008, p. 1.
236. Actually, IMF documents deal with both the short- and the long-term reforms to the international financial system. Nevertheless, for the purpose of this book, the focus is solely on the proposed long-term measures.
237. See, also, IMF, 2009d, p. 9 e 12.
238. Securities Industry and Financial Markets Association (SIFMA), the American Securitization Forum (ASF), the European Securitization Forum (ESF), and the Australian Securitization Forum (AuSF), 2008, p. 5.
239. See, for instance, the recommendations issued by the G20, 2009c, p. xiii.
240. The EU also approved a new regulation that will raise standards for the issuance of credit ratings used in the Community. More information is available at the EU website; in particular, see EU Commission, 2009.
241. As reported in Luce and Freeland, 2009.
242. See, for instance, Gapper, 2009.
243. See, for instance, Financial Stability Board, 2009a.
244. G20, 2009b. The G20 also expressed interest in exploring mechanisms of 'market borrowing by the IMF to be used if necessary in conjunction with other sources of financing, to raise resources to the level needed to meet demands.'
245. The legislation in question is the final Supplemental Appropriations Act 2009, which was passed by the House on 16 June and the Senate on 18 June.
246. Congress also authorized the Treasury to bring forward the governance reform of the IMF, giving more voice to less represented countries and allowing for a one-time allocation of the special drawing rights (SDR), the IMF reserve currency.
247. As reported in *The Economist*, 2009b. Mexico secured a $47 billion credit line from the IMF in April 2009 drawing from the FCL.
248. As reported in Merli, 2009, p. 12.
249. As quoted in Ikenberry, 1992, p. 296.

7   Conclusions: Past and Future of International Financial Governance

250. The literature on the influence of economic ideas on institutional outcomes is huge and references to this literature have been provided throughout the book. The following references are therefore only illustrative of some of the main areas of research. For an analysis of the influence of economic ideas on domestic economic policies, see Blyth, 2002, and Berman, 1998. For the influence of ideas within the European Union, see Parsons, 2003, and McNamara, 1998. For contributions on the influence of ideas in the security domain, see Acharya, 2004. For contributions on the influence of ideas on monetary policies, see Widmaier, 2007, and Maman and Rosenhek, 2007.

251. On the recognition that mass publics can be a source of institutional change, see Widmaier, Blyth, and Seabrooke, 2007, and in particular, Seabrooke, 2007a.
252. IMF, 'A Changing IMF—Responding to the Crisis,' Factsheet, July. Available at http://www.imf.org/external/np/exr/facts/changing.htm, date accessed 7 August 2009.
253. See, for instance, the account in *The Economist*, 2008.
254. The World Bank, for instance, assists member countries in the design and implementation of policies that strengthen the domestic financial system and help countries in identifying risks in this system. The BCBS, the IOSCO, and the IAIS, in turn, provide specialized knowledge by setting the standards in the field of banking supervision, securities, and insurance supervision respectively.

Bibliography

Abdelal, R. (2007) *Capital Rules: The Construction of Global Finance* (Cambridge, MA: Harvard University Press).

Acharya, A. (2004) 'How ideas spread: Whose norms matter? Norm localization and institutional change in Asian regionalism,' *International Organization*, 58, 2, 239–75.

Adler, E. (1991) 'Cognitive evolution: A dynamic approach for the study of international relations and their progress,' in Emanuel Adler and Beverly Crawford, eds *Progress in Postwar International Relations* New York: Columbia University Press, 43–88.

Akerlof, G., and R. Shiller (2009) *Animal Spirits: How Human Psychology Drives the Economy, and Why It Matters for Global Capitalism* (Princeton: Princeton University Press).

Armella, P. A. (1995) Conference Address 'Fifty years after Bretton Woods: The future of the IMF and the World Bank,' Madrid, Spain, 29–30 September.

Atkins, R. (1995) 'Sun rises on eastern insurance markets – Financial services liberalisation deal is a boost for European insurers,' *Financial Times*, 8 August.

Baker, A. (2005) *The Group of Seven: Finance Ministries, Central Banks and Global Financial Governance* (London: Routledge).

Bank for International Settlements (2008) 'Annual Report: The unsustainable has run its course and policymakers face the difficult task of damage control,' 30 June.

Barnett, M. N., and M. Finnemore (2004) *Rules for the World: International Organizations in Global Politics* (Ithaca: Cornell University Press).

Bela Belassa ed. (1986) *Towards Renewed Economic Growth in Latin America* (Washington, D.C: Institute for International Economics).

Benoit, B. (2008) 'Berlin may go it alone on bank regulations,' *Financial Times*, 6 February.

Berger, F. C. (2003) 'Preface,' in P.-P. Kuczynski and J. Williamson, eds *After the Washington Consensus: Restarting Growth and Reform in Latin America* (Washington, DC: Institute for International Economics).

Berman, S. (1998) *The Social Democratic Model: Ideas and Politics in the Making of Interwar Europe* (Cambridge: Harvard University Press).

Best, J. (2003) 'Moralizing finance: The new financial architecture as ethical discourse,' *Review of International Political Economy*, 10, 3, 578–603.

Best, J. (2005) *The Limits of Transparency: Ambiguity and History of International Finance* (Ithaca: Cornell University Press).

Bhagwati, J. (1998) 'The capital myth: The difference between trade in widgets and dollars,' *Foreign Affairs*, 77, 3, 7–12.

Bierkester, T. J. (2002) 'State, sovereignty and territory,' in W. Carlsnaes, T. Risse and B. A. Simmons, eds *Handbook of International Relations* (London: Sage).

Bini Smaghi, Lorenzo. (2004) 'A Single EU Seat in the IMF?' *Journal of Common Market Studies*, 42, 2, 229–248.

Bloom, D. E., and J. G. Williamson (1998) 'Demographic transitions and economic miracles in emerging Asia,' *World Bank Economic Review*, 12, 3, 419–55.

Blundell-Wignall, A., P. Atkinson, and S. H. Lee (2008) 'The current financial crisis: causes and policy issues,' *OECD Financial Market Trends*, 2, 1–28.

Blustein, P. (1994) 'Pact a milestone in march of capitalism; Indonesia's Suharto, in political shift, led forum to open trade,' *Washington Post*, 16 November.

Blyth, M. (2002) *Great Transformations. Economic Ideas and Institutional Change in the Twentieth Century* (Cambridge: Cambridge University Press).

Boorman, J. (1998) 'Press conference – Seminar on capital account liberalization,' IMF Meeting Hall, Washington DC, US, 10 March.

Boorman, J. (2002) 'Sovereign debt restructuring: Where stands the debate?' Speech given at the conference cosponsored by the CATO Institute and *The Economist*, New York, 17 October.

Boorman, J. (2003) 'IMF explains capital flows proposal,' *New Straits Times (Malaysia)*, 3 February.

Boorman, J. (2004) 'Some challenges confronting the IMF.' Address at the Institute of International Finance, *Understanding Country Risk* seminar, London, 17 November.

Boorman, J. (2006) Author's interview, Director, Policy Development and Review Department, International Monetary Fund (1990–2001), Washington, DC, 23 March.

Boorman, J. et al., (2000) 'Managing financial crises: The experience in East Asia,' IMF Working Paper No. 00/107, Washington, DC: International Monetary Fund.

Boughton, J. M. (2000) 'Michel Camdessus at the IMF: A retrospective,' *Finance & Development*, 37, 1, 2–6.

Boughton, J. M. (2001) *Silent Revolution: The International Monetary Fund, 1979–1989* (Washington, DC: International Monetary Fund).

Boughton, J. M. (2002) 'Why white, not Keynes? Inventing the post-war international monetary system,' IMF Working Paper No. 02/52, Washington, DC: International Monetary Fund.

Boughton, J. M. (2006) 'American in the shadows: Harry Dexter White and the design of the International Monetary Fund,' IMF Working Paper No. 06/6, Washington, DC: International Monetary Fund.

Boughton, J. M., and S. K. Lateef, eds (1995) *Fifty Years After Bretton Woods: The Future of the IMF and the World Bank* (Washington, DC: International Monetary Fund).

Braithwaite, T., and F. Guerrera (2009) 'US reveals sweeping regulatory overhaul,' *Financial Times*, 26 March.

Brealy, R. (1999) 'The Asian crisis: Lessons for crisis management and prevention,' *Bank of England Quarterly Bulletin*, 39, 3, 196–285.

Broome, A. J. (2008) 'The importance of being earnest: The IMF as a reputational intermediary,' *New Political Economy*, 13, 2, 125–51.

Broome, A. J. (forthcoming a) 'Standardizing currency practices: Transforming current account convertibility into a global policy norm,' in S. Park and A. Vetterlein, eds *Owning Development: Creating Global Policy Norms in the World Bank and the IMF* (Cambridge: Cambridge University Press).

Broome, A. J. (forthcoming b) *The Currency of Power: The IMF and Monetary Reform in Central Asia* (Basingstoke: Palgrave).

Broome, A., and L. Seabrooke (2007) 'Seeing like the IMF: Institutional change in small open economies,' *Review of International Political Economy*, 14, 4, 576–601.

Bryant, C. (2009) 'EU leaders push sweeping regulations,' *Financial Times*, 22 February.

Buiter, W. (2008) 'The end of American capitalism as we knew it.' 17 September. Available at http://blogs.ft.com/maverecon/2008/09/the-end-of-american-capitalism-as-we-knew-it/

Calomiris, C. (1998) 'The IMF's imprudent role as lender of last resort,' *The Cato Journal*, 17, 3, 275–95.

Calvo, G. A., L. Leiderman, and C. M. Reinhart (1995) 'Capital inflows to Latin America with reference to the Asian experience,' in S. Edwards, ed. *Capital Controls, Exchange Rates, and Monetary Policy in the World Economy* (Cambridge: Cambridge University Press).

Calvo, G. A., and E. G. Mendoza (1996) 'Petty crime and cruel punishment: Lessons from the Mexican debacle,' *American Economic Review, Papers and Proceedings*, 86, 2, 170–75.

Camdessus, M. (1994) 'International cooperation for high-quality growth: The role of the IMF at 50.' Address at the Complutense University, Madrid, Spain, 21 December.

Camdessus, M. (1995a) Address at the Conference on Banking Crises in Latin America, organized by the Inter-American Development Bank and the Group of 30, Washington, DC, 6 October.

Camdessus, M. (1995b) 'Closing statements,' in J. M. Boughton and S. K. Lateef, eds *Fifty Years After Bretton Woods: The Future of the IMF and the World Bank* (Washington, DC: International Monetary Fund).

Camdessus, M. (1995c) 'Drawing lessons from the Mexican crisis: Preventing and resolving financial crises – The role of the IMF.' Address at the 25th Washington Conference of the Council of the Americas on 'Staying the Course: Forging a Free Trade Area in the Americas,' Washington, DC, 22 May.

Camdessus, M. (1995d) 'Global perspectives on the issues,' in J. M. Boughton and S. K. Lateef, eds *Fifty Years After Bretton Woods: The Future of the IMF and the World Bank* (Washington, DC: International Monetary Fund).

Camdessus, M. (1995e) 'The IMF and the challenges of globalization – The Fund's evolving approach to its constant mission: The case of Mexico.' Address at the Zurich Economics Society, Zurich, Switzerland, 14 November.

Camdessus, M. (1995f) 'The IMF in a globalized world economy – The tasks ahead,' Third Annual Sylvia Ostry Lecture, Ottawa, Canada, 7 June.

Camdessus, M. (1995g) 'Income distribution and sustainable growth: The perspective from the IMF at fifty,' Opening remarks to the conference on 'Income Distribution and Sustainable Growth,' Washington, DC, 1 June.

Camdessus, M. (1995h) 'Prospects and challenges in our globalized world economy.' Address at the Wharton School of the University of Pennsylvania, Philadelphia, 4 April.

Camdessus, M. (1996a) 'Argentina and the challenge of globalization.' Address at the Academy of Economic Science, Buenos Aires, Argentina, 27 May.

Camdessus, M. (1996b) 'Challenges facing the IMF and Malaysia.' Address at a Meeting of Financial and Business Leaders, Kuala Lumpur, Malaysia, 15 July.

Camdessus, M. (1996c) 'The International Monetary Fund: Increasing economic opportunities and meeting the challenges in the global economy,' Remarks at the Mid-America Committee, Chicago, 11 April.

Camdessus, M. (1996d) 'Promoting safe and sound banking systems: An IMF perspective,' Remarks at the Conference on 'Safe and Sound Financial Systems: What Works for Latin America,' Inter-American Development Bank, Washington, DC, 28 September.

Camdessus, M. (1996e) 'Sustaining macroeconomic performance in the ASEAN countries.' Address at at the Conference on 'Macroeconomic Issues Facing ASEAN Countries', Jakarta, Indonesia, 7 November.

Camdessus, M. (1997a) Joint Press Conference of Philippe Maystadt, Chairman, Interim Committee and Michel Camdessus, Managing Director, International Monetary Fund, Washington, DC, 28 April.

Camdessus, M. (1997b) 'The agenda for global financial cooperation.' Address to the Association of Japanese Business Studies, Washington, DC, 13 June.

Camdessus, M. (1997c) 'The Asian crisis and the international response.' Address at the Institute of Advanced Business Studies (IESE) of the University of Navarra, Barcelona, Spain, 28 November.

Camdessus, M. (1997d) 'The Asian financial crisis and the opportunities of globalization.' Address at the Second Committee of the United Nations General Assembly, New York, 31 October.

Camdessus, M. (1997e) 'Do we still need the IMF in an era of massive private capital flows?' Remarks at the Economic Club of New York, 6 June.

Camdessus, M. (1997f) 'Lessons from Southeast Asia,' Remarks at a Press Briefing, Singapore, 13 November.

Camdessus, M. (1997g) 'Rebuilding confidence in Asia,' Remarks at the ASEAN Business Forum, Kuala Lumpur, Malaysia, 2 December.

Camdessus, M. (1998) 'Reflections on the crisis in Asia.' Address to the Extraordinary Ministerial Meeting of the Group of 24, Caracas, Venezuela, 7 February.

Camdessus, M. (2000) 'Statement by IMF Managing Director Michel Camdessus on the death of Manuel Guitián,' News Brief No. 00/9, 8 February.

Campbell, J. L. (2001) 'Institutional analysis and the role of ideas in political economy,' in J. L. Campbell and O. K. Pederson, eds *The Rise of Neoliberalism and Institutional Analysis* (Princeton: Princeton University Press).

Campbell, J. L. (2004) *Institutional Change and Globalization* (Princeton: Princeton University Press).

Campbell, J. L., and O. K. Pederson, eds (2001) *The Rise of Neoliberalism and Institutional Analysis*. (Princeton: Princeton University Press).

Capano, G. (2009) 'Understanding policy change as an epistemological and theoretical problem,' *Journal of Comparative Policy Analysis: Research and Practice*, 11, 1, 7–31.

Carvajal, A., et al., (2009) 'The perimeter of financial regulation,' Staff Position Note No. 09/07, Washington, DC: International Monetary Fund.

Chwieroth, J. M. (2007) 'Testing and measuring the role of ideas: The case of neoliberalism in the International Monetary Fund,' *International Studies Quarterly*, 51, 1, 5–30.

Chwieroth, J. M. (2009) *Capital Ideas: The IMF and the Rise of Financial Liberalization* (Princeton: Princeton University Press).

Cline, W. R. (1983) *International Debt and the Stability of the World Economy* (Washington, DC: Institute for International Economics).

Cline, W. R. (1984) *International Debt: Systemic Risk and Policy Response* (Washington, DC: Institute for International Economics).

Cline, W. R. (1995) *International Debt Reexamined* (Washington, DC: Institute for International Economics).

Clinton, B. (1993a) 'First Inaugural Address,' Washington, DC, 20 January.

Clinton, B. (1993b) 'State of the Union Address,' Washington, DC, 17 February.

Committee on IMF Governance Reform (2009) 'Final Report,' Washington, DC: International Monetary Fund, 24 March.

Cottrell, M. P. (2009) 'Legitimacy and institutional replacement: The convention on certain conventional weapons and the emergence of the Mine Ban Treaty,' *International Organization*, 63, 2, 217–48.

Crockett, A. (1996) 'Lessons from the Mexican crisis,' in G. A. Calvo, M. Goldstein, and E. Hochreiter, eds *Private Capital Flows to Emerging Markets after the Mexican Crisis* (Washington, DC: Institute for International Economics; Vienna: Austrian National Bank).

Culpepper, P. D. (2008) 'The Politics of common knowledge: Ideas and institutional change in wage bargaining,' *International Organization*, 62, 1, 1–33.

Cutler, C. A., V. Haufler, and T. Porter, eds (1999) *Private Authority and International Affairs* (Albany: State University of New York Press).

Cyert, R. N., and J. G. March (1963) *A Behavioral Theory of the Firm* (Englewood Cliffs: Prentice-Hall).

Dawson, T. C. (2002) 'The IMF's role in Asia: Part of the problem or part of the solution?.' Prepared text for remarks at the Institute of Policy Studies and Singapore Management University Forum, Singapore, 10 July.

de Laroisiere, J. (2009) 'The high level group on financial supervision in the EU,' Brussels, 25 February.

De Rato, R. (2006) 'New priorities for an era of globalisation,' *The Banker*, 2 January.

De Vries, M. G. (1969) 'Exchange restrictions,' in K. J. De Vries, ed. *The International Monetary Fund 1945–1965* (Washington, DC: International Monetary Fund), 217–228.

De Vries, M. G. (1986) *The IMF in a Changing World: 1945–1985* (Washington, DC: International Monetary Fund).

Delong, J. B., and B. Eichengreen (2004) 'Between meltdown and moral hazard: The international monetary and financial policies of the Clinton administration,' in J. A. Frankel and P. R. Orszag, eds *American Economic Policy in the 1990s* (Cambridge: MIT Press).

Dodd, R., and P. Mills (2008) 'Outbreak: US subprime contagion,' *Finance & Development*, 45, 2, 14–18.

Dornbusch, R., and A. Werner (1994) 'Mexico: Stabilization, reform, and no growth,' *Brookings Paper on Economic Activity*, 1, 253–315.

Draghi, M. (2008) 'Combating the global financial crisis – The role of international cooperation,' Distinguished Lecture delivered at the Hong Kong Monetary Authority, 16 December.

Duffie, D., and C. Zhou (2001) 'Credit risk derivatives in banking: Useful tools for managing risk?' *Journal of Monetary Economics*, 48, 1, 25–54.

The Economist (1994) 'Recalled to life: A survey of international banking,' 30 April.
The Economist (1998) 'The perils of global capital,' 9 April.
The Economist (2000a) 'The right boss for the Fund,' 2 March.
The Economist (2000b) 'Köhler's quest,' 27 July.
The Economist (2008) 'Financial regulation: Repairs begin at home,' 31 January.
The Economist (2009a) 'The G20 and the IMF banking on the Fund,' 8 April.
The Economist (2009b) 'The IMF: Mission possible,' 8 April.
The Economist (2009c) 'The inefficiency of markets: Slaves to some defunct economist,' 11 June.
The Economist (2009d) 'Regulating banks: Basel brush,' 2 April.
The Economist (2009e) 'What went wrong,' 6 March.
Edwards, M. S. (2009) 'Public support for the international economic organizations: Evidence from developing countries,' *Review of International Organizations*, 4, 2, 185–209.
Eichengreen, B. (1996) *Globalizing Capital: A History of the International Monetary System* (Princeton: Princeton University Press).
Eichengreen, B. (2006) 'Financial stability,' Paper commissioned by the Secretariat of the International Task Force on Global Public Goods, Stockholm, Sweden.
Eichengreen, B. (2009) 'Out of the box thoughts about the International Financial Architecture,' IMF Working Paper No. 09/116, Washington, DC: International Monetary Fund.
Eichengreen, B., et al., (1999) 'Liberalizing capital movements: Some analytical issues,' Economic Issues No. 17, Washington, DC: International Monetary Fund.
Esdar, B. (2006) Author's interview, Executive Director, Germany [1997–2001], International Monetary Fund, Washington DC, 23 May.
EU Commission (2008) 'Credit rating agencies: Frequently asked questions,' Brussels, European Community, 12 November. Available at http://europa.eu/rapid/pressReleasesAction.do?reference=MEMO/08/691&format=HTML&aged=0&language=EN&guiLanguage=fr
EU Commission (2009) 'Approval of new Regulation will raise standards for the issuance of credit ratings used in the Community,' Brussels, European Community, 23 April. Available at http://europa.eu/rapid/pressReleasesAction.do?reference=IP/09/629&format=HTML&aged=0&language=EN&guiLanguage=en
European Central Bank (2009) 'The Euro Area bank lending survey,' 6 February.
European Securitization Forum (2008) 'Securitization Data Report Q4,' London: European Securitization Forum.
Feinberg, R. (1992) 'Latin America: Back on screen,' *International Economic Insights*, 3, 4, 2–6.
Feldstein, M. (1998) 'Refocussing the IMF,' *Foreign Affairs*, 77, 2, 20–33.
Fidler, S. (1988) 'IMF and World Bank meetings; World Bank threatens to usurp IMF role,' *Financial Times*, 30 September.
Fidler, S. (1994) 'Survey of Latin American finance,' *Financial Times*, 11 April.
Financial Stability Board (2009a) 'Principles for sound compensation practices,' 2 April. Available at http://www.fsforum.org/publications/r_0904b.pdf

Financial Stability Board (2009b) 'Report of the Financial Stability Forum on addressing procyclicality in the financial system,' 2 April. Available at http://www.fsforum.org/publications/r_0904a.pdf

Financial Stability Forum (2000) 'Issues paper of the task force on implementation of standards,' 25–6 March. Available at http://www.fsforum.org/publications/Issues_Paper_Standards00.pdf

Finnemore, M., and K. Sikkink (1998) 'International norm dynamics and political change,' *International Organization*, 52, 4, 887–917.

Fischer, S. (1995a) 'Globalization of the world economy: Its impact on trade and security.' Address at the National Press Club, Washington, DC, 24 April.

Fischer, S. (1995b) 'The IMF after fifty years and the Mexican crisis,' *The Banker*, May.

Fischer, S. (1995c) 'What does the Halifax communique imply for the international financial system?' Lecture at the Korea Institute of Finance, 20 May.

Fischer, S. (1997a) 'Capital account liberalization and the role of the IMF,' Paper prepared for the International Monetary Fund's Seminar on 'Asia and the IMF,' Hong Kong, 19 September.

Fischer, S. (1997b) 'How to avoid international financial crises and the role of the International Monetary Fund.' Address at the 15th Annual Cato Institute Monetary Conference, Washington DC, 14 October.

Fischer, S. (1998a) 'The Asian crisis: A view from the IMF.' Address at the Midwinter Conference of the Bankers' Association for Foreign Trade, Washington, DC, 22 January.

Fischer, S. (1998b) 'Capital-account liberalization and the role of the Fund,' in S. Fischer, ed. *Should the IMF Pursue Capital-Account Convertibility?* (Princeton: Princeton University Press).

Fischer, S. (1998c) 'Crisis prevention and crisis management: The role of the IMF,' Deutsche Bank conference on 'Emerging Markets: Can They be Made Crisis Free?' 3 October.

Fischer, S. (1998d) 'Press conference – Seminar on capital account liberalization,' IMF Meeting Hall, Washington DC, 10 March.

Fischer, S. (1999a) 'The Asian crisis: The beginning of the end?' Address at at the Asia Society's 10th Annual Corporate Conference, 'Asia's Choice: Open Markets or Government Control,' Manila, February.

Fischer, S. (1999b) 'Reforming the international financial system,' *The Economic Journal*, 109, 459, 557–76.

Financial Service Authority (2009a) 'The FSA publishes "The Turner Review": A wide-ranging review of global banking regulation,' FSA/PN/037/2009, 18 March. Available at http://www.fsa.gov.uk/pages/Library/Communication/PR/2009/037.shtml

Financial Service Authority (2009b) 'The Turner Review: a regulatory response to the global banking crisis,' March. Available at http://www.fsa.gov.uk/pubs/other/turner_review.pdf

Financial Stability Forum (2009) Press Release. Financial Stability Forum re-established as the Financial Stability Board. 2 April.

Frieden, J. A. (2006) *Global Capitalism: Its Fall and Rise in the Twentieth Century* (New York and London: W.W. Norton & Company).

G7 (1994) Ministers of the Group of Seven. Naples Summit Communiqué, 20th Meeting, 8–9 July.

G7 (1995) Ministers of the Group of Seven. Halifax Summit Communiqué, 21th Meeting, 16 June.

G8 (2009) Statement of G8 Finance Ministers. Lecce, Italy. 13 June.

G20 (2008) 'Declaration: Summit on financial markets and the world economy,' Washington DC, 15 November.

G20 (2009a) Communiqué from the London Summit, London, 2 April.

G20 (2009b) 'Declaration on delivering resources through the international financial institutions,' London, 2 April. Available at http://www.g20.org/ Documents/Fin_Deps_IFI_Annex_Draft_02_04_09_-__1615_Clean.pdf

G20 (2009c) 'Enhancing sound regulation and strengthening transparency, Final Report,' 25 March.

G24 (1993) Ministers of the Intergovernmental Group of Twenty-Four on International Monetary Affairs, Communiqué, Washington, DC, 25 September.

G30 (2009) 'Financial reform: A framework for financial stability. Group of thirty, prepared by the Financial Reform Working Group'. Available at http:// www.group30.org/pubs/reformreport.pdf

Gapper, J. (2009) 'How banks learnt to play the system,' *Financial Times*, 6 May.

Geithner, T. F. (2009) Remarks before The Economic Club of Washington, Washington DC, 22 April.

Gephardt, R., D. Bonior, N. Pelosi, B. Frank, M. Waters, and E. E. Torres (1998) 'Letter to the Honourable Robert E. Rubin, Secretary, Department of the Treasury,' 1 May.

Giles, C. (2007) 'Wrong lessons from Asia's crisis,' *Financial Times*, 1 July.

Gilpin, R. (1981) *War and Change in World Politics* (Cambridge: Cambridge University Press).

Goldstein, J. (1993) *Ideas, Interests, and U.S. Trade Policy* (Ithaca: Cornell University Press).

Goldstein, M. (1998) *The Asian Financial Crisis: Causes, Cures, and Systemic Implications* (Washington, DC: Institute of International Economics).

Goldstein, M., and G. A. Calvo (1996) 'What role for the official sector?' in G. A. Calvo, M. Goldstein and E. Hochreiter, eds *Private Capital Flows to Emerging Markets After the Mexican Crisis* (Washington, DC: Institute for International Economics; Vienna: Austrian National Bank).

Goldstein, M., and D. Folkerts-Landau (1993) 'International capital markets: Part II. Systemic issues in international finance,' IMF World Economic and Financial Surveys, Washington, DC: International Monetary Fund.

Goldstein, M., et al., (1991) 'Determinants and systematic consequences of international capital flows,' IMF Occasional Paper No. 77, Washington, DC: International Monetary Fund.

Goldstein, M., et al., (1993) 'International capital markets: Part I. Exchange rate management and international capital flows,' IMF World Economic and Financial Surveys, Washington, DC: International Monetary Fund.

Golup, P. S. (2004) 'Imperial politics, imperial will and the crisis of US hegemony,' *Review of International Political Economy*, 11, 4, 763–86.

Gonzales-Paramo, J. M. (2008) Speech read at the Global ABS Conference, Cannes, France, 1 June.

Gorton, G., and G. Pennacchi (1995) 'Banks and loan sales marketing nonmarketable assets,' *Journal of Monetary Economics*, 35, 3, 389–411.

Gourevitch, P. A. (1986) *Politics in Hard Times: Comparative Responses to International Economic Crises* (Ithaca: Cornell University Press).

Guitián, M. (1992) 'The unique nature of the responsibilities of the International Monetary Fund,' IMF Pamphelet Series No. 46, Washington, DC: International Monetary Fund.

Guitián, M. (1995) 'Capital account liberalization: Bringing policy in line with reality,' in S. Edwards, ed. *Capital Controls, Exchange Rates, and Monetary Policy in the World Economy* (Cambridge: Cambridge University Press).

Guitián, M. (1996) 'The issue of capital account convertibility: A gap between norms and reality,' in S. M. Nsouli and M. Guitián, eds *Currency Convertibility in the Middle East and North Africa* (Washington, DC: International Monetary Fund).

Haas, E. B. (1990) *When Knowledge is Power: Three Models of Change in International Organizations* (Berkeley: University of California Press).

Haas, P. M. (1992a) 'Introduction: Epistemic communities and international policy coordination,' *International Organization*, 46, 1, 1–35.

Haas, P. M., ed. (1992b) *Knowledge, Power, and International Policy Coordination* (Columbia: University of South Carolina Press).

Haggard, S. (2000) *The Political Economy of the Asian Financial Crisis* (Washington, DC: Institute for International Economics).

Hall, B., A. Barker, and C. Bryant (2009) 'Sarkozy claims credit on tighter regulation,' *Financial Times*, 2 April.

Hall, B., and J. Mackintosh (2009) 'France to call for hedge fund crackdown,' *Financial Times*, 12 February.

Hall, P. A., ed. (1989) *The Political Power of Economic Ideas: Keynesianism across Nations* (Princeton: Princeton University Press).

Hall, R. B., and T. J. Biersteker, eds (2002) *The Emergence of Private Authority in Global Governance* (Cambridge: Cambridge University Press).

Hanna, N. K., S. Boyson, and S. Gunaratne (1996) 'The East Asian miracle and information technology: Strategic management of technological learning,' World Bank Discussion Paper No. 326, Washington, DC: World Bank.

Hay, C. (1999) 'Crisis and the structural transformation of the state: Interrogating processes of change,' *British Journal of Politics and International Relations*, 1, 3, 317–44.

Hay, C. (2001) 'The "crisis" of Keynesianism and the rise of Neoliberalism in Britain: An ideational institutionalist approach,' in J. L. Campbell and O. K. Pederson, eds *The Rise of Neoliberalism and Institutional Analysis* (Princeton: Princeton University Press).

Helleiner, E. (1994) *States and the Reemergence of Global Finance: From Bretton Woods to the 1990s* (Ithaca and London: Cornell University Press).

Higgott, R. A., G. Underhill, and A. Bieler, eds (2000) *Non-State Actors and Authority in the Global System* (London: Routledge).

Horsefield, J. K. (1969) *The International Monetary Fund, 1945–1965: Twenty Years of International Monetary Cooperation* (Washington, DC: International Monetary Fund).

IEO (2004) 'The IMF and recent capital account crises: Indonesia, Korea, and Brazil,' Evaluation Report, Washington, DC: Independent Evaluation Office.

IEO (2005) 'The IMF's approach to capital account liberalization,' Evaluation Report, Washington, DC: International Monetary Fund.

Ikenberry, J. G. (1992) 'A world economy restored: Expert consensus and the Anglo-American postwar settlement,' in P. M. Haas, ed. *Knowledge, Power, and International Policy Coordination* (Columbia: University of South Carolina Press).

IMF (1994a) 'IMF supports Mexico's exchange rate action,' News Brief No. 94/18, 22 December.

IMF (1994b) 'World economic outlook,' Washington, DC: International Monetary Fund, October.

IMF (1995a) 'International capital markets: Developments, prospects, and key policy issues,' Washington, DC, International Monetary Fund, August.

IMF (1995b) 'World economic outlook,' Washington DC, International Monetary Fund, May.

IMF (1996a) 'International capital markets: Developments, Prospects, and key policy issues,' Washington, DC: International Monetary Fund, September.

IMF (1996b) 'World economic outlook,' Washington, DC: International Monetary Fund, May.

IMF (1997a) 'Annual report,' Washington, DC: International Monetary Fund.

IMF (1997b) 'World economic outlook: "Globalization: opportunities and challenges",' Washington, DC: International Monetary Fund, May.

IMF (1997c) 'World economic outlook: Interim assessment,' Washington, DC: International Monetary Fund, December.

IMF (1998a) 'International capital markets: Developments, prospects, and key policy issues,' Washington, DC: International Monetary Fund, September.

IMF (1998b) 'Seminar discusses the orderly path to capital account liberalization,' *IMF Survey*, 27, 6, 81–4.

IMF (1998c) 'World economic outlook,' Washington, DC: International Monetary Fund, May.

IMF (1999) 'IMF tightens defenses against financial contagion by establishing contingent credit lines,' 25 April.

IMF (2000) 'IMF: a virtually universal institution. Camdessus years marked by progressive process of harnessing globalization benefits for all members,' *IMF Survey. Special Supplement*, February.

IMF (2008a) 'Global financial stability report,' Washington, DC: International Monetary Fund, April.

IMF (2008b) 'Global financial stability report,' Washington, DC: International Monetary Fund, October.

IMF (2009a) 'Global financial stability report,' Washington, DC: International Monetary Fund, January.

IMF (2009b) 'Initial lessons of the crisis,' Washington, DC: International Monetary Fund.

IMF (2009c) 'Initial lessons of the crisis for the global architecture and the IMF,' Washington, DC: International Monetary Fund.

IMF (2009d) 'Lessons of the financial crisis for future regulation of financial institutions and markets and for liquidity management,' Washington, DC: International Monetary Fund.

IMF (2009e) 'The recent financial turmoil – Initial assessment, policy lessons, and implications for fund surveillance,' Washington, DC: International Monetary Fund.

IMF Archives, BUFF/94/106, 'Concluding remarks by the acting chairman for the seminar on issues and developments in the international exchange and payments system,' 16 November 1994.

IMF Archives, BUFF/96/50, 'Summing up by the Chairman: Standards for the dissemination of economic and financial statistics to the public by member countries and implementation of the SDDS,' 15 April 1996.

IMF Archives, EBM/95/30, Minutes of Executive Board Meeting. 'Mexico – Review under stand-by arrangement,' 29 March 1995.

IMF Archives, EBM/95/73, Minutes of Executive Board Meeting. 'Capital Account Convertibility – Review of Experience, and Implications for Fund Policy,' 28 July 1995.

IMF Archives, EBM/97/38, Minutes of Executive Board Meeting. 'Capital account convertibility – Consideration of possible amendment of Articles of Agreement – Further considerations,' 15 April 1997.

IMF Archives, EBM/97/66, Minutes of Executive Board Meeting. 'Capital movements under an amendment of the Articles of Agreement – Concepts of "International Capital Movement" and "Restrictions",' 30 June 1997.

IMF Archives, EBM/97/87, Minutes of the Executive Board. 'Capital movements under an amendment of the Articles of Agreement – Transitional arrangements, approval Policies, and implications for financing; and legal aspects of capital movements – Further considerations,' 26 August 1997.

IMF Archives, EBM/97/93, Minutes of Executive Board Meeting. 'Capital movements under an amendment of the Articles – Draft Report of Executive Board to Interim Committee,' 8 September 1997.

IMF Archives, EBM/98/38, Minutes of Executive Board Meeting. 'Liberalization of capital movements under an amendment of Articles – Statement by the Managing Director,' 2 April 1998.

IMF Archives, EBS/98/44, 'Review of members' policies in the context of surveillance – Lessons for surveillance from the Asian crisis.' Prepared by the Policy Development and Review Department, 9 March 1998.

IMF Archives, EBM/98/103, Minutes of Executive Board Meeting. 'Strengthening the architecture of International Monetary System; strengthening financial systems; and orderly capital account liberalization – Draft Reports of Managing Director to Interim Committee.' 23 September 1998.

IMF Archives, MD/Sp/98/5, 'Capital account liberalization and the role of the Fund.' Remarks by Michel Camdessus, Managing Director of the International Monetary Fund. IMF Seminar on Capital Account Liberalization, Washington, DC, 9 March 1998.

IMF Archives, SM/94/202, 'Issues and developments in the international exchange and payments systems,' Prepared by the Monetary and Exchange Affairs Department. 1 August 1994.

IMF Archives, SM/95/164, 'Capital account convertibility: Review of experience and implications for fund policies.' Prepared by the Monetary Affairs and Exchange Department. 7 July 1995.

IMF Archives, SM/95/164, Sup. 1, 'Capital account convertibility – Review of experience and implications for Fund policies – Background paper'. 10 July 1995.

IMF Archives, SM/97/32, 'Capital account convertibility and the role of the Fund-review of experience and consideration of a possible amendment of the

Articles.' Prepared by the Legal, Monetary and Exchange Affairs, and Policy Development and Review Departments. 5 February 1997.

IMF Archives, SM/97/32 Supplement 1, 'Review of experience with capital account liberalization and strengthened procedures adopted by the Fund.' Prepared by Monetary and Exchange Affairs, Policy Development and Review, and Research Departments. 6 February 1997.

IMF Archives, SM/97/86, 'Capital account convertibility and a possible amendment of the Articles – Further considerations.' 25 March 1997.

IMF Archives, SM/97/146, 'Capital movements under an amendment of the Articles: Concepts of "international capital movements" and "restrictions".' 10 June 1997.

IMF Archives, SM/97/173, 'Capital account convertibility: Transitional arrangements, approval policies and financing under an amendment.' 1 July 1997.

IMF Archives, SM/98/75, 'Summary of the seminar on capital account liberalization.'25 March 1998.

IMF Archives, SM/98/172, 'Developments and issues in the international exchange and payments system.' Prepared by the Monetary and Exchange Affairs Department. 7 July 1998.

IMF Archives, SM/98/233, 'Draft Report by the Managing Director on strengthening financial systems and orderly capital account liberalization.' 21 September 1998.

Institute of International Finance (1999a) 'Executive summary,' Washington, DC, IIF Working Group on the Liberalization of Capital Movements, Institute of International Finance, 20 January.

Institute of International Finance (1999b) 'Final report,' Washington, DC, IIF Working Group on the Liberalization of Capital Movements. Institute of International Finance, 20 January.

Institute of International Finance (2008a) 'Final Report of the IIF Committee on market best practices: Principles of conduct and best practice recommendations. Financial services industry response to the market turmoil of 2007–2008,' Washington, DC, Institute of International Finance, July. Available at http://www.iif.com/press/press+75.php

Institute of International Finance (2008b) 'Final Report by its Committee on market best practices,' Washington, DC: Institute of International Finance, 17 July. Available at http://www.iif.com/press/press+75.php

Institute of International Finance (2009) 'Capital flows to emerging market economies,' Washington, DC: Institute of International Finance, 27 January.

Interim Committee (1994) 'Press communiqué and declaration on cooperation to strengthen the global expansion composition,' Madrid, Spain, 2 October.

Interim Committee (1997) 'Statement of the Interim Committe on the liberalization of capital movements under an Amendment of the Articles.' Attached to the Communiqué of the Interim Committee of the Board of Governors of the International Monetary Fund, Hong Kong, 21 September.

Interim Committee (1998) 'Press communiqué.' Washington, DC, 4 October.

International Financial Institution Advisory Commission (2000) 'Final Report and transcripts of meetings and hearings,' Washington, DC.

Irvine, S. (1997) 'Worth the paper it's printed on?' *Euromoney*, 48–50.

Ito, T. (2007) 'Asian currency crisis and the IMF, ten years later: Overview,' *Asian Economic Policy Review*, 2, 1, 16–49.

James, H. (1995) 'The historical development of the principle of surveillance,' *IMF Staff Papers* 42, 4, 762–91.

James, H. (1996) *International Monetary Cooperation Since Bretton Woods* (New York and Oxford: Oxford University Press).

John Williamson (1990) *The Progress of Policy Reform in Latin America*, (Washington, D.C: Institute for International Economics).

Kapstein, E. B. (1996) 'Shockproof,' *Foreign Affairs*, 75, 1, 2–8.

Katzenstein, Peter J. (1996) *Cultural Norms and National Security: Police and Military in Postwar Japan* (Ithaca NY: Cornell University Press).

Kaufmann, D. (2009) 'The G-20 and the end of ideology: From Washington to London to New York,' Washington, DC: The Brookings Institution.

Keck, M. E., and K. Sikkink (1998) *Activists Beyond Borders: Advocacy Networks in International Politics* (Ithaca: Cornell University Press).

Kirshner, J. (1999) 'Keynes, capital mobility and the crisis of embedded liberalism,' *Review of International Political Economy*, 6, 3, 313–37.

Klotz, A. (1995) *Norms in International Relations: The Struggle Against Apartheid* (Ithaca: Cornell University Press).

Kratochwil, F. V. (2006) 'History, action and identity: Revisiting the "second" great debate and assessing its importance for social theory,' *European Journal of International Relations*, 12, 1, 5–29.

Kristof, N. D., and D. E. Sanger (1999) 'How U.S. wooed Asia to let cash flow in,' *The New York Times*, 16 February.

Kristof, N. D., and S. Wudunn (1999) 'Of world markets, none an island,' *New York Times*, 17 February.

Kristof, N. D., and E. Wyatt (1999) 'Who went under in the world's sea of cash,' *The New York Times*, 15 February.

Krueger, A. O. (2001) 'International financial architecture for 2002: A new approach to sovereign debt restructuring.' Address given at the National Economists' Club Annual Members.' Address delivered at the American Enterprise Institute, Washington DC, 26 November.

Krueger, A. O. (2002) 'New approaches to sovereign debt restructuring: An update on our thinking.' Address given at the Conference on 'Sovereign Debt Workouts: Hopes and Hazards,' Institute for International Economics. Washington DC, 1 April.

Krugman, P. (1994) 'The myth of Asia's miracle,' *Foreign Affairs*, 73, 6, 62–78.

Krugman, P. (1995) 'Dutch tulips and emerging markets,' *Foreign Affairs*, 74, 4, 28–44.

Krugman, P., (1998a) 'Saving Asia: It's time to get radical,' *Fortune*, 7 September.

Krugman, P. (1998b) 'What happened to Asia?' in G. Irwin and D. Vines, eds *Financial Market Integration and International Capital Flows* (Cheltenham, UK: Edward Elgar).

Krugman, P. (1999) 'Capital control freaks: How Malaysia got away with economic heresy,' *Slate Magazine*, 27 September.

Kuczynski, P.-P., and J. Williamson, eds (2003) *After the Washington Consensus: Restarting Growth and Reform in Latin America* (Washington, DC: Institute for International Economics).

Kuhn, T. (1962) *The Structure of Scientific Revolutions* (Chicago: University of Chicago Press).

Lane, T., et al., (1999) 'IMF-supported programs in Indonesia, Korea, and Thailand: A preliminary assessment,' IMF Occasional Paper No. 178, Washington, DC: International Monetary Fund.

Legro, J. W. (1997) 'Which norms matter? Revisiting the "failure" of internationalism,' *International Organization*, 51, 1, 31–63.

Leiteritz, R. J., and M. Moschella (forthcoming) 'The International Monetary Fund and capital account liberalization: A case of failed norm institutionalization,' in S. Park and A. Vetterlein, eds *Owning Development: Creating Global Policy Norms in the World Bank and the IMF* (Cambridge: Cambridge University Press).

Levy, J. (1994) 'Learning and foreign policy: Sweeping a conceptual minefield,' *International Organization*, 48, 2, 279–312.

Lippman, T. W. (1994) 'Pacific summit agrees on vast free market,' *The Washington Post*, 16 November.

Lombardi, D. (2009) 'After the fall: Re-asserting the International Monetary Fund in the face of global crisis,' Washington, DC: The Brookings Institution.

Luce, E., and C. Freeland (2009) 'Summers backs state action,' *Financial Times*, 8 March.

Maman, D., and Z. Rosenhek (2007) 'The politics of institutional reform: The "Declaration of Independence" of the Israeli Central Bank,' *Review of International Political Economy*, 14, 2, 251–75.

Marchesi, S., and J. P. Thomas (1999) 'IMF conditionality as a screening device,' *Economics Journal*, 109, 454, 111–25.

Mckenna, B. (1998) 'U.S. reads the riot act to Indonesia. Economic crisis deepens: Suharto shoulders blame,' *The Globe and Mail*, 10 January.

McNamara, K. R. (1998) *The Currency of Ideas: Monetary Politics and the European Union* (Ithaca: Cornell University Press).

Meltzer, A. H. (1998) 'Asian problems and the IMF,' *The Cato Journal*, 17, 3, 267–74.

Merli, A. (2009) 'Europa dell'Est, così si è evitato il collasso,' *Il Sole24 ore*, May.

Minsky, H. (1992) 'The financial instability hypothesis,' Working Paper No. 74, New York: Levy Economics Institute.

Mohamad, M. Bin (1998) Opening remark at the 6th ASEAN Summit. Hanoi, Vietnam, 15 December.

Momani, B. (2004) 'American politicization of the International Monetary Fund,' *Review of International Political Economy*, 11, 5, 880–904.

Momani, B. (2005a) 'Limits on streamlining fund conditionality: The International Monetary Fund's organizational culture,' *Journal of International Relations and Development*, 8, 2, 142–63.

Momani, B. (2005b) 'Recruiting and diversifying IMF technocrats,' *Global Society*, 19, 2, 167–87.

Momani, B. (2007) 'IMF staff: Missing link in fund reform proposals,' *Review of International Organization*, 2, 39–57.

Moschella, M., and L. Seabrooke (2008) 'Policy feedback and the politics of economic reform: The IMF and institutional change in East Asia,' Paper presented at the 2nd Global International Studies Conference, World International Studies Committee (WISC), Slovenia.

Mosley, L. (2003) 'Attempting global standards: National governments, international finance, and the IMF data regime,' *Review of International Political Economy*, 10, 2, 331–62.

Naim, M. (1995) 'Latin America the morning after,' *Foreign Affairs*, 74, 4, 45–61.

Nielson, D. L., M. J. Tierney, and C. A. Weaver (2006) 'Bridging the rationalist-constructivist divide: Re-engineering the culture of the World Bank,' *Journal of International Relations and Development*, 9, 2, 107–39.

Noble, G. W., and J. Ravenhill, eds (2000) *The Asian Financial Crisis and the Architecture of Global Finance* (Cambridge: Cambridge University Press).

OECD (1995) 'Multilateral agreement investment report by the committee on international investment and multinational enterprise and the committee on capital movements and invisible transactions.' Meeting of the OECD Council at Ministerial Level, Paris, 24 May.

Park, S. (2005) 'Norm diffusion within international organizations: A case study of the World Bank,' *Journal of International Relations and Development*, 8, 2, 111–41.

Park, S., and A. Vetterlein, eds (forthcoming) *Owning Development: Creating Global Policy Norms in the World Bank and the IMF* (Cambridge: Cambridge University Press).

Park, Y. C. (1996) 'East Asian liberalization, bubbles, and challenge from China,' *Brookings Papers on Economic Activity*, 2, 357–71.

Parker, G., C. Giles, and E. Luce (2009) 'G20 leaders hail crisis fightback,' *Financial Times*, 2 April.

Parsons, C. (2003) *A Certain Idea of Europe* (Ithaca: Cornell University Press).

Paulson, H. (2007) 'Current housing and mortgage developments,' Paper presented at the Georgetown Univeristy Law Center, 16 October.

Pauly, L. W. (1997) *Who Elected the Bankers? Surveillance and Control in the World Economy* (Ithaca: Cornell University Press).

Pauly, L. W. (1999) 'Good governance and bad policy: The perils of international organizational overextension,' *Review of International Political Economy*, 6, 4, 401–24.

Pisani-Ferry, J., and I. Santos (2009) 'Reshaping the global economy,' *Finance & Development*, 46, 1, 8–12.

Porter, A., R. Winnett, and T. Harnden (2009) 'Gordon Brown, G20 summit: Gordon Brown announces "new world order",' *Telegraph*, 3 April.

Porter, T. (2005) *Globalization and Finance* (Cambridge: Polity).

Prasad, E. S., and R. Rajan (2008) 'A pragmatic approach to capital account liberalization,' *Journal of Economic Perspectives*, 22, 3, 149–72.

Prasad, E. S., K. Rogoff, S.-J. Wei, and A. M. Kose (2003) 'Effects of financial globalization on developing countries: Some empirical evidence,' IMF Occasional Paper No. 220, Washington, DC: International Monetary Fund.

Quirk, P. J. (1994) 'Capital account convertibility: A new model for developing countries,' IMF Working Paper No. 94/81, Washington, DC: International Monetary Fund.

Quirk, P. J., Hernàn Cortés, Kyung-Mo Huh, Barry R. Johnston, Arto Kovanen, Dmitri Menchikow, Hiroshika Nishikawa, Christopher Ryan, Virgilio Sandoval (1995) 'Issues in international exchange and payments systems,' World Economic and Financial Surveys, Washington, DC: International Monetary Fund.

Bibliography 203

Radelet, S., and J. D. Sachs (1998) 'The East Asian financial crisis: Diagnosis, remedies, prospects,' *Brookings Papers on Economic Activity*, 1, 1–74.

Rodrik, D. (1998) 'Who needs capital-account convertibility?' in S. Fischer, ed. *Should the IMF Pursue Capital-Account Convertibility?* (Princeton: Princeton University Press).

Rodrik, D., (2009) 'A Plan B for global finance,' *The Economist*, 12 March.

Rojas-Suàrez, L. (1991) 'Risk and capital flight in developing countries,' in M. Goldstein, D. J. Mathieson, and T. Lane, eds *Determinants and Systemic Consequences of International Capital Flows*, IMF Occasional Paper No. 77 (Washington, DC: International Monetary Fund).

Rothstein, B., and S. Steinmo (2002) 'Restructuring politics: Institutional analysis and the challenges of modern welfare states,' in B. Rothstein and S. Steinmo, eds *Restructuring the Welfare State: Political Institutions and Policy Change* (New York: Palgrave).

Roubini, N. (2009) 'Anglo-Saxon model has failed,' *Financial Times*, 9 February.

Rubin, R. E., and J. Weisberg (2003) *In an Uncertain World: Tough Choices from Wall Street to Washington* (New York: Random House).

Ruggie, J. G. (1982) 'International regimes, transactions, and change: Embedded liberalism in the postwar economic order,' *International Organization*, 36, 2, 379–415.

Ryan, T. (2009) 'Wall Street is a willing partner in financial reform,' *Financial Times*, 8 June.

Sachs, J. (1998) 'Fixing the IMF remedy,' *The Banker*, February.

Sachs, J., A. Tornell, and A. Velasco (1996) 'The collapse of the Mexican peso: What have we learned?' *Economic Policy*, 22, 15–56.

Sanger, D. E. (1995) 'Do fickle markets now make policy?' *The New York Times*, 19 March.

Schadler, S., M. Carkovic, A. Bennett, and R. Kahn (1993) 'Recent experiences with surges in capital inflows,' IMF Occasional Paper No. 108, Washington, DC: International Monetary Fund.

Schwartz, A. J. (1998) 'Time to terminate the ESF and the IMF,' Cato Foreign Policy Briefing No. 48.

Seabrooke, L. (2007a) 'The everyday social sources of economic crises: From "great frustrations" to "great revelations" in interwar Britain,' *International Studies Quarterly*, 51, 4, 795–810.

Seabrooke, L. (2007b) 'Legitimacy gaps in the world economy: Explaining the sources of the IMF's legitimacy crisis,' *International Politics*, 44, 2–3, 250–68.

Seabrooke, L. (2007c) 'Varieties of economic constructivism in political economy: Uncertain times call for disparate measures,' *Review of International Political Economy*, 14, 2, 371–85.

Securities Industry and Financial Markets Association (SIFMA), the American Securitization Forum (ASF), the European Securitization Forum (ESF), and the Australian Securitization Forum (AuSF) (2008) *Restoring Confidence in the Securitization Markets*. 3 December 2008.

Sikkink, K. (1991) *Ideas and Institutions: Developmentalism in Argentina and Brazil* (Ithaca: Cornell University Press).

Smith, J. R., and C. Chandler (1995) 'Peso crisis caught U.S. by surprise,' *The Washington Post*, 13 February.

Smythe, E. (2000) 'State authority and investment security: non-state actors and the negotiation of the Multilateral Agreement on Investment at the OECD,' in R. A. Higgott, G. Underhill, and A. Bieler, eds *Non-State Actors and Authority in the Global System* (London: Routledge).

Soros, G. (1998) *The Crisis of Global Capitalism: Open Society Endangered* (New York: Public Affairs).

Southey, C. (1995) 'EU pushes Japan, S Korea on financial services,' *Financial Times*, 12 July.

Steinmo, S. (2003) 'The evolution of policy ideas: Tax policy in the 20th century,' *British Journal of Politics and International Relations*, 5, 2, 206–36.

Stiglitz, J. E. (2002a) *Globalization and its Discontents* (London: Penguin Books).

Stiglitz, J. E. (2002b) 'How the IMF became part of the problem,' *The Times*, 22 June.

Stiglitz, J. E., and A. Charlton (2005) 'The strategic role of the IMF: Risks for emerging market economies amid increasingly globalized financial markets.' Paper prepared for the G24 Technical Group Meeting, 15–16 September.

Strauss-Kahn, D. (2009a) 'Crisis management and policy coordination: Do we need a new global framework?' Speech delivered at Oesterreichische Nationalbank, Vienna, Austria, 15 May.

Strauss-Kahn, D. (2009b) 'Multilateralism and the role of the International Monetary Fund in the global financial crisis.' Speech delivered at the School of Advanced International Studies, Washington, DC, 23 April.

Suchman, M. C. (1995) 'Managing legitimacy: Strategic and institutional approaches,' *The Academy of Management Review*, 20, 3, 571–610.

Summers, L. (1998) 'Remarks before the International Monetary Fund,' US Treasury Press Release RR-2286, Washington DC, 9 March.

Surel, Y. (2000) 'The role of cognitive and normative frames in policy-making,' *Journal of European Public Policy*, 7, 4, 495–512.

Swedberg, R. (1986) 'The doctrine of economic neutrality of the IMF and the World Bank,' *Journal of Peace Research*, 23, 4, 377–90.

Tarullo, D. K. (2008) *Banking on Basel: The Future of International Financial Regulation* (Washington, DC: Peterson Institute for International Economics).

Tett, G. (2008) 'Big freeze part 1: How it began,' *Financial Times*, 3 August.

Tett, G. (2009) 'Insight: Big steps taken to reform Wall Street,' *Financial Times*, 14 May.

Thacker, S. C. (1998) 'The high politics of IMF lending,' *World Politics*, 52, 1, 38–75.

Thirkell-White, B. (2004) 'The International Monetary Fund and civil society,' *New Political Economy*, 9, 2, 251–70.

Thirkell-White, B. (2005) *The IMF and the Politics of Financial Globalization* (Basingstoke: Palgrave Macmillan).

Tirole, J. (2002) *Financial Crises, Liquidity, and the International Monetary System* (Princeton: Princeton University Press).

Truman, E. M., ed. (2006) *A Strategy for IMF Reform*, Policy Analyses in International Economics 77 (Washington DC: Institute of International Economics).

US Congress (1998a) House of Representatives. Hearing Before the Subcommittee on General Oversight and Investigations of the Committee on Banking and Financial Services. *An Examination of the Russian Economic Crisis and the*

International Monetary Fund Aid Package. 105th Cong. 10 September 1998. Washington, DC: U.S. Government Printing Office.

US Congress (1998b) House of Representatives. Hearing before the Subcommittee on General Oversight and Investigations of the Committee on Banking and Financial Services. *Review of the Operations of the International Monetary Fund*. 105th Cong. 21 April 1998. Washington, DC: US Government Printing Office.

USTR (1996) 'National Trade Estimate Report on Foreign Trade Barriers, 11th annual report by the Office of the U.S. Trade Representative,' 1 April.

Vetterlein, A. (2007) 'Economic growth, poverty reduction, and the role of social policies: The evolution of the World Bank's social development approach,' *Global Governance*, 13, 4, 513–33.

Vetterlein, A. (2008) 'Lacking ownership: The IMF and its engagement with social development as a global policy norm,' in S. Park and A. Vetterlein, eds *Owning Development: Creating Global Policy Norms in the World Bank and the IMF* (Cambridge: Cambridge University Press).

Viñals, J. (2009) 'Keynote remarks by José Viñals, Financial Counsellor and Director Monetary and Capital Markets Department, IMF Brussels Economic Forum,' 15 May.

Wade, R., and F. Veneroso (1998) 'The Asian crisis: The high debt model versus the Wall Street-Treasury-IMF complex,' *New Left Review*, 228, 3–22.

Walter, A. (2000) 'Globalisation and policy convergence: The case of direct investment rules,' in R. A. Higgott, G. Underhill, and A. Bieler, eds *Non-State Actors and Authority in the Global System* (London: Routledge).

Walter, A. (2002) 'Financial liberalization and prudential regulation in East Asia: Still perverse?' Working Paper, Institute of Defence and Strategic Studies, Singapore.

Walter, A. (2008) *Governing Finance: East Asia's Adoption of International Standards* (Ithaca: Cornell University Press).

Wayne, L. (1994) 'Global mutual funds: Expectations are high,' *The New York Times*, 3 January.

Weaver, C. (2007) 'The world's bank and the bank's world,' *Global Governance*, 13, 4, 493–512.

Weaver, C. (2008a) *Hypocrisy Trap: The World Bank and the Poverty of Reform* (Princeton: Princeton University Press).

Weaver, C. (2008b) 'The strategic social construction of the World Bank's gender and development agenda,' in S. Park and A. Vetterlein, eds *Owning Development: Creating Global Policy Norms in the World Bank and the IMF* (Cambridge: Cambridge University Press).

Weber, M. (1978) *Economy and Society: An Outline of Interpretive Sociology* (Berkeley: University of California Press).

Weir, M. (1992) 'Ideas and politics of bounded innovation,' in S. Steinmo, K. Thelen, and F. Longstreth, eds *Structuring Politics: Historical Institutionalism in Comparative Analysis* (Cambridge: Cambridge University Press).

Wendt, A. (1999) *Social Theory of International Relations* (Cambridge: Cambridge University Press).

Widmaier, W. W. (2007) 'Where you stand depends on how you think: Economic ideas, the decline of the council of economic advisers and the rise of the federal reserve,' *New Political Economy*, 12, 1, 43–59.

Widmaier, W. W., M. Blyth, and L. Seabrooke (2007) 'Exogenous shocks or endogenous constructions? The meanings of wars and crises,' *International Studies Quarterly*, 51, 4, 747–59.

Williamson, J. (1983) *Prospects for Adjustment in Argentina, Brazil, and Mexico: Responding to the Debt Crisis* (Washington, DC: Institute for International Economics).

Williamson, J., ed. (1990a) *Latin American Adjustment: How Much Has Happened?* (Washington, DC: Institute for International Economics).

Williamson, J. (1990b) 'What Washington means by policy reform?' in J. Williamson, ed. *Latin American Adjustment: How Much Has Happened?* (Washington, DC: Institute for International Economics).

Williamson, J. (1994a) 'In search of a manual for Technopols,' in J. Williamson, ed. *The Political Economy of Policy Reform* (Washington, DC: Institute for International Economics).

Williamson, J., ed. (1994b) *The Political Economy of Policy Reform* (Washington, DC: Institute for International Economics).

Williamson, J. (2003) 'Costs and benefits of financial globalization: Concepts, evidence and implications,' in G. R. D. Underhill and X. Zhang, eds *International Financial Governance Under Stress. Global Structures versus National Imperatives* (Cambridge: Cambridge University Press).

Williamson, J. (2004) 'The Washington consensus as policy prescription for development.' Lecture delivered at the World Bank, Washington, DC, 13 January.

Williamson, J., and M. Mahar (1998) *A Survey of Financial Liberalization* (Princeton: Princeton University Press).

Wolf, M. (2009) 'This crisis is a moment, but is it a defining one?' *Financial Times*, 19 May.

Woods, N. (2006) *The Globalizers: The IMF, the World Bank, and their Borrowers* (Ithaca and London: Cornell University Press).

Woods, Ngaire, and Domenico, Lombardi (2006) 'Uneven patterns of governance: How developing countries are represented in the IMF.' *Review of International Political Economy*, 13, 3, 480–515.

Wyplosz, C. (1999) 'International financial instability,' in I. Kaul, I. Grunberg, and M. Stern, eds *Global Public Goods* (New York: Oxford University Press).

Yoon, Y. (2007) 'Policy failure was at the root of the Asian financial crisis,' *Financial Times*, 10 July.

Index